D0853288

Living Constitution, Dying Faith

AMERICAN IDEALS AND INSTITUTIONS SERIES

Robert P. George, series editor

Published in partnership with the James Madison Program in American Ideals
and Institutions at Princeton University, this series is dedicated to the exploration
of enduring questions of political thought and constitutional law; to the promo-
tion of the canon of the Western intellectual tradition as it nourishes and informs
contemporary politics; and to the application of foundational Western principles
to modern social problems.

ALSO IN SERIES:

Robert H. Bork, *A Time to Speak: Selected Writings and Arguments*
Elizabeth Fox-Genovese, *Marriage: The Dream That Refuses to Die*
David Novak, *In Defense of Religious Liberty*

Living Constitution, Dying Faith

Progressivism and the

New Science of Jurisprudence

Bradley C. S. Watson

Wilmington, Delaware

Copyright © 2009 ISI Books

All rights reserved. No part of this publication may be reproduced or transmitted in any form or by any means, electronic or mechanical, including photocopy, or any information storage and retrieval system now known or to be invented, without permission in writing from the publisher, except by a reviewer who wishes to quote brief passages in connection with a review written for inclusion in a magazine, newspaper, or broadcast.

Watson, Bradley, C. S., 1961–

    Living Constitution, dying faith : progressivism and the new science of jurisprudence / Bradley C. S. Watson. —Wilmington, Del. : ISI Books, c2009.

        p. ; cm.
        (American ideals and institutions series)

        ISBN: 978-1-933859-70-5
        Includes bibliographical references.

        1. Political questions and judicial power—United States.
2. Judge-made law—United States. 3. Constitutional law—United States. 4. Progressivism (United States politics) 5. Culture and law. I. Title. II. Series.

KF5130 .W38 2009   2008928733
347.73/12—dc22   0901

ISI Books
Intercollegiate Studies Institute
Post Office Box 4431
Wilmington, DE 19807-0431
www.isibooks.org

Manufactured in the United States of America

I dedicate this book to the memory of my parents,
Charles W. and Nelsie Watson—
the all resistless hurricane has swept over them

Contents

Let us have faith that right makes might, and in that faith, let us, to the end, dare to do our duty as we understand it.

—*Abraham Lincoln*

Ever in the making, as law develops through the centuries, is this new faith which silently and steadily effaces our mistakes. . . . [W]e worry ourselves overmuch about the enduring consequences of our errors. . . . The future takes care of such things.

—*Benjamin N. Cardozo*

Acknowledgments

No book springs fully formed from the mind of its author alone, and this one is certainly no exception. I owe many debts of gratitude to those who helped me think through my topic, and then commit my thoughts to paper. Most recently, I have been blessed by my association with the James Madison Program in American Ideals and Institutions at Princeton University, which allowed me to spend a year in residence in Princeton's Department of Politics, where I worked primarily on this book. The program provides Princeton—and the nation—with a unique center for the study of American political institutions and principles and their relationship to the great moral, cultural, and philosophic problems of our time and all times. To speak of the program is necessarily to speak also of its founder and director, Professor Robert P. George. His boundless energy—and dedication to promoting the moral and intellectual virtues to the glory of God—ought to be an inspiration to the entire academic world.

I am also grateful too to Bradford P. Wilson, the Madison Program's associate director, who works tirelessly on behalf of the interests of the visiting research scholars, and who commented on various parts of this book in the manuscript stages.

While at Princeton, I benefited enormously from the regular intellectual stimulation and generous advice offered by the other visiting scholars of the Madison Program. And I must say too that I benefited from the occasional gauntlets laid down by them: Alan Gibson, Matthew Holland, Carson Holloway, Catherine McCauliffe, and Paul Moreno—all of whom I now call friends. When I presented a part of the present work as a public paper at Princeton, I was fortunate enough to have in the audience Walter F. Murphy, whose penetrating questions led me to clarify my arguments on the nature of the American founding, and in particular Lincoln's interpretation of it.

Less proximately, but no less importantly, I am thankful for the extraordinary environment of the political philosophy program at the Claremont Graduate School, where, more than a decade ago, I finished my doctorate. It was there that my interest in and appreciation of progressivism as an enduring force in American politics was born. I owe special thanks to Charles R. Kesler, who introduced me to the thought of so many of the progressives with whom I am now dealing in this volume.

Though I am formally identified as a political scientist, I do not especially embrace this identification, at least in its current significations. I consider myself rather a teacher, and student, of great books. The fact that this aspiration has remained largely a reality is due very much to my home institution, Saint Vincent College. Gary M. Quinlivan, the dean of the academic division of Saint Vincent in which I reside—the Alex G. McKenna School of Business, Economics, and Government—faces the daunting task of harmonizing the theoretical and the practical, and strives mightily not to stint the former for the sake of the latter. At Saint Vincent, supported and protected against many of the most fashionable and pernicious trends in contemporary higher education, I am free to be a guide for my students—as best I can be—to the complex and fascinating relationships between ideas and action. I am free also to dwell on the eternal questions of politics and human life—right and wrong, justice and injustice, good and evil. The extent to which I can successfully do these things is subject only to my own—not institutional—limitations.

Unfortunately, I always find writing a painful struggle. As usual, my family—Barbara, Victoria, Charles, and James—bore the brunt of my absences as I struggled to complete this volume. I am grateful to them.

It should go without saying—but I will say it anyway—that errors and oversights in this work are faults of mine, and not of those who have instructed, advised, or inspired me.

Introduction

Some might consider constitutional interpretation to be arid ground traversed solely by legal specialists, and even then, only at the risk of death by boredom. I hope this book will convince them otherwise. Constitutional interpretation is a vital window into the world of ideas and moral-political action. Most attentive citizens intuit this, at least now and then. The curtains covering this window are occasionally lifted during Senate confirmation hearings for Supreme Court justices. These hearings have, since the 1980s, become popular spectator sports, one part partisan politics, and one part morality play. Still, a significant number of Americans seem baffled by what happens in them, uncertain as to the kinds of questions that should be asked by the senators, and uncertain as to the kinds of answers that should be forthcoming from the nominees.

In many ways, the judiciary, and in particular the Supreme Court of the United States, has become the most politically controversial branch of government. It has undoubtedly become the locus of attention for those concerned with what are often referred to as the "culture wars." How and why this has come to be the case is a fascinating story. It is a story that finds its beginnings in the transformation of American political thought that commenced in the late nineteenth century, and it has continued apace throughout the twentieth and twenty-first. This transformation led, in a word, to progressivism, and it continues to inform contemporary notions of a living or organic Constitution. My aim is to elucidate the connection that American progressivism as a philosophical movement and political ideology, has with American legal theory and practice, showing how the philosophical currents that dominated American political thinking in the second half of the nineteenth century played out, and continue to play out, in the realm of jurisprudence.

While I certainly touch on conventional arguments as to what contemporary jurisprudence isn't—for example, the fact that it is not "originalist" or "textualist"—this is not really the heart of my argument. Rather, I seek to elucidate what contemporary jurisprudence *is,* that is, to explicate it on its own terms, and to show why and how such a jurisprudence is destined to be destructive of any and all claims of fixed moral or political truth. That is to say, contemporary historicist jurisprudence is not only hostile to the liberal constitutionalism of the American Founders, but to any moral-political philosophy that allows for the possibility of a truth that is not time-bound. Therefore, while concentrating on American progressive thought, the book is also a meditation on political thought more generally, as well as an examination of legal history and the intellectual origins of modern constitutional interpretation.

In particular, I examine the confluence of two strains of historicist thinking—social Darwinism and pragmatism—and the metamorphosis of these twin doctrines into a powerful intellectual progressivism. These doctrines could and did mean different things to different people, and each spawned "right" and "left" versions. But together they decisively undermined the classical understanding of politics as that understanding had manifested itself in the new world through such organizing documents as the U.S. Constitution and through such writings as *The Federalist*. Of course, an older confidence in progress, including a new science of politics, had deep roots in America, but these roots never grew into a doctrine, or a philosophy of history. They could not support the growth of intellectual progressivism, which first manifested itself a century after the founding and was exemplified by such political thinkers as John Dewey, W. E. B. DuBois, William James, Francis Lieber, William Graham Sumner, and Lester Frank Ward, and such political actors as Theodore Roosevelt and Woodrow Wilson. At its high water mark, this progressivism argued openly for an overturning of the principled Madisonian constitutionalism of natural rights and limited and dispersed power, in favor of an organic, evolutionary model of the Constitution and regime that, today, is clearly evident in constitutional jurisprudence.

Progressivism continues to exist largely as legal theory. Woodrow Wilson had argued, in various ways and with varying degrees of candor, against what he understood to be the anachronistic Madisonian constitutionalism that he saw as an obstacle in the path of historical unfolding. This degree of historical consciousness, this overt suspicion of traditional American political institutions, has been uncommon among political actors since then. However, it has not been uncommon among Supreme Court justices. It is to the Court and its key decisions, particularly in the area of "civil rights," that we must look to see most clearly progressivism's continuing hold on American public life. The American constitutional landscape has changed dramatically over the past century. The most obvious facets of change are as apparent to those who embrace the new landscape as to those who have their doubts about it. They include the dramatic enlargement of national power at the expense of the states; courts of law increasingly asserting themselves as policy makers and implementers; judges becoming increasingly sensitive to the alleged historical exigencies of their time when interpreting the Constitution; and individual and group claims against the larger polity gaining increasing traction in the judicial system.

The early progressive justices, particularly Oliver Wendell Holmes, Louis Brandeis, and Benjamin Cardozo, show us the extent of the progressive era's influence on our understanding of the Constitution and constitutionalism. Their progressivism caused them—and so many who followed in their footsteps—to fluctuate wildly and often randomly between two aspirations: to make decisions perceived to be "legitimate" in the eyes of the community (because they respond to the "felt necessities" of the age), and to make decisions that counter what they claimed to be illegitimate majority will. The difficulty is that neither aspiration is rooted in constitutional text, tradition, logic, or structure. Rather, each is rooted in the judge's view of where we are in the ever-flowing river of History. It is our place in this river, rather than the metes and bounds of the formal Constitution, that determines which necessities are most deeply felt and which manifestations of majority will are illegitimate. This organic, historically conditioned view of constitutionalism has, over the past century, effectively triumphed, although it must still exist within a constitutional structure that is formally hostile to it.

In chapter 1, I sketch the meaning and implications of the "living" or "organic" Constitution, partly by showing its pervasiveness as a metaphor for contemporary constitutional interpretation. It is a metaphor that would have been profoundly alien to the Founders, whose understanding of law was structured around the idea of a knowable, unchanging moral order, to which human law and the Constitution—and therefore constitutional interpretation—were subservient. With Socrates in Plato's *Minos*, the Founders would have agreed that law aims to be a discovery of *what is*. With Saint Thomas Aquinas, they would have agreed that all human law, to be law, cannot contradict the natural law that reflects the divine reason. The well-known cases to which I aver in this chapter engage major cultural controversies and seek to "resolve" them judicially in a way that would have been unimaginable to the Founders, given their understandings of common-law constitutionalism—and indeed would be unimaginable in many a common-law courtroom outside the United States today. Many justices evidence their faith in a philosophy of History, with a capital H. They share a notion of historical unfolding—History as more than a mere record of events—and they conjoin this with an understanding of the judiciary's role in History. That is to say, they see the Court as the governmental institution on the cutting edge of an inexorable process, one that guides and "fine tunes" History. For today's legal elites, constitutional interpretation lives—as does the Constitution itself—but the unchangeable and unshakable faith behind it is dead.

Reconsidering the Founders' constitutionalism helps us to understand just how far we have come over the last two centuries. In chapter 2, I deal squarely with this constitutionalism, and its authoritative latter-day interpretation by Abraham Lincoln. I seek to highlight the tension between historicism and the Founders' view of limited and dispersed powers serving the "laws of nature and nature's God." I also seek to show the importance both the Founders and Lincoln placed on reverence for things past, and faith in the enduring principles of the regime. By laying this groundwork, my aim is to show, in later chapters, the disjunction between the Founders' understandings of constitutionalism and common-law reasoning, and the progressive jurisprudence whose foundations were laid after the Civil War. The Founders' understanding took the reasoning of common-law judges to be an accessory to political liberty, not the apotheosis of it. Unlike the new science of jurisprudence, the old science of jurisprudence largely limited itself to a careful application of existing law and attended to particular circumstances. Advocates of the new science of jurisprudence are therefore mistaken insofar as they argue that the contemporary evolutionary understanding of the Constitution in fact reflects traditional, organic, common-law reasoning.

In chapter 3 I trace the intellectual origins of the historicism explicit in the new science of jurisprudence through the schools of thought and thinkers mentioned above, as well as others. I argue that our contemporary lack of belief or faith in a merely "legalistic" Constitution parallels the decline of faith in the laws of nature and nature's God, which succumbed long ago, at least for legal elites, to the blows of Darwinism and pragmatism.

In chapter 4, I show how this historicism came to dominate political thinking by the early twentieth century. Two of the century's greatest presidents—Theodore Roosevelt and Woodrow Wilson—laid the groundwork, through both the theory and practice of vigorous presidential leadership, for the institutionalization of progressive thought in all branches of government, including especially the judiciary.

It is to the courtroom in particular that I turn in chapter 5. I show in detail the relationship of this dominant current of American political thought to constitutional jurisprudence. And I examine the jurisprudence of Brandeis, Holmes, and Cardozo in an inductive effort to sketch the legal theory implied by progressivism, including its links to sociological and realist jurisprudence. This "new science of jurisprudence" continues to have profound implications for our own day.

In chapter 6, I show how the progressive tide swept through key academic disciplines, especially law and political science. From Francis Lieber—America's first political scientist—to Woodrow Wilson—the first political scientist to become president—the new approach to regime phenomena and therefore constitutional jurisprudence illustrates not only the merger of disciplines but also of "left" and "right" under the banner of an organicism of historical process and progress. Of necessity, this organicism was marked by a declining faith in eternal verities. As it dominated the government, so it quickly came to dominate the university, which in turn helped to institutionalize further the new way of thinking and solidify its hold on the minds of legal and political elites. As early progressivism came to define political science at its disciplinary birth (a fact to which Wilson alluded in his inaugural address on becoming president of Princeton University), so it also found a home—and ultimately a more enduring one—in American law schools.

In the final chapter, I return to the most compelling contemporary manifestations of the new science of jurisprudence, including the postmodern "right to a noun" that is indicated by same-sex marriage decisions. I thereby conclude with reflections on the importance of political ideas to the current and future state of our jurisprudence, and, in turn, the importance of jurisprudence to furthering particular moral-political understandings of the nature of things. The new science of jurisprudence will attempt to perpetuate itself because of its own premises. Progressivism emphasizes motion and growth, to which the only alternative is stasis and death. Therefore, court decisions will continue to be understood as the engines of History and social growth, just as incremental genetic mutations are the engines of organic growth.

The argument of this book stands on its own. Nevertheless, I conceive of the volume as a companion to my earlier book, *Civil Rights and the Paradox of Liberal Democracy* (1999). In that book I examined the unfolding of human consciousness with respect to fundamental moral-political categories relevant to legal reasoning. I argued that liberal democracy must necessarily be grounded in certain understandings of natural moral truths, which understandings by their very nature become unstable in liberal democracies. Much constitutional change initiated and enforced by courts is a byproduct of new understandings of nature and a denial of the old understandings of natural truth. It therefore carries with it great regime-level risks. The earlier volume outlined a philosophical psychology of judicial reasoning that remained aloof from many particularities in the development and application of these new understandings. In this book, I magnify a moment—or series of moments—in the unfolding of human consciousness from which the previous volume, by design, abstracted. What the earlier volume did in macrocosm, the present volume does in microcosm. In the end, I hope this book reaffirms the notion that ideas rule the world. The question we always face is which ideas we are to use as our guiding stars and compasses.

1

The Organic Constitution

More than a century ago, Supreme Court justice Oliver Wendell Holmes, dissenting in the famous case of *Lochner v. New York* (1904)[1], endorsed "the right of a majority to embody their opinions in law," claiming that a constitution does not incorporate a particular economic theory that can overcome democratic prerogative. In that case, Holmes was rejecting a laissez-faire theory of economics and the strong theory of individual rights that went with it. It was a theory arguably relied upon by the Court's majority, and it indeed "matched the conception of the constitutional order entertained by a prominent sector of the bench and bar in the United States at the turn of the century."[2] In rejecting a theory putatively unlinked to the Constitution, Holmes played the role of strict constructionist, unwilling to impose his—or anyone else's—preferences on the true Constitution. And yet, in other circumstances, Holmes was willing to impose theoretical understandings of the American constitutional order even more distant from constitutional text, tradition, logic, or structure than the majority's opinion in *Lochner*. Of course, Holmes did not admit this in his judgments. He instead adopted the pose—as judges are wont to do—of impartial interpreter of the Constitution, unencumbered by theoretical attachments and philosophical insights at odds with neutral detachment and disinterested interpretation.

Holmes's unattributed intellectual debts are to progressivism, and the debts are not only Holmes's. Nor are they limited to other prominent jurists of his day. American jurisprudence of the twentieth and twenty-first centuries has, time and time again, drifted from its roots in the common law and Madisonian constitutionalism toward a progressive vision of history. The manifestations of this drift are various. As many leading scholars have observed, the "values" the Supreme Court has chosen to enforce have changed radically over the last century—from a substantive due-process enforcement of economic rights to a new form of substantive due process in support of personal liberties or civil rights.[3] But behind the imposition of these substantive values are both a philosophy of history and a theory of the Court's role in history. This view of history grows out of the twin, late nineteenth-century doctrines of social Darwinism and pragmatism. As such, it is alien to the American constitutional order as the Founders conceived it.

This book is largely about the nature of, and the philosophical reasons behind, this new science of jurisprudence, and their implications for American constitutionalism. My argument emphasizes deep continuities, at least from the late nineteenth century to the present, more than disjunctions. Progressive jurisprudence nowadays has, rhetorically at least, largely divorced itself from its Darwinian roots, even as these roots have spread and supported many developments throughout elite legal circles, to the point where the progressive synthesis is rarely if ever identified as or recognized for what it is: something deeply and ineradicably hostile to the American Constitution. Because of this hostility, progressivism as legal theory is unable to claim legitimacy in the eyes of the American people. It must therefore lurk in the shadows of law schools; in many judicial chambers, it generally remains an unstated or even unrecognized ground of constitutional interpretation. When it does make its most public appearances, in the form of controversial Supreme Court decisions, it must cloak itself in the robes of common-law judging and in the language of traditional legal formalism. But it is rooted in neither.

In the early 1990s, the plurality opinion of the U.S. Supreme Court in *Planned Parenthood v. Casey* (1992)[4] famously asserted or reasserted an individual right to be "free from unwarranted governmental intrusion into matters so fundamentally affecting a person as the decision whether to bear or beget a child." It went on to add that such "intimate and personal choices" are "central to personal dignity and autonomy" and to the liberty protected by the due-process clause of the Fourteenth Amendment, which has at its heart "the right to define one's own concept of existence, of meaning, of the universe, and of the mystery of human life," beliefs that "define the attributes of personhood." Affirming this language a decade later, Justice Anthony Kennedy, writing for the majority in *Lawrence v. Texas* (2003),[5] also asserted the importance of an "emerging recognition" of new rights worthy of judicial protection, in this case concerning homosexuality. "In all events," he claimed, "we think that our laws and traditions in the past half-century are of most relevance here. These references show an emerging awareness that liberty gives substantial protection to adult persons in deciding how to conduct their private lives in matters pertaining to sex." Only through recognition of such liberty, argued Justice Kennedy, can we avoid stigmatizing and demeaning the autonomous choices of individuals, whose dignity is revealed in time. In fact,

> Had those who drew and ratified the Due Process Clauses of the Fifth Amendment or the Fourteenth Amendment known the components of liberty in its manifold possibilities, they might have been more specific. They did not presume to have this insight. They knew times can blind

us to certain truths and later generations can see that laws
once thought necessary and proper in fact serve only to
oppress. As the Constitution endures, persons in every
generation can invoke its principles in their own search
for greater freedom.

In striking down the state statutes at issue—one placing
limits on abortion, the other on homosexual conduct—these
decisions relied on purported substantive due-process protections of the Fourteenth Amendment—in Justice Kennedy's
phrasing, the "due process right to demand respect for conduct
protected by the substantive guarantee of liberty." But in so doing, they also put forth particular, interlocking understandings
of constitutionalism, individuality, and a dynamic of historical
unfolding—or History, conceived as more than a mere record of
events. Along with these understandings is a theory, adopted *sub
silentio,* of the judiciary's role in History.

This theory was adopted explicitly by the late Justice William J. Brennan when he claimed that judges must recognize that
"the genius of the Constitution rests not in any static meaning it
might have had in a world that is dead and gone, but in the adaptability of its great principles to cope with current problems and
current needs."[6] According to Brennan, the "vision of our time"
is destined to be different from the vision of other times, and a
central part of the judicial role is to act as visionary. Although the
Constitution is in some degree a "structuring text" marking out
the bounds of government, it is, more fundamentally, a visionary
document demanding ever more democracy and respect for individual dignity.[7] To inject meaning into these terms, the judge will
eschew "a technical understanding of the organs of government"
in favor of "a personal confrontation with the wellsprings of our
society."[8] Asserting that individual dignity is the most important
of all political values, Brennan sees the judge's job as articulating
its meaning as that meaning reveals itself in time.

This revelation is aided by the full play of ideas. The reason for the protection of "broad and deep rights of expression"[9] is that they are related to the intellectual and spiritual growth over time that lends dignity to the human creature. Citing approvingly Justice Brandeis's dictum in *Whitney v. California* (1927)[10] that the state has no end beyond ensuring the full development of human faculties, Brennan avers that the "demands of human dignity will never cease to evolve."[11] Dignity is not fixed—it has no principles or laws beyond those governing its internal evolutionary dynamic. In fact, the very act of looking for fixed principles or laws is regressive, for in so acting we cast a glance toward a past wherein dignity was, always and everywhere, less developed and more stultified. A corollary of this view is that the scope and power of government—whether state or national— are in principle unlimited, because of the need to support human dignity and the constant development of human faculties. Courts merely adjudicate at the "collision points" between state and society, and they must be on guard against anything that stifles salutary development.[12] The task of judging is therefore itself protean and consists of accurately reading and responding to the constant flux of human aspiration.[13] The Supreme Court has the last word on constitutional interpretation, but the last word for any one time cannot be the last word for all time, or the Constitution "falls captive" to the "anachronistic views of long-gone generations."[14] The Constitution is timeless only because its interpretations are time-bound; its genius lies in its recognition of the inevitability of the "evolutionary process."[15] Adaptation to the "ever-changing conditions of national and international life"[16] is the *sine qua non* of constitutionalism, and the navigational system of this organic process, if not its motor, is the judicial branch.

One of Brennan's colleagues on the Court, the late Justice Thurgood Marshall, also pointedly claimed that the meaning of the Constitution was not fixed in Philadelphia or anywhere else.[17]

The Constitution that emerged from Philadelphia was merely "a product of its times,"[18] as is the Constitution we now have. The changes we have witnessed in our constitutional fabric were not, and could not have been, foreseen or accepted by those who gathered in 1787 to draft the document.[19] The constitutional text itself lies dead in a vault in the National Archives.[20] The views of our own time are all that lives. Constitutional interpretation involves perceiving and clearly articulating the direction of evolutionary change for an organic document that serves the needs of an organic state. Those who possess an insight into History must redefine outdated notions of liberty, justice, and equality. Their aim is to aid a process that is outside the full control of any one individual or institution. The historical process is an immense struggle for survival of the good over the bad, and good fortune is indispensable to a proper unfolding of History.[21]

On some questions, History moves rapidly. It is the job of the wise majority of the Court to recognize its direction and clear the obstacles, which often take the form of state laws, that stand in its way. The rapidity of historical change is illustrated by the difficulty even the Court has in keeping up with it. Certain minority opinions gain majority status in remarkably short periods of time. It took only seventeen years for *Lawrence* to overturn *Bowers v. Hardwick* (1986),[22] in which a 5–4 majority of the Supreme Court upheld a Georgia anti-sodomy statute. According to Justice Kennedy in *Lawrence,* even as *Bowers* was being decided, there was an "emerging recognition" of the substantial liberty of adult persons to choose freely in "matters pertaining to sex." The Court's majority in *Bowers* failed by remaining blind to the stamp of approval that History had already placed on homosexual conduct—but this historical fact was not lost on the *Bowers* dissenters. For example, Justice Harry Blackmun quoted approvingly Oliver Wendell Holmes in condemning a rule of law whose grounds "have vanished long since." Such "blind imitation of the past"[23] is senseless, because the ethical grounds upon which such statutes were based have shifted radically over time. According to Blackmun, in our time, at least, "much of the richness of a relationship will come from the freedom an individual has to *choose* the form and nature" of that relationship. Human personality must be allowed to develop by keeping the state out of the business of restricting "intimate associations." The asserted primacy of freedom of choice thus allows us to define our natures as we see fit, subject only to the requirement of mutual consent. The process of redefinition is, in principle, virtually unlimited. It will continue to unfold as new understandings of human personality manifest themselves in History.

A mere eight years before *Lawrence*, in *Hurley v. Irish-American Gay, Lesbian, and Bisexual Group of Boston* (1995),[24] the Court had held unanimously that a privately organized parade could exclude groups that wished to convey a message contrary to that favored by the parade organization, thus protecting the organization's First Amendment rights. However, just five years later in *Boy Scouts of America v. Dale* (2000),[25] the Court could only muster a slim 5–4 majority for the proposition that an open homosexual did not have a right to join the Boy Scouts as an adult leader because his presence in the organization would convey a message contrary to the one the Boy Scouts wished to convey. What had happened in the intervening five years?[26] The dissent in *Boy Scouts*, penned by Justice John Paul Stevens, gives us some clues. For him, unfavorable views of homosexuals are rooted in ancient prejudices, best likened to the "equally atavistic opinions about certain racial groups" or other opinions "nourished by sectarian doctrine." Only "habit, rather than analysis" grounds the man–woman distinction. Thus does Justice Stevens, in a single paragraph, take on and dismiss both revelation and classical moral reasoning. He goes on, in the same paragraph, to substitute for them History and historical progress, including the findings of social science as revealed in History:

> Over the years . . . interaction with real people, rather
> than mere adherence to traditional ways of thinking
> about members of unfamiliar classes, have modified
> these opinions. A few examples: The American Psychi-
> atric Association's and the American Psychological Asso-
> ciation's removal of "homosexuality" from their lists of
> mental disorders; a move toward greater understanding
> within some religious communities; Justice Blackmun's
> classic opinion in *Bowers;* Georgia's invalidation of the
> statute upheld in *Bowers;* and New Jersey's enactment of
> the provision at issue in this case. Indeed, the past month
> alone has witnessed some remarkable changes in attitudes
> about homosexuals.

Justice Stevens's reasoning, not coincidentally, bears a close resemblance to the reasoning of the unanimous Court in *Brown v. Board of Education* (1954),[27] wherein sociological jurisprudence, in the form of reliance on psychological studies, took the place of constitutional or common-law reasoning. As Chief Justice Earl Warren then wrote, what is true, or at least fashionable, "in these days" is sufficient warrant for the Court to lay down an enduring constitutional principle. This is a sensible course of action if, and only if, History is reliably progressive, steadily revealing new and legally relevant "truths" in time.

A series of "right to die" cases further illustrates the centrality of historical reasoning to some members of the Court. In *Cruzan v. Missouri Department of Health* (1990),[28] the 5–4 majority of the Court held that a competent person has a constitutionally protected Fourteenth Amendment liberty interest in refusing unwanted medical treatment, but that the state of Missouri could require clear and compelling evidence of an incompetent person's wishes concerning the withdrawal of lifesaving medical treatment. Justice Antonin Scalia, in a concurring opinion, would have had the Court stand back from "right to die" questions entirely, for the Constitution is silent on the matter, and indeed it has never been the case that states have been prohibited from interfering with such a purported right, the contours of which "are neither set forth in the Constitution nor known to the nine Justices of this Court any better than they are known to nine people picked at random from the Kansas City telephone directory." But in considering right-to-die cases non-justiciable on constitutional grounds, Scalia was a minority of one.

In *Washington v. Glucksberg* (1997),[29] the Court upheld a Washington state statute that outlawed assisted suicide. In writing for the majority, Chief Justice William Rehnquist noted the cases in which the Court held that the Fourteenth Amendment's due-process clause offers substantive protections of liberty going beyond fair procedure. These have included, among other things, the right to marry, the right to marital privacy, and, in *Casey,* the right to abortion. But Rehnquist also asserted the reluctance of the Court to expand substantive due process to other areas because of the fundamentally political nature of the enterprise, and because of the superiority of legislative debate, experimentation, and compromise to judicially imposed substantive standards. However, in a concurring judgment, Justice David Souter claimed that the experimentation of the legislative process is to be preferred only for the present. "The Court should accordingly stay its hand to allow reasonable legislative consideration. While I do not decide for all time that respondents' claim should not be recognized, I acknowledge the legislative institutional competence as the better one to deal with that claim at this time." For Souter, judicial intervention is not called for until it is. Facts revealed as History unfolds, rather than common-law or constitutional principles, determine the justiciability of fundamental moral-political questions.

Souter offered a similar concurrence in *Vacco v. Quill* (1997),[30] which was heard in conjunction with *Glucksberg.* In *Vacco,* an equal-protection claim was raised against a New York law that allowed competent patients to refuse medical treatment but made it a crime to assist a competent person to commit suicide, including by prescription of lethal medication. The argument in favor of striking down the law alleged that this resulted in different treatment for similarly situated patients, one subset of whom chose suicide by refusal of treatment, the other by ingestion of medication. Justice Rehnquist, for the Court, maintained as rational the distinction between refusal of treatment and assisting with suicide—the former resulting in death from "an underlying fatal disease or pathology," the latter involving the intention on the part of a doctor that "the patient be made dead." In his concurrence, Justice Souter would only say that he did "not conclude that assisted suicide is a fundamental right entitled to recognition at this time." According to Justice Souter's reasoning, for the time being—but only for the time being—the state statutes in *Glucksberg* and *Vacco* are not unconstitutional under either the due-process standard or the equal-protection standard. But History will be the ultimate judge.

The Transformation of American Political Thought

More than any other branch of government, our courts have adopted the historical view of the Constitution and constitutionalism. This view is not simply that we have, of necessity, an interpretable Constitution, but rather one that must be interpreted in light of a particular understanding of the historically situated, contingent nature of the state, the individual, society, and constitutionalism itself. This understanding contradicts an earlier American constitutionalism of limited and dispersed powers serving the "laws of nature and nature's God." As Herman Belz has noted,

> The conception of the constitution as a formal legal instrument or code giving existence to government and

prescribing and limiting the exercise of its powers, rather
than as the basic structure of the polity, not consciously
constructed but growing organically through history, was
one of the distinctive achievements of the American Revolution, and oriented constitutional description and analysis in the early republic toward a legalistic approach.[31]

The modern historical, as opposed to legalistic, approach
has been embraced by the judicial appointees of different presidents from different decades, including both Democrats and
Republicans, "liberals" and "conservatives." A major transformation in American political thought was necessary to bring
such a diverse cast of characters to embrace an organic view of
the Constitution. This transformation is little understood. Legal
historians have preferred to concentrate on legal education or
legal theory narrowly construed, rather than the philosophical
categories that animate thought and action.[32] Political theorists
have, for the most part, not filled the gap. We can only begin
to assess the new constitutionalism—as well as the new science
of jurisprudence that is its handmaiden—by tracing its philosophical origins.[33]

Of course, in tracing philosophical origins it is always difficult to know where and when to begin. The burden of my argument is to show that the proximate causes of the new constitutionalism are social Darwinism and philosophical pragmatism.
Both represent a radical critique of the foundations of the American regime and, indeed, an attack on the Constitution itself.
But, of course, a case can be made—and it is a case I concede—
that these strains of thought were themselves the products of,
or heavily influenced by, other philosophical currents. So some
qualifications are in order.

As social Darwinism borrowed occasionally from its intellectual first cousin, Hegelianism, so pragmatism leaned heavily on utilitarianism. Social Darwinists grafted a philosophy

of history onto a theory of evolution and a science of biology. Likewise, pragmatists coupled a utilitarian calculus with a faith in social experiments to show the true path to growth. William James, one of the fathers of American pragmatism, dedicated his collection of lectures published under the title *Pragmatism* to the great English utilitarian John Stuart Mill.[34] The connection is not insignificant. As Roger Kimball has argued, "Together with Rousseau, Mill supplied nearly all of the arguments and most of the emotional fuel—the texture of sentiment—that have gone into defining the progressive vision of the world."[35] The essence of Mill's philosophy of politics was in many ways experimental inquiry. By this means, he wished to discover which paths are best for human growth and adaptation to an ever-changing environment. Results are observed and assessed, and further experimental inquiry takes place. *On Liberty* argues famously for "experiments in living." Freedom of speech, formerly viewed as a natural right of human beings, becomes in Mill expressive freedom, justified not as something rooted in nature or in ultimate purposes, but in light of its consequences for social development. Challenge, experiment, and struggle validate hypotheses, and broad expressive freedom allows these conflicts to play out, with the "strong" surviving.

In addition, by the early twentieth century American progressives evinced a belief in Weberian bureaucratic rationality—that is, in the desirability of a coterie of "experts" whose job is to guide the ship of state down a river of evolutionary growth. Far from being free-spirited social experimenters, or the unconscious agents of History (as Hegel understood world-historical men), these more ordinary political actors would be trained experts in administrative technique, able to identify and clear logjams in the river. In 1916, leading progressive thinker Herbert Croly, one of the founders of the *New Republic*, idealized a world in which "administrative courts" would engage in work of "positive and formative character," representing the "collective will for the accomplishment of a social program" and thereby being "reasonable," though not "impartial."[36] In Croly's view, common-law courts, so wedded to individual rights, were unlikely to be able to serve social policy; they would exist in parallel beside administrative courts, with which they would occasionally "fight out" their claims according to "liberal public opinion."

The protection of individual rights, according to Croly, will remain a "phase" of social justice for "an indefinite future," but only "as long as such protection is necessary" will common-law courts be able to subject "the more inspiring work" of administrative courts to review.[37] Croly thus seems to anticipate something akin to the earlier merger, in both the United Kingdom and the United States, of courts of equity with courts of common law. For Croly, the merger will be between the extant common-law courts and administrative bodies, or perhaps simply occur via the staffing of the former with expert custodians of "social purpose" and "scientific method."[38] As Croly remarks,

In the past, common-law justice has been appropriately symbolized as a statuesque lady with a bandage over her eyes and a scale in her fair hands. The figurative representation of social justice would be a different kind of woman equipped with a different collection of instruments. Instead of having her eyes blindfolded, she would wear perched upon her nose a most searching and forbidding pair of spectacles, one which combined the vision of a microscope, a telescope, and a photographic camera. Instead of holding scales in her hand, she might perhaps be figured as possessing a much more homely and serviceable set of tools. She would have a hoe with which to cultivate the social garden, a watering-pot with which to refresh it, a barometer with which to measure the pressure of the social air, and the indispensable typewriter and filing cabinet with which to record the behavior of

society. . . . [H]aving within her the heart of a mother and
the passion for taking sides, she has disliked the inhuman
and mechanical task of holding a balance between verbal
weights and measures.[39]

Still, notwithstanding these qualifications, it is fair to say
that the uniquely American expressions of what were essentially
nineteenth-century European ideas came under the rubrics of
social Darwinism and pragmatism. By the late nineteenth century, Darwinism had in many ways begun to dominate American political thought. Transmitted by thinkers such as William
Graham Sumner and Lester Frank Ward, it was being freely
applied to all aspects of social science and philosophy.[40] While
Sumner represented "right" social Darwinism and Ward "left"
social Darwinism, there were deep continuities to their thinking. "Right" social Darwinism has long since withered, but the
"left" or progressive version was quickly assimilated by leading
thinkers and would eventually be applied to social policy and
become a guiding force for twentieth-century jurisprudence.

For several decades, Darwinism was on the move and on the
make. It was understood in one or both of two main senses. It
could be viewed as a rigid evolutionary and biological doctrine
that was directly analogous to the actual process of social development, or it could be conceived more loosely as an exemplar of
a natural scientific method destructive of traditional prejudices, philosophical certitudes, and faith in a divine order.[41] Most
forms of intellectual idealism, and even much religious sentiment, were soon co-opted, even as most ordinary Americans no
doubt clung to their faith in moral and political absolutes.

Over roughly the same time period, pragmatism too was a
growing force in American intellectual life. Even more self-con-
sciously than the Darwinists, the pragmatists had in mind an
undermining of moral and political certitudes. From its founding by Charles Sanders Peirce, to its popularization by William

James, through its development in the hands of John Dewey, pragmatism played off Darwinian concepts as it applied its thoroughgoing philosophical skepticism to all areas of thought. Together with their direct offshoots, social Darwinism and pragmatism had, by the early twentieth century, coalesced into the potent political and intellectual cocktail of progressivism. I refer not to progressivism as it is often taught in history books, i.e., capital-p Progressivism as a political and social movement. Rather, I mean progressivism as an intellectual movement and set of intellectual attachments; more particularly, a complex web of theoretical insights into human nature, history, state, and society. Progressivism so understood is characterized by a set of ideas that have at their core a marked historicism—which is to say, the belief that truth is always and everywhere relative to its time and place. The progressive intellectual synthesis emphasizes evolution, experimentation, pragmatic and instrumental reason, and individualism as the keys to understanding and guiding the inevitable processes of social growth.

Not coincidentally, these emphases are also evident in much contemporary American jurisprudence, beginning with Oliver Wendell Holmes, a boyhood friend of James. Writing in dissent in a 1921 case, Holmes refers to state legislatures as "laboratories" for social experimentation.[42] Just two years earlier, Holmes had argued for the invalidation of federal legislation that he claimed violated the First Amendment—also on the grounds of the importance of experimentation. Indeed, the Constitution itself is "an experiment, as all life is an experiment."[43] The personal-rights revolution in American jurisprudence can thus be said to have commenced well before the 1940s or 1950s, the decades most often associated with it. The jurisprudence on which it depends—deference not to legislative judgments, but to the principle of experimentation in the service of organic growth—traces its roots directly to the progressive (or Darwinian-pragmatic) era of American political thought. Legal scholar and federal judge Richard Posner has recently noted, with considerable sympathy, that Darwin undermined what he calls the orthodox philosophic tradition of Platonism.[44] For him, the central insight of Darwin is the notion of intellect as a method of dealing with adaptation and change, rather than as a vehicle for gaining metaphysical insight. The judicial process, like the evolutionary process, is experimental and pragmatic in its efforts to ensure the triumph of the stronger or, loosely speaking, "best" variants of social, political, and jurisprudential growth. Posner seems to be in full agreement with Franklin Delano Roosevelt's suggestion, made during his 1932 presidential campaign, that the country needs "bold, persistent experimentation."

Despite the efforts of Justice Holmes—notably in his dissent in *Lochner*—to portray the conservative Court of the very early twentieth century as wedded to "right" social Darwinism, there is little evidence that this was the case. It is true that the Supreme Court of that era had moved to alter "the institutional balance of American government. On one front it helped shift power from the states to the nation, and on another front it expanded the power of the federal judiciary over all other branches of government—over state courts and over the legislative and executive branches of both state and nation."[45] Substantive due process, together with the contract and commerce clauses, and, to a lesser extent, the Fourth and Fifth Amendments, provided the vehicles for a forceful reconfiguration of the doctrine of judicial review.[46] However, it is useful to compare Justice David Brewer—who, more than any other single figure, personified the Court's concern with protecting economic rights—with Justice Holmes. Sitting on the Court from 1890 to 1910, Brewer shared with Holmes a deep suspicion of populism, but unlike Holmes he conceived the judge's role in more activist terms when it came to defending property from democratic leveling, and market forces from dangerous political interference. In doing this, he pledged fealty to inalienable rights. Thanks to Holmes, he and the Court he represented are generally seen as sharing many of the assumptions of "right" social Darwinism. But, in fact, Brewer, like most other justices of his day, believed in a providential order of the universe, including fixed and immutable principles of truth beyond human invention, principles that constrained government. He was therefore profoundly at odds with historicist thinking.[47]

· Brewer, in many ways, represented the typical understanding of both the intelligent citizen and the political and jurisprudential leaders of his day. As Mark Warren Bailey has observed, "that the justices apparently possessed an abiding faith in the existence of God and in the tenets of Christianity was unsurprising, in light of their upbringings and religious inclinations. For example, Justice Stephen J. Field and his nephew, Justice David J. Brewer, were both reared in a strict Congregationalist setting. John Marshall Harlan received a thoroughly religious education . . . [as did] Justice William Strong. . . ."[48] Antebellum moral philosophy was uniform and ubiquitous in the colleges,[49] and lawyers and jurists especially imbibed it. Even after *The Origin of Species* was first published in 1859, this philosophy was not rapidly replaced.[50] Brewer was certainly no friend of unbridled capitalism or materialism, which were to him "false gods."[51] In fact, the "predilection for seeing the hand of Providence at work in the natural order and the belief that reason or an innate moral sense was capable of discerning the dictates of natural and absolute justice predisposed educated Americans to accept a system of thought that appeared to explicate and systematize those principles."[52] The old science of jurisprudence was such a system of thought. Ideas, not environmental or material conditions, inspired the conservative thought—including jurisprudence—of the late nineteenth century. The Court's conservatism was no more determined by social conditions or material interests than Holmes's attempts to overcome it, and it was not determined at all by evolutionary categories.

Only cutting-edge thinkers such as Holmes seemed to reject the earlier moral philosophy root and branch, though it was
far from the simple-minded syllogistic thinking he so derided.[53]
Ironically, when Holmes condemned the *Lochner*-era Court for
its alleged reliance on social Darwinist principles, he was the
only social Darwinist on the Court. It was only when substantive due process together with a variety of other judicial doctrines were used for consciously progressive purposes, in the
hands of justices such as Holmes, that they became inextricably
linked to a philosophy of History that continues to leave its mark
on American jurisprudence. One of the reasons why we no longer see this clearly is because the history of the progressive era is
largely progressive history.

Law and Politics in the Progressive Age

Although I am concentrating on intellectual progressivism
and its influence on jurisprudence, it is important to note that
"movement" Progressivism supported the growth of intellectual
progressivism in significant ways. The progressive movement
represented a complex amalgam of labor, farm, consumer,
middle-class, and, to a certain degree, business interests, all
of whom shared the view that the rapid industrialization of
America in the late nineteenth and early twentieth centuries
created problems that only the regulatory state, relying on
administrative expertise, could solve. According to many
progressives, the legislative branch—state or federal—was best
equipped to investigate social problems, collect expert evidence,
design and fund programmatic solutions, and hold accountable
the expert administrators of these programs to the democratic
will. The power of government was to be brought to bear for
the sake of the "little man," and in this sense regulation and
administration were understood to be democratic activities. By
century's turn, various state legislatures had enacted antitrust

laws and were exercising regulatory control over labor matters and transportation—particularly railroad—industries. When Congress passed the Interstate Commerce Act of 1887 and the Sherman Anti-Trust Act of 1890, it signaled the federal government's willingness to ride the progressive wave. As the new century dawned, regulatory efforts on both the state and national levels increased.

So, from the late nineteenth century to 1937 (when the Supreme Court moved in a reliably progressive direction), progressives and populists enjoyed the most leverage in Congress and state legislatures and had to fend off challenges to progressive legislation in the courts—particularly the U.S. Supreme Court, which was then the most "conservative" branch of government. The progressives of that era came rightly to see the federal courts as friends of private property and corporate interests, particularly those operating across state lines. For the early progressives, national and state regulatory authority had to be reasserted against an imperial, and politically tendentious, judiciary. In their eyes, legislatures held the key to effective, efficient reform. A new science of legislation, informed by social-science expertise, was seen as the key to resolving the economic and political problems of the day. Courts, by contrast, were seen as the enemies of reform and, in the words of a young Felix Frankfurter, ignorant of "facts and events"[54] and therefore prone to speculative and counterproductive reasoning. According to Edward Purcell,

> Conservatives portrayed the courts—especially the federal courts—as the institutional embodiment of the ideals of law, reason, and justice. They examined the legislative branch, in contrast, with cold and unforgiving eyes, focusing on every corruption, failing, and flaw. Progressives, conversely, pictured legislatures and their expert administrative agencies relatively abstractly and as they

wished them to be, as authentically popular, problem-solving, and even "scientific" branches of government. They scrutinized the courts, in contrast, with a searing realism that revealed judicial work as ill-informed and socially biased.[55]

In the 1896 presidential election, the political orientation, and activism, of the Supreme Court became an issue for the first time since the election of 1860.[56] As courts—and particularly federal courts—began to intervene to protect property and economic rights (albeit hardly for social Darwinist reasons), the stage was set, for the first time in American history, for a conflict between the legislative and judicial branches (and between legal scholars) on the constitutionality of perceived judicial supremacy. As Clement Vose has noted,

> The Populists of the 1890s and the Progressives in the twentieth century brought into public life a "new morality," not readily accommodated under the police power. The new morality saw capitalist and industrialist, rather than gambler, pimp and bootlegger, as sinning against society. Factory conditions were deplorable, city slums loathsome, housing horrendous, the legal rights of children, women and all workers in dangerous industries virtually nonexistent. A social movement emerged in the 1890s to study these conditions and act against them. The movement was led by not one person but was, rather, an amalgamation of brilliant critics like Lincoln Steffens and Upton Sinclair; dedicated young women like Florence Kelley and Jane Addams; able lawyers like Clarence Darrow and Louis D. Brandeis; and politicians like Robert LaFollette and Hiram Johnson—all innovators creating new social institutions, novel legislation, sophisticated sanctions and inducements and changing conceptions of constitutional law.[57]

Prominent opponents of what was seen as a progressive assault on the independence of the federal judiciary included William Howard Taft, who, as president, advocated narrow procedural reforms over altering the substantive direction of constitutional interpretation.[58] This "middle position" found favor with a growing nonprogressive reform movement within the legal community, a movement with which even progressives could find common ground.

The echoes of this conflict remain very much with us. As the politically conservative—some might say reactionary— courts embraced substantive due process, they were supported by conservative forces elsewhere. The American Bar Association, in particular, consistently opposed progressive reforms. Then as now, the legal community, with the obvious exception of the progressives, tended to view common-law courts as sober and narrow expositors of the law. By contrast, they saw legislatures as partisans of radical social and economic thinking. Lawyers tended to defend the courts as the forums in which political and constitutional reasonableness was most likely to be found—for reasons of expertise, not to mention power and self-interest.

Over the past century, the institutional allegiances of the legal class have not changed, though its politics have. Some sixty-five years before Raoul Berger penned *Government by Judiciary*,[59] attacking the use of the Fourteenth Amendment's equal-protection clause to override democratic legislative authority in order to suit judges' policy preferences, the progressive lawyer Louis B. Boudin wrote an article of the same title that attacked the use of the amendment's due-process clause in service of the same end.[60] By the late twentieth century, limitation of judicial power was a major goal of moral and political conservatives rather than progressive thinkers. Thus, the view of courts and legislatures held by conservatives of the progressive era is the view that today is held by liberals, and the view of these institutions held by the early progressives is today held by conservatives. Since 1937, we have witnessed a perfect role reversal.

The doctrines that account for these shifting allegiances—History, intelligence, evolution, and growth—found particularly fertile ground in the politically unaccountable and intellectually elite body that is the U.S. Supreme Court. While the Court has stopped enforcing "economic" rights, it has often enforced various species of individual or personal "noneconomic" rights since the first progressive justices began hearing cases. For almost a century, the Court has been torn less by a choice over whether or not to exercise self-restraint in judicial review—though as a tactical matter progressives argued for it during the era of economic substantive due process—and more over the nature and scope of the individual rights and substantive values it chooses to enforce. In the name of a newfound judicial "restraint," the post-1937 Roosevelt Court shied away from challenging legislative judgments on economic or commercial matters, but it set the stage for the explosive growth of rights in keeping with "left" or progressive social Darwinism. In light of this consistency, we would do well to remind ourselves of the dangers the judicial branch poses to constitutional forms and republican government, dangers that the Anti-Federalist writer Brutus foresaw so long ago. His warning seems especially apt for an age in which judges are under the spell of a philosophy of History that denies in principle the notion of fixed truth or a morally ordered universe:

> There is no power above them, to controul any of their decisions. There is no authority that can remove them, and they cannot be controuled by the laws of the legislature. In short, they are independent of the people, of the legislature, and of every power under heaven. Men placed in this situation will generally soon feel themselves independent of heaven itself.[61]

2

The Constitution of the Fathers

Brutus's fears were expressed in the context of the ratification debate over the U.S. Constitution. These fears of overweening judicial power were not misplaced. If anything, the concerns Brutus and other Anti-Federalists expressed have been made more pressing in light of a philosophy of History that was unknown to the founding generation, Anti-Federalists included. Before further examining the nature and origins of this philosophy, it is useful to return to the founding moment, and then to the political thought of its most able nineteenth-century interpreter—Abraham Lincoln. We will then be in a position to understand better the breadth and depth of the challenges to the Constitution of the fathers that were unleashed by the intellectual and political climate that followed so quickly on Lincoln's death.

The nature and implications of the American founding, and the Constitution that was its product, are notoriously matters of dispute.[1] Nevertheless, when we examine the founding, two fundamental facts emerge that show the nature of the divergence from founding principles that commenced with the emergence of historical categories. The first is that America's Founders had a principled understanding of natural rights, which were held not to be culturally determined or time-bound or subject to infinite incremental growth, but applicable to all men everywhere and final. The second is that the American Founders saw America also as an outgrowth of inherited or customary understandings, but this historical inheritance reflected a working out of principles that pointed toward ultimate, trans-historical truth. Historical change was not understood by the Founders to be an unending series of evolutionary improvements to principles, institutions, or modes of political life, but as a series of movements toward the principles of constitutional liberty that, once worked out, would fix the ends and constrain the means of government.

Put another way, from the perspective of the Founders, America had a "creedal" or universal side, and a "cultural" or particular side, but the two were expressions of the same truth. America was understood to be rooted in philosophic principle *and* incremental historical development, but neither of these twin roots was seen to be incompatible with a deep rational attachment to, and Judeo-Christian faith in, eternal verities. The creedal understanding of America relied heavily on John Locke's plain teaching, while the cultural understanding relied heavily on America's inheritances from, most broadly, the Judeo-Christian tradition and, more specifically, the English common-law tradition.[2] The American Founders themselves borrowed freely and non-dogmatically from both creedal and cultural sources— from ideas rooted in both principled and historical understandings of the foundations of political life—and so must we if we are to understand these roots.

Creed and Its Critics

The word "creed" derives from the Latin for "belief" (*credo*) and is commonly understood to mean a formal, authoritative statement of doctrine. In the present context, it refers to a philosophic, systematic account of fundamental beliefs or principles that define America, because they are ideas to which Americans look to understand and articulate their purposes as a nation. Used in this sense, we can indeed say that the American experience, especially at the founding—but also since—has in fact been quite principled or creedal. The American creed, by the common assent of supporters and detractors, is most notably expressed in the second paragraph of the Declaration of Independence with the assertion that we "hold these truths to be self-evident, that all men are created equal."

Of course, there have been many disputes over the meaning of this universal formulation of American principles—most notably the Civil War. It is impossible to deny that a creedal or principled interpretation of America was central to the thinking of Abraham Lincoln, and, in some important ways, that triumphed, at least temporarily. For Lincoln, as we will see, Americans are a people—as are *all* people—endowed with certain inalienable natural rights. Natural rights stem from a fact of nature—our being equal human beings. By "equal," we can only mean *politically* equal, not the self-evident falsehood that men are equal in all respects.

But how do we know we are politically equal? We use our reason to observe ourselves and others and come to the rational conclusion that no man is so markedly superior to another, or specifically marked out by God, so as to be entitled to rule without the consent of the ruled. We exist as in-between beings, as neither beasts nor gods. Consent—and therefore the formation of government by social contract—is an inexorable conclusion of an observable fact of nature, independent of all customs, conventions, traditions, and cultures. And indeed, all liberal democratic forms of government recognize, if not explicitly then at least implicitly, the fundamental fact of human equality, for not to recognize it is to argue for another form of government—a non liberal-democratic form.

All this, of course, can be gleaned from Locke's *Second Treatise of Government*.[3] The influence of Lockean ideas is quite evident not only in the Declaration of Independence and Jeffersonian thought, but also in the thinking of most other prominent Founders, representing a wide spectrum of views of the founding era. It is also evident in some sermons of the founding era, in various ratification debates over state constitutions, and in various state constitutional documents.[4]

None of this is to deny that particular grievances, and Christian piety, moved the hearts of Americans during the founding era. But the intellectual coherence for this era is provided by a principled, social contractarian formulation. One way to express this principled formulation is that America was founded as a nation of Lockean natural rights. That America and many of the most prominent Americans have dedicated themselves to this proposition is clear—it remains the eight-hundred-pound gorilla in the living room of American politics. It also remains the central reason why the notion of a living or organic Constitution sits uneasily with so many Americans outside the elite intellectual classes.

We see the powerful influence of this proposition even today. For example, in the context of the war on terrorism, George W. Bush claimed that freedom is not America's gift to the world, but God's gift to all mankind. This might sound like Wilsonian progressivism, but as a statement of principle, duly limited by prudent statesmanship as to what is actually attainable, it is quite compatible with the American creed. In particular, it is compatible with a theory of natural rights that shows that rights exist in nature, the bequest not of a government, but of an omnipotent, just God.[5]

Lockean natural-rights theory was stillborn in Europe, due in no small part to the attacks launched by David Hume, its greatest critic. In America, by contrast, the doctrine lived—albeit it fought for its life at times—through the early twentieth century.

It succumbed (notwithstanding occasional restatements by figures as diverse as Calvin Coolidge, Martin Luther King Jr., Ronald Reagan, and George W. Bush) only to the dogma of historical progress on which rested the combined forces of social Darwinism, pragmatism, twentieth-century progressivism, and modern liberalism. Such longevity is difficult to account for except by recourse to the importance of the creed to the American founding, and the importance of the founding to later Americans.

The natural-rights interpretation of the American founding has many critics on both the left and the right—the left critics owing much to the progressive vision of the necessity of continuous evolution and organic social growth. Common to the left-liberal critiques are several intertwined concerns. Political and economic statists fear natural-rights doctrines because they see them tied up with property (as Locke indeed says they are), and therefore as standing in the way of the growth and flourishing of the administrative state. Multiculturalists attack natural-rights doctrines because natural rights emphasize what is *common* to human beings, as opposed to what divides them, and argue that the commonalities overwhelm the differences. Such an argument—especially if true—deprives multiculturalists of power. Moral skeptics, in alliance with multiculturalists, claim that natural rights do not in fact simply exist, because no morality does. Meanwhile, the atheist strain of left-liberalism will not countenance anything being God-given, much less rights that might stand as principled bulwarks in the path of certain political, economic, and cultural goals.

Some traditionalist conservatives evince other suspicions of natural-rights doctrines. For them, natural-rights language has a revolutionary, universalistic appeal (which they see in the rhetoric of George W. Bush). In this view, universal natural-rights principles applying to all quickly lead away from the preservation of the rights of citizens in actual political communities—to a kind of fervent, radical, French-revolutionary style of politics dedicated to theoretical abstractions. These traditionalists prefer to see America as a continuation of a certain religious inheritance and of Anglo-American traditions and governmental forms. For them, continuities—not discontinuities—are what define the American founding, and therefore America. They see American rights as outgrowths of distinctly British (as opposed to natural) rights. Another, overlapping type of conservative critique—what we might call the "classical republican" variant of conservatism—sees an emphasis on rights, natural or otherwise, as undermining something more important to the maintenance of a decent civil society—*virtue*, and indeed *citizenship*, as opposed to mere aggressive individualism.[6] But from the Founders' point of view, as we shall see, these suspicions are misplaced.

Our Culture as an Intellectual Inheritance

"Culture" is derivative from the Latin *cultura* or *colo*, meaning to care for, refine, grow, or raise up, especially in an agricultural sense. When applied to public questions, culture is commonly understood to have an organic, as opposed to a principled, philosophic, or creedal connotation. Cultural conditions are the soil and fertilizer in which political systems take root and grow and out of which they define themselves with reference to particulars, rather than philosophical universals: *this land* and *this people*, as opposed to *the cosmos*.

The American creed reveals itself in the context of a particular history and culture. Indeed, if we grant that natural rights principles are universal, this by no means implies they can be implemented universally, or even recognized by all. Cultural traditions often cut against the acknowledgment of natural rights. Even in the United States, one can say that constitutional democracy was by no means inevitable. The American Founders thought and acted with great originality and boldness and had broad sympathy for the nascent principles of liberty. But had America not been settled largely by Englishmen, or at least those familiar with the English conception of liberty, it would, without question, have been a very different country. American understandings and institutions simply would not have taken the shape they did, had not the Founders been profoundly influenced by the constitutional history, political philosophy, and common-law doctrines originating in England.

For many of the Founders, the constitutional history of England was the story of the gradual limitation of royal power, from Magna Carta (1215), to the Petition of Right (1628), to the development of the common-law and independent courts, to the "Glorious Revolution" of 1688–89. Of this latter event, Locke's *Second Treatise* gave a theoretical account, arguing that legitimate sovereign power comes only from a compact among the people, acting through parliament, and limiting the prerogatives of the king.[7] By the mid-1760s, this social-compact theory was explicitly influencing many members of the founding generation and was being voiced in the pulpits and in pamphlets. As Henry Steele Commager has argued, what united the Founders—even Jefferson and Hamilton—far outweighed what divided them.[8] Beyond English constitutional history, they were steeped in a uniquely American Enlightenment, which drew on a great wellspring of common ideas and historical events, from classical to modern times. This background was the soil in which a vigorous Whig history took root. In expounding and institutionalizing certain philosophic principles, the Founders relied on a historically situated narrative, that led to their—the American—creed. In other words, natural rights and social-compact theory do not exhaust the Founders' understanding of founding.

The Founders understood well that philosophical premises could inform Americans only because they were made plain in a particular tradition. And the Founders knew yet more: that the *realization* of natural rights happens not in accordance with philosophical reasoning in the here-and-now. Rather, the extent and limits of rights—and obligations—are marked out in time, though nature provides both a floor and a ceiling to legitimate rights claims.

Our Culture as Accretion

We are thus led to another sense of culture. That is, culture or tradition not as an explicit intellectual borrowing and building, but as a more inchoate set of inheritances and the incremental articulations of these inheritances. Here, I am speaking of traditions that are understood, in many cases, pre-rationally. That is, they are understood as things that are given, imbibed, or revealed rather than argued for. They might well have a kind of collective rationality arising from usage and long experience, but they are not understood this way by most people—they are simply accepted. They include traditions that predate Lockean natural-rights liberalism, or anything that directly led to it, and they do not necessarily argue—at least unequivocally—for equality and consent as organizing principles of just societies.

One way to express this cultural or organic formulation is to suggest that America is less a Lockean and more a Humean nation—that is, one that can be understood along the customary lines suggested by David Hume.[9] But even such customary lines do not rely on a philosophy of History, or a sense of inexorable forward locomotion. Hume's claim is simply that man's moral and political senses come not from reason but from sentiment rooted in experience with the moral and political things—with culture. For him, there are few, if any, absolutes or universal principles that can define our loyalties or guide our actions. We rely less on reason than on cultural memory for our sense of the just. Therefore, the act of political founding relies on the fixing of sentiments around certain ideas and political forms rather than on abstract philosophic reasoning—and certainly the maintenance of these forms depends on a unity of sentiment or cultural consensus. Hume notes that people actually understand their allegiances in terms of historical accident rather than rational principles. To hold open the possibility of uprooting habitual ways of thinking and being by recourse to either a principle or a philosophy of History would be radically destabilizing, not only for politics or public morality, but for private morality as well. Government's job is to tame the most destructive passions rather than to inflame them by reliance on abstractions. For a decent politics, spontaneous order is far more crucial than philosophic, or modern scientific, reason.

There is indeed something to be said for the importance of this view to the Founders' thinking. One can find universal, liberal principles embedded throughout the founding, but so can one find genuinely conservative principles. Reason and custom were blended in a set of ideas and institutions that were understood to rely on prescription for their force.

Even the Declaration of Independence pointedly notes that "*Prudence,* indeed, will dictate that Governments *long established* should not be changed for light and transient Causes; and accordingly all *Experience* hath shewn, that Mankind are more disposed to suffer, while Evils are sufferable, than to right themselves by abolishing the Forms to which they are accustomed." (The emphases are mine.) If there be outrage in the Declaration, it comes not from a dangerous attachment to abstractions, but from a set of very particular grievances that are grievous only by comparison. A particular notion of constitutionalism—only later to be written down—is embedded in the Declaration. As James R. Stoner has noted, "The outrage comes from a hidden premise: the English constitutional tradition, or at least the common-law rights and liberties of that tradition, which the Americans claim as their rightful heritage."[10] This is a tradition that contains within it something it has not yet fully achieved, and what it has achieved, it has not yet transferred to America. The Declaration looks forward only because it can look backward.

In *Federalist* 2 we find an argument that veers far from social-compact theory. John Jay claims that "[t]his country and this people seem to have been made for each other, and it appears as if it was the design of Providence that an inheritance so proper and convenient for a band of brethren, united to each other by the strongest ties, should never be split into a number of unsocial, jealous, and alien sovereignties." Here we see a markedly Humean understanding of founding: one that emphasizes culture and deemphasizes reason, or at least suggests that our creed cannot be separated from our culture.

In the constitutional scheme, the Founders attached great importance to the slow development of public sentiments, sometimes uniting for common purposes, other times placing checks on destructive passions. Reason, or high philosophic principle, cannot much aid in this process, which occurs by the coalescing and dividing of public opinion in a large republic that is suspicious of hastily arrived at or shoddily interpreted doctrines and dogmas. This process certainly cannot be promoted through reliance on an elite class of philosopher kings not accountable to public sentiment. The Founders understood, with Plato, that full philosophic wisdom was unlikely to be available, and they certainly did nothing to suggest that it might be found in one or another of the branches of the national government.

We might be created equal, but society naturally articulates itself into interests, opinions, and passions that must be tempered by allowing them to compete for a hold on public attention.[11] Private rights and the public good are promoted not through recourse to high principle, but spontaneously. Destructive impulses are controlled, and collective reason asserts itself, incrementally. In *Federalist* 49, Madison argues against Jefferson's plan to turn constitutional controversies over to the people because of the dangers of agitating popular passions and making constitutional government unlovable. Despite the apparent consonance of Jefferson's plan with the principle of consent, the

Constitution recognizes that all functioning consensual mechanisms require the support of prejudice and habit. And of course, many other particular mechanisms and institutions (such as the Senate) were designed to act as decisive checks on immediate, unreflective popular sovereignty—with the aim, among other things, of preventing radical swings of public mood from affecting public policy. Responsibility to the people can mean long-term responsibility.

Even Jefferson, writing in his *Notes on the State of Virginia* several years before the Constitutional Convention, plainly displayed his view that abstract philosophical doctrines are insufficient to ground a well-functioning government. Speaking of the defects of the Virginia state constitution, he writes, "This constitution was formed when we were new and inexperienced in the science of government. . . . No wonder then that time and trial have discovered very capital defects in it."[12] He goes on to say that "173 despots would surely be as oppressive as one. . . . As little will it avail us that they are chosen by ourselves. An *elective despotism* was not the government we fought for."[13] He clearly states his desire to correct these defects, and he indicates that the rights of man can only be guaranteed through prudent institutional mechanisms.

The Constitution reflects such prudence. As Madison in *Federalist* 9 suggests, there are lessons to be drawn from history, but we have also come to a point where a "new science of politics" can permanently inform our efforts to create just government. Partly by dint of theoretical insight and partly from a careful study of history, we are now in a position to understand and create institutional mechanisms such as the distribution and separation of powers, as well as an extended sphere of politics and society that will prevent concentrated, factional opinions from dominating the whole of the republic. But these are merely means to a fixed end, which is the preservation of the permanent rights of creatures who are made in the image of God. As Madison writes in *Federalist* 10, a well-constructed union must break and control the violence of faction, because even governments based on the principle of consent can fail to protect the rights of citizens. In more contemporary terms, democracies can err, and even majorities can choose to govern against the true, long-term interests of themselves and their political order insofar as they choose to undermine the natural rights of others—which natural rights provide the only possible foundation for consensual government to begin with. Remaining true to the form of popular government while preventing, in the interests of justice, an "overbearing majority" from governing in its sole interest is not an easy task. Hence the need to allow many factions—rooted in the different interests, opinions, and passions of citizens—to check each other.

As Madison makes clear in *Federalist* 51, this competition of factions in the general populace occurs in much the same way that ambition is allowed to counteract ambition when the branches of government check and balance each other. The Constitution creates a system, as Madison writes, wherein the interests of the man are connected to the constitutional rights of the place. The Constitution consciously tries to blend good government and liberty with the republican form, because republicanism alone is not sufficient to guarantee either. Consent, or more democracy, is *not* equivalent to more freedom, from the Founders' point of view. The real purpose of the separation of powers is not just to protect the people from the government, or the branches from each other. It is to moderate the people's claim to rule—including their ability to rule unreasonably—without contradicting that claim.

Earlier, *The Federalist* told its readers that the secret to good representation was size, in the form of the extended sphere. But by *Federalist* 51 it is clear that this must be supplemented by the independent wills of the branches and states. The wills of the various branches and levels of government are ultimately derived from the people but still independent of them in an immediate sense. The argument for the extended sphere in *Federalist* 10 was insufficient because it understated the power of *opinion*. Popular opinions can sweep across even an extended sphere in relatively short order. It is far more difficult for them to sweep quickly across branches of government, each of which has a will of its own. And in the end, according to Publius, government is not only about expressing the will of the people. On the contrary, "Justice is the end of government. It is the end of civil society. It ever has been and ever will be pursued until it be obtained, or until liberty be lost in the pursuit. In a society under the forms of which the stronger faction can readily unite and oppress the weaker, anarchy may as truly be said to reign as in a state of nature, where the weaker individual is not secured against the violence of the stronger." Like Jefferson, the founding Federalists feared elective despotism.

The competitive processes of the extended sphere and the system of separation of powers in large measure rely on the "low" impulses of man, but these impulses are directed always to the preservation of the highest manifestations of human dignity, including the right to continuing consent to government and treatment according to the rules of justice, each of which presupposes that we are beings of a certain kind with rights inherent in our nature. As Publius argued, people of many *interests* could with zeal support the new Constitution and the republic it created precisely because it would be effectually dedicated to the preservation of fixed natural rights in a way that the preexisting confederacy of states was not. The rights of citizens are preserved not through constant recourse to philosophical principle handed down from on high, but from our natures, high and low. As we are understood as beings capable of choice, so we must be allowed to exercise our choice, bearing in mind the natural limits of choice.

And apart from, or rather assumed by, the constitutional framework are all the things the Founders did not change, despite their "new science of politics." The Founders rarely doubted the centrality of the Christian religion and Christian morality to the success of the American experiment. They believed that reason and revelation were true guides to human affairs, and that they pointed in the same direction on questions of natural rights and moral conduct. Despite this comity, George Washington in his Farewell Address makes plain his view that traditional religion, more than philosophy, can reliably instruct and discipline the many.

The English common law, too, was accepted by the Founders, who were steeped in it through their readings of Sir Edward Coke and William Blackstone. In his *Institutes of the Laws of England*, Coke saw the common law as a working out and application of fundamental law in English circumstances. Law emerges slowly, incrementally, but the law of nature—God's law—is always in the background, preceding, grounding, and restricting all human law. Human law grows out of the soil—out of the culture of the nation—as it confronts practical problems, but long experience and the prescriptive wisdom of past generations move the law toward perfection, such that English positive law, rooted in this wisdom, reflects divine reason. Hence the glory of the common law—it confronts problems individually and specifically without excessive reliance on grand-vision theorizing. For Coke, law does not rely on an unrooted "natural" reason that can be used to upend traditional arrangements. Rather, the reason of things reveals itself in the details. For the Founders, the inherent value of the rule of law comes to sight through this deeply conservative understanding of the common law.[14]

By the 1790s, Blackstone's relatively new *Commentaries on the Laws of England* had outstripped Coke as the definitive expositor of common-law principles for the Americans. Blackstone, unlike Coke, concerned himself with modern liberal rights theory and its relationship to the common law. In other words, there is more Enlightenment liberalism in Blackstone, who was writing a century later. The point of political community for Blackstone is to preserve the rights of each individual member, though he does not subscribe to a state of nature theory as does Locke. Blackstone is able to put Lockean and Humean ideas together and weave them into a common-law constitutionalism. In reading Blackstone, the Founders came to see natural rights and social compact as congruent with the common law. As Michael Zuckert has argued, they therefore did not, like the French, feel the need to throw out their ancient legal code, for it was at once both ancient and modern, protecting the rights not only of Englishmen, but of men simply. "Partly because of Blackstone, the Americans could at once think of political society as a rationalist product of a social compact and as an entity shaped and governed by a law built on custom, deriving its authority from its antiquity and 'grown' character."[15]

All these things point to the inherent caution and prudence of the Founders, and their understanding of the necessity of relying, to some degree, on Burkean species wisdom. The Founders intentionally, and sometimes unintentionally, blended and blurred Lockean individualism and Humean traditionalism. At the very end of *The Federalist,* Alexander Hamilton is moved to quote Hume:

> To balance a large state or society . . . on general laws, is a work of so great difficulty that no human genius, however comprehensive, is able, by the mere dint of reason and reflection, to effect it. The judgments of many must unite in the work: Experience must guide their labor: Time must bring it to perfection: And the feeling of inconveniences must correct the mistakes which they inevitably fall into in their first trials and experiments.[16]

But in this blending and blurring, the Founders' belief in eternal truths—either stated abstractly or revealed in history—

never wavered. While truth might be incrementally revealed in history, it was not created in or by History or beholden to it. The truth was indeed "out there," and the Americans' new science of politics, in both its creedal and cultural facets, represented a sustained effort to approximate it.

Not coincidentally, this same task of bringing republican government into line with unchanging principles of natural right confronted America's greatest statesman, Abraham Lincoln, as he attempted to deal with the unfinished business of the founding era. The task discloses a naturally recurring problem for republican forms of government; it is a problem that History can never solve. It might be added that it is certainly not a problem that the judiciary—the least republican branch of government—can solve, partly because it *is* the least republican.

Abraham Lincoln and Natural Rights

The political rhetoric and actions of Lincoln remain among the greatest affirmations that there are such things as natural rights that do not change with time, that the American Constitution is dedicated to preserving them, and that the role of great political actors, while responding to urgent necessities, is to look backward rather than forward.[17] For him, the state is more formal than organic, History is not destined to unfold in a democratic direction, and republican institutions, because of their indissoluble link with the passions, are always in peril. Moral and political regress are as likely as, perhaps more likely than, progress. Furthermore, there are certain fixed principles beyond which progress is impossible. From relatively early in his adult life, through the coming and prosecution of the Civil War, Lincoln exemplified this belief in formal constitutionalism, overlaid with the complementary belief in the necessity of active statesmanship for preserving it, where statesmanship is understood as prudential political activity at the highest level in circumstances where positive law cannot be a comprehensive guide. Sharing with Plato and Aristotle the view that negative regime change is an ever-present possibility, Lincoln was profoundly wary of the very notion of progress. Evolution and growth were not part of his political vocabulary.

In 1863, Lincoln declared that America "was conceived in liberty, and dedicated to the proposition that all men are created equal." This proposition was grounded in the laws of nature and nature's God, and Lincoln understood it to be the central truth of the American political experiment. It was a proposition that unequivocally condemned chattel slavery as illegitimate for his time, and for all time. In the cause of opposing slavery, Lincoln represented the apotheosis of the founding natural rights understanding of the American constitutional order and the political principles it enshrined. Both were, in Lincoln's view, handed down by the Founding Fathers for later generations to preserve.

In Lincoln's interpretation, the theory of individual natural rights, as refracted through the thinking and institutions of the Founders, serves as a brake on demagogic egalitarianism and nihilistic individualism. This is because natural rights are self-limiting. They point to *nature*. One can know what human nature *is*—what type of creature one is referring to when one says "man"—and therefore what is appropriate to this type of creature by nature. This knowledge is necessary to begin, and ultimately to end, the discussion of rights and their concomitant obligations. Rights are things that can be reasoned about. They do not, and cannot, depend on mere will, or tradition, or History, for will is fickle and tradition and history sometimes indefinite—and sometimes simply wrong. For Lincoln, natural rights provide the ground for a manly assertiveness in pursuit of something beyond individual satisfaction.[18]

This is not to say that memory, tradition, and prejudgments do not serve as great aids to attaching later generations' love to the creed of the regime. And even the most strident critics of the

Founders do not accuse them of moral libertinism. The case can be made that the Founders were steeped in the notions of moral limits and virtue, public and private, from their Christian roots and their reading of the classics. But whether Lincoln speaks of rational philosophic doctrines or the deep-seated attachments of the American people, he conceives of them as mutually reinforcing and as things that must not change, come what may. To embrace the Founders truly, we must embrace their sense of the eternal and the sacred.

In Lincoln's day, as in the Founders', liberalism and conservatism were foreign terms. Like the Founders themselves, Lincoln emphasized both universals and particulars within a natural-rights "creed" supported by cultural traditionalism. In other words, his "liberal" universalism was quite unlike the liberalism that would follow, which was based on the doctrine of progress toward an ever more democratic future (which meant eschewing the past), combined with a faith in administrative and scientific expertise to help take us there. The political corollary of this more contemporary understanding of liberal progress is "leadership." And leadership in a positive sense was alien to the old political vocabulary. Lincoln, like the Founders, viewed such a concept with suspicion because of its obvious kinship with demagoguery. Each relies on a relative lack of institutional constraints. For the founding Federalists, "leadership" cannot be respectable after the Constitution is in place. The desire for leaders creates followers, and as Tocqueville so eloquently noted, it is not clear that a nation of followers is capable of self-government. However, Lincoln, like the Founders, did imagine that there would be a place for statesmanship in a republican regime, i.e., for the prudential regime-level activities of great men who could re-ground and "re-found" the nation in its unchanging principles.

Nowhere is Lincoln's conception of the eternal verities and the duty of the statesman to preserve them more comprehensively worked out than in his "Lyceum Address" of 1838.[19] The subject of Lincoln's remarks at the Springfield, Illinois, Lyceum was "the perpetuation of our political institutions." This very title, of course, suggests that American political institutions were in danger, that they are not self-perpetuating. Lincoln claims that the glorious scenes of the Revolution "smothered and rendered inactive" for a time the "jealousy, envy, and avarice, incident to our nature." During the Revolution, destructive impulses were directed outward toward a common enemy, rather than inward toward fellow citizens and the regime itself. While the revolutionary generation persisted, "a *living history* was to be found in every family," marked by the scars of battle, and readily understandable to all. "But *those* histories are gone. They *can* be read no more forever. They were a fortress of strength; but, what invading foemen could *never do,* the silent artillery of time *has done.*" The fall of a republican people from grace comes gradually, not precipitously; it comes not from an act, but from a slow loss of collective memory.

Passion, in Lincoln's view, cannot be an enduring friend to decent politics. At best, it can be an aid to such politics only in fleeting moments. "Reason, cold, calculating, unimpassioned reason, must furnish all the materials for our future support and defence. Let those materials be moulded into a *general intelligence, sound morality* and, in particular, *a reverence for the constitution and laws.*" But such a reason does not take hold unless citizens are acculturated in a certain way. The Founders' new science of politics is thus as much a science of statesmanship as it is of machinery. The effort required to save the republic cannot be reduced to a mechanistic pursuit of self-interest among citizens and leaders, wherein the passions check and cancel each other automatically. In fact, one might say that no governmental structure, however cleverly crafted, can sustain a regime indefinitely. Ultimately, instruction in the unchanging principles of the regime, and statesmanship aimed at guiding the regime back to those principles, are needed.

Lincoln speaks first of the dangers he apprehends from the lowest political manifestation of human passions—the passions of the mob. In their wild, unrestrained quest for justice, mobs could satisfy their passions as they saw fit and get away with it. And inevitably, the mob confuses its passion with what is politically right. America of the 1830s suffered from the confusion of passion with right, due directly to the all-too-human tendency to assume that what one desires one has a right to. In a regime that forgets the permanent limitations of justice, individuals fall back on claims that their "rights"—reduced to desires or concerns—must be satisfied. While the pursuit of individual self-interest might, in gentler times, lead to apathy, in Lincoln's time it led to mob rule. This is a natural development, according to Lincoln, in the absence of a continuing moral-political education. In a manner reminiscent of Plato, Lincoln reminds us that without reverence for law, we no longer have citizens or politics. Instead, we have individuals engaged in rational-choice analysis, which can lead to mob violence. It might equally lead to an attenuated society in which nobody is ever willing to sacrifice.

As the Founders themselves faded into memory, so, Lincoln claims, has the memory of their sacrifices faded, and with it the most salutary patriotic checks on the popular passions. When the mob substitutes its judgment for the sober judgment of deliberative institutions, not only are the innocent subject to the most horrendous injustices, but "the lawless in spirit are encouraged to become lawless in practice," and good men "become tired of, and disgusted with, a Government that offers them no protection." The "mobocratic spirit" thus breaks down the "strongest bulwark of any Government . . . the *attachment* of the people."

Echoing the same themes as so many of the Founders, Lincoln argues that something more than reason is needed to attach a people firmly to a republican regime. He proposes a "political religion" for the nation, whereby every American would "swear by the blood of the Revolution" never to violate the laws. Rever-

ence for the laws—including America's constitutional forms—
must constantly be reinforced to everyone, from the "lisping
babe" to the legislator and judge. Going beyond the signers of
the Declaration, Lincoln declares that *every* American must
"pledge his life, his property, and his sacred honor." Life can and
must be risked for the sake of a ruling principle. This proposition would be quite unintelligible to a model of politics based on
self-interest, personal growth, or individual freedom alone. That
natural or human rights must be maintained by recourse to a
political religion, requiring continuing sacrifice upon its altars,
is a way of saying that reason needs to be maintained by faith.
Far from being an oxymoron, this understanding is consistent
with the conservatism of the Founders in their desire to fix the
prejudices—literally, the prejudgments—of citizens to the Constitution. Put another way, regimes need the prejudices of the
community on their side.

To those who would maintain that politics must not rely on
a trans-historical conception of the greatest human goods, Lincoln suggests that the lack of such a conception results in chaos.
A society cannot be maintained if it is dedicated to ignorance
about the good for man *qua* man, or if this good is understood
by the many to depend on their preferences or the place of the
regime in History. At the broadest level, if we define political
right not in accordance with a nature that transcends and limits
human choice, but rather in accordance with the satisfaction of
passions, we run into the problem of immediate gratification.[20]
If individuals are taught not to control passion, or to elevate unlimited freedom of choice, then there is no incentive to postpone
gratification, assuming that unjust actions in pursuit of such
gratification can be gotten away with. The ethic of gratification
of passion is ultimately contradictory; it cannot sustain political
order. Self-interest logically collapses into self-indulgence. The
self-interested passions exist everywhere, in all regimes, as *The
Federalist* rightly notes, so people must be taught to attach their

passions to the public interest. According to Lincoln, an individualist analysis of human life is incompatible with the perpetuation of political institutions, even in—perhaps especially in—a republican regime. But for any regime, love must overcome fear, and stasis must undergird all incremental change.

For Lincoln, blood sacrifice is part of the primal bond of the nation. Everyone must at least *imagine* himself a descendant of those who fought in 1776 for the Declaration. Lincoln's dark reflections on the reality of mob rule turn out to be arguments for the control of passion through faith, which supports the timeless reason of American constitutional forms. Lincoln's political religion thus cuts across the church–state and public–private distinctions that were to become so central to American political life in the twentieth century. He argues for a political orthodoxy that is incompatible with a self-interested model of politics.

In his "Temperance Address" of 1842,[21] Lincoln again calls for reason over passion, and also for faith in and reverence for the Constitution and laws and those who embody them. "Washington is the mightiest name on earth—*long since* mightiest in the cause of civil liberty; *still* mightiest in moral reformation. On that name, an eulogy is expected. It cannot be. To add brightness to the sun, or glory to the name of Washington, is alike impossible. Let none attempt it. In solemn awe pronounce the name, and in its naked deathless splendor, leave it shining on." In his deep reverence for things past, and in his attempt to reorient public opinions and passions around the constitutional forms of yesterday, Lincoln of course argues that such things and such forms are not artifacts of a dead past whose meaning must evolve according to the dictates of History.

Lincoln's civil or political religion is far from idolatry. It in fact serves as a supplement to revealed religion, for it is aimed at illuminating the moral and political things that do not change. Lincoln can apply categories of reason and faith in his discussion of civil religion precisely because the citizens to whom he

speaks are so steeped in these categories. Whatever their devia-
tions from the spirit and letter of the founding moment, they
have been formed by that moment and cannot shake its hold on
their reason or emotions.

As we have seen, the call for civil religion first appears as an
attempt to control passions manifesting themselves in the form
of mobocratic rule. But Lincoln points to a yet greater danger
to popular government. There is a more deadly manifestation
of the view that politics can be reduced to transient passions,
opinions, or interests. If we so lower our political horizons, we
not only fail to check the passions of the many, but we also fail
to take sufficient account of the passions of the few—those especially talented and ambitious individuals who exist in most
regimes and belong to "the family of the lion and the tribe of the
eagle." Viewed from above as well as below, regimes, and perhaps
especially republican regimes, are always in peril. The argument
for self-interest will lead some to demand that their *will* become
law. These are individuals who will not bow before someone
else's religion, because they wish to be gods themselves. As the
threat from the mob came from below, so this threat comes from
above. These "lions" and "eagles" feed on the lesser animals in a
reflection of natural hierarchy. The implication is that the rule of
such individuals is by natural right, unlike the rule of the mob.
Towering genius "thirsts and burns for distinction; and, if possible, it will have it, whether at the expense of emancipating slaves,
or enslaving freemen." Here we see the tension between Lincoln's
belief in formal equality and his dark reflection on the qualita-
tive difference between certain rulers and the ruled.

The reduction of politics to passion or self-interest cannot
solve the problem of a Caesar figure who cannot stand being
treated as an equal. He is always a potential tyrant. Indeed he
might well mask his tyranny with the cloak of republican politics until he can subvert the republic. To reduce the threat from
above, the greatest and most ambitious minds must find a role

in the renewal of the republic rather than in its subversion. They must reconcile their greatness with the doctrine of human equality. They must use their powers and ambition to create, through statesmanship, space for a new birth of freedom.

Lincoln tells us that we must never forget the role of magnanimous men in history. Republican government is no machine, and it is not moving in a reliably progressive direction. The abilities of a Caesar must be placed in the service of republican principles if those principles are to survive, but it is in those principles that Lincoln finds righteousness, not in Caesarism itself.[22] A political savior must needs come for a people who have exhausted their political religion and who cannot themselves save their republic. With acts of statesmanship in turn comes a reinvigoration of that political religion for future generations, with the statesman joining the pantheon of the republic's civic gods. There is therefore a deep symbiotic relationship between democracy, or republicanism, and statesmanship.

The experiment in republican government is never fully successful because it is never over. As Lincoln argued in his 1854 speech on the Kansas-Nebraska Act,[23]

> Our republican robe is soiled, and trailed in the dust. Let us repurify it. Let us turn and wash it white, in the spirit, if not the blood, of the Revolution. Let us turn slavery from its claims of "moral right." . . . Let us return it to the position our fathers gave it; and there let it rest in peace. Let us re-adopt the Declaration of Independence, and with it, the practices, and policy, which harmonize with it.

Each generation must be re-familiarized with the eternal truths on which republican government rests, but also with the memory of great men and deeds past. Its members must be taught how to be *citizens* again, whereas mere individualism requires no education. This intellectual and moral education can never be stinted, for true progress—toward the full realization of republican ideas—requires regular glances backward. The desire to be as gods, whether on the part of the people or statesmen, requires for its check an even greater desire to revere the rational principles on which republicanism is founded. But such desire cannot come from reason alone, for reverence always transcends the reasons for it.

In the Gettysburg Address,[24] Lincoln dedicates the nation to "a new birth of freedom" and issues another call for a civil religion thus revealing his continued reverence for "our fathers" who had brought forth the nation four score and seven years ago. He invokes a community defined by a special mission, conceived in liberty, and dedicated to a proposition. His reverence for the "fathers" indeed seems to give them a moral authority over us the living—an authority that limits consent and individual rights. Gettysburg is the final resting place for those who were moved not only by a formal principle of equality, but who "gave their lives that that nation might live." They dedicated themselves to something beyond equality, and beyond even survival.

In speaking of this "new birth of freedom," Lincoln does not suggest that the founding be transcended, but rather that it be completed. He does not exhibit a suspicion of founders, which suspicion is characteristic of modern liberalism and social contract theory. Social-contractarian man could not have undertaken such a thing as the Civil War; such an undertaking requires eyes that have seen glories beyond contractarian formulations. For Lincoln, the Founders are worthy of respect, and command obedience, precisely because such respect and obedience cement the attachments of the people to the regime that the Founders created, and that subsequent generations merely inherited. The Founders are first among equals because human beings crave not only formal equality, but also models of greatness for emulation. It is through collective memory that citizens are reminded of the limits of equality, and it is through this that their passions are molded to serve the common good. Lincoln thus exhibits deep sympathies for both the "creedal" and "cultural" facets of the founding.

Statesmanship, by its nature, knows no method in the strict sense of rules or doctrines. Persuasion, as Lincoln implies in the Temperance Address, forms a part of the statesman's art. But the *sine qua non* of the statesman is prerogative—or actions that cannot, by definition, be bound by rules. Clearly, there is much about Lincolnian statesmanship that would have troubled many in the founding generation, particularly the Anti-Federalists, who saw government first and foremost as the province of the ordinary man—of formally and substantively equal citizens. But Lincolnian statesmanship does betray a certain kinship to the Federalist view, which emphasized a government partly divorced from the people precisely in order to allow greater men to rule. The extent to which this was actively contemplated by many Federalists is obscured by their intentional deemphasis, in the interests of getting the Constitution ratified, of the necessity for statesmanship. Such indirection was a dictate of prudence in an age deeply suspicious of centralized and potentially demagogic power. How, after all, does one tell the difference in the secular world between a savior and a devil, a statesman and a demagogue? By what criteria might one distinguish those bent on saving republican government from those bent on destroying it? Both have talent and ambition. Ultimately, an unchanging criterion of political right is needed. The statesman is he who argues correctly what the law *is* and plausibly as to how he will uphold it. This, of course, raises the problem of interpreting whose argument is right, and whether the person making it can be taken seriously. And this problem is not formally soluble. But a people who live in the shadow of a bygone age of greatness, and who have not completely stepped outside that shadow, enjoy the greatest odds of remaining true to their principles, with the free gift of statesmanship to aid them.

Natural Rights and Common-Law Constitutionalism

In his oration on the occasion of the Fourth of July 1852, the former slave and great abolitionist Frederick Douglass praised the "solid manhood" of the fathers of the Constitution, who "seized upon eternal principles" to create a "glorious liberty document," that contained not "a single pro-slavery clause" on its "plain reading."[25] Just five years later, the U.S. Supreme Court handed down what was, and remains by wide acclamation, one of the worst decisions in its history. In *Dred Scott* (1857),[26] the Court's majority notoriously held slaves to be property.

It is a decision that should stand as a reminder of the limits and dangers of a politicized judging that would aim to move the nation in a direction that it has not chosen to move. Yet it seldom reminds us of this. Instead, because of the progressive desire to utilize courts in the service of social change, we are constantly reminded not of *Dred Scott* but of *Marbury v. Madison,* in which Chief Justice Marshall allegedly framed a broad power of judicial review of legislation. But as Robert Lowry Clinton has argued, *Marbury* established no such thing and was not cited as providing authority for such a power for most of its history:

> In essence, *Marbury* has become a myth—one which, like Plato's noble lie, imparts the flavor of time-honored truth to what is really a modern idea of judicial guardianship. Consider the significance of a mythology which enables a small group of fallible persons to impose policies on others to whom they are politically unaccountable; or entertain for a moment the discard of the myth, leaving modern judicial review grounded on what would be its primary progenitor were it not for *Marbury*'s existence: *Dred Scott v. Sandford,* the first case in which the Supreme Court set aside a national law on substantive policy grounds alone.[27]

It is the mythical *Marbury* that was accepted by a number of prominent early progressives,[28] and is accepted by virtually all progressive thinkers today. An activist Supreme Court, relying on substantive due process, is now essential to the progressive agenda. The theories that justify such activism are largely incompatible with constitutional principles or constitutional statesmanship as the Founders and Lincoln conceived them.

Dred Scott was the first time that the Court "invalidated national legislation in a case unequivocally not of a judiciary nature."[29] That courts might occasionally make decisions as dreadful as this should not be surprising in light of the fallibility of human nature. What does appear surprising, from the perspective of the twentieth and twenty-first centuries, is the vehemence of the reaction against the decision and the principled critique of it offered by someone who would soon become president. Chief Justice Roger Taney's decision held, among other things, that slaves were property and that a federal government of enumerated powers could not override this property interest in areas under its jurisdiction. The judgment had the effect of repealing the Missouri Compromise and preempting federal legislation aimed at stopping the spread of slavery. For Lincoln, the equal natural rights embraced at the founding made slavery in principle illegitimate, but in practice the Founders had no power to eliminate it. The right did not change with time, but the means to enforce it could and would. The means to fixed ends are always subject to prudential deliberations which occur in the arena of practical politics. The existence of natural rights is not put into question by the fact that they cannot immediately be realized. As Lincoln argued in his speech on *Dred Scott*,[30] the authors of the Declaration of Independence

> did not mean to assert the obvious untruth, that all were then actually enjoying that equality, nor yet, that they were about to confer it immediately upon them. In fact,

they had no power to confer such a boon. They meant simply to declare the right, so that the enforcement of it might follow as fast as circumstances should permit. They meant to set up a standard maxim for free society, which should be familiar to all, and revered by all; constantly looked to, constantly labored for, and even though never perfectly attained, constantly approximated. . . . They knew the proneness of prosperity to breed tyrants, and they meant when such should re-appear in this fair land and commence their vocation they should find left for them at least one hard nut to crack.

In his withering attack on the *Dred Scott* decision, Lincoln indicates that he will offer no resistance to it but puts into radical question its value as precedent. He notes that "[j]udicial decisions are of greater or less authority as precedents, according to circumstances. That this should be so, accords with both common sense, and the customary understanding of the legal profession." He then goes on to set down a remarkable list of qualifications on the precedential value of judicial decisions:

If this important decision had been made by the unanimous concurrence of the judges, and without any apparent partisan bias, and in accordance with legal public expectation, and with the steady practice of the departments throughout our history, and had been in no part, based on assumed historical facts which are not really true; or, if wanting in some of these, it had been before the court more than once, and had there been affirmed and re-affirmed through a course of years, it then might be, perhaps would be, factious, nay, even revolutionary, to not acquiesce in it as a precedent.

But when, as it is true we find it wanting in all these claims to the public confidence, it is not resistance, it is not

factious, it is not even disrespectful, to treat it as not having
yet quite established a settled doctrine for the country. . . .

In the depth of his moral and constitutional reasoning, Lincoln was certainly a prodigy among presidents. But in the act simply of interpreting the meaning of the Constitution, and of necessity staking out the limits of the Supreme Court's authority in this regard, Lincoln was not doing anything out of the ordinary:

> Before the Civil War all three branches of the federal government . . . interpreted the Constitution. The great debates in Congress were over the meaning of important constitutional provisions. The antebellum congressional record is filled with speeches asserting the legislators' duty to interpret the Constitution rightly and in accordance with accepted canons of construction. In the 1790s, debates in Congress on the meaning of key provisions in Articles I, II, and II shaped the contours of the federal government for a century-and-a-half. At the same time, early presidential vetoes of congressional acts were exercised almost solely on constitutional grounds. . . .[31]

It was not until decades later that, to paraphrase Woodrow Wilson, the machinery of government would be considered so delicate, and so in need of rarefied expertise, that no rustics—whether in the form of public opinion or conceived as the political branches of government—could be entrusted with its care. The new disdain for constitutional politics would be integrally linked with a philosophy of History that would come to justify unbridled judicial power. This philosophy would make the aberration that was *Dred Scott* the norm. At the same time, it would delegitimize Lincoln's arguments against judicial power freed from constitutional constraint.

For the Lincoln Republicans, the drawing of the sword and the national fratricide that went along with it was the price ultimately worth paying for the preservation of the constitutional order as they understood it, which involved a re-grounding in unchanging principles. The attainment of power was important for particular constitutional ends, and its exercise was thus limited. Political power was not something to be used for its own sake, or for ever-evolving purposes. In claiming that slavery cannot be neither good nor bad—it has to be one or the other—Lincoln and the Republicans joined an "absolutist" morality to politics.

There is no "science of politics," new or old, that can give a mechanical answer to the question of what constitutes statesmanship. Any answer must come out of the deepest moral and regime analysis, which Lincoln himself undertook. Lincoln reminds us that there can be no binding "legal" rules untethered from unchanging principles of right. At the highest level of statesmanship, the argument is precisely over what the law is—but not over the fact that there is law. Furthermore, once the law is determined, whether it is to be applied categorically must be dictated by prudence, taking account of the full range of experience and practical possibilities. The political science of Aristotle, *The Federalist,* and Lincoln recognized this fact and did not look for a formal solution to these problems or to the problem that people will sometimes fight when they disagree. In the 1850s and '60s, statesmanship was a necessity for justice, i.e., to bring consent and majority rule back into line with equal natural rights. Lincoln in effect maintained a deep sympathy with the sentiments expressed by Edmund Burke when he claimed, "The effect of liberty to individuals is, that they may do what they please: we ought to see what it will please them to do, before we risk congratulations."

3

The Social Darwinist Moment

In the America of the late nineteenth century, the old understanding of the nature and permanent limits of politics was dead or dying. The death of this understanding was necessarily linked to a reevaluation and reconfiguration of the American Founders' political categories and their conception of the regime they had created. The death was hastened, and arguably caused, by the arrival on the intellectual scene of the various doctrines and philosophic assumptions commonly (though only subsequently) associated with the phrase "social Darwinism." The time was ripe for such a movement. Social Darwinism began to dominate American thinking just as transcendentalism was on the wane, but before pragmatism and another form of historicism, this one linked to Hegelian idealism, had fully matured.[1] Hegelianism would indeed prove to be a first cousin, or perhaps even an alter ego, to social Darwinism by the early twentieth century.

Richard Hofstadter has claimed that, in the three decades after the Civil War, almost every American thinker of first or second rank had to confront social Darwinism.[2] "In some respects the United States during the last three decades of the nineteenth and at the beginning of the twentieth century was *the*

55

Darwinian country."[3] For example, Princeton's James McCosh made a bow to evolution or the "development hypothesis"[4] in his *Christianity and Positivism* in 1871. "By the 1880s, the lines of argument that would be taken in the reconciliation of science and religion had become clear. Religion had been forced to share its traditional authority with science, and American thought had been greatly secularized."[5] This secularization was reflected in the Social Gospel movement, whose leaders shared a basic belief "in an inevitable progress toward a better order on earth—the Kingdom of God," which belief was "fortified by evolutionary dogma."[6] Historically, social Darwinism first stormed the universities, then churches, where "evolution won its chief victories among the intellectually alert members of the more liberal Protestant denominations."[7] As Herbert Hovenkamp has noted,

> Only a few ideas in intellectual history have been so powerful and captivating that they have overflowed the brim of the discipline from which they came and spilled over into everything else. The theory of evolution is unquestionably one of these. In fact, evolution was an idea so powerful that it seemed obvious when Charles Darwin offered it. After all, there were prominent evolutionists a century before Darwin. Charles Darwin merely presented a model that made the theory plausible. It was a model, though, that infected everything, and one that appeared to answer every question worth asking, no matter what the subject.[8]

The model of natural selection was seen as an all-purpose explanatory tool that could put the human sciences, especially politics and jurisprudence, on a parallel track with modern natural science.

On the foundation laid by the social Darwinists and those in allied philosophical movements, many of the most influential

American political thinkers and actors through the twentieth century came to share six core, overlapping understandings of the nature of politics and constitutional government.

First, that there are no fixed or eternal principles that govern, or ought to govern, the politics of a decent regime. Old political categories are just that, and Lincoln's understanding of the Founders' Constitution, to the extent it is worthy of any consideration at all, is a quaint anachronism.

Second, that the state and its component parts are organic, each involved in a struggle for never-ending growth. Contrary to the Platonic ideal of stasis, and contrary, too, to the Aristotelian notion of natural movement toward particular ends, the new organic view of politics suggests that movement itself is the key to survival and what can perhaps loosely be termed the political "good."

Third, that democratic openness and experimentalism, especially in the expressive realm, are necessary to ensure vigorous growth—they are the fertilizer of the organic state. Such experimentalism implies a particular sort of consequentialism or utilitarianism when judging institutions and laws.

Fourth, that the state and its component parts exist only in History, understood as an inexorable process, rather than as a mere record of events.

Fifth, that some individuals stand outside this process and must, like captains of a great ship, periodically adjust the position of this ship in the river of History—to ensure that it continues to move forward, rather than run aground and stagnate. Politics demands an elite class possessed of intelligence as a method, or reason directed to instrumental matters rather than fixed truth. This elite class springs into action to clear blockages in the path of historical progress, whether in the form of anachronistic institutions, laws, or ideas. These blockages will form in the path of the ship of state when openness or experimentalism proves inadequate.

Sixth, and a direct corollary to the strong historicism just mentioned, that moral-political truth or rightness of action is always relative to one's moment in History, or the exact place of the ship in the river of time.

According to the social Darwinists and those who would follow in their footsteps, a new social science was indebted to Darwin, whose organic, genetic, and experimental logic could be brought to bear on an array of human problems heretofore considered insoluble, or at least perennial. Darwin comes to be understood less as a biologist and more as a political philosopher or political scientist rejecting old modes and orders. No one more clearly explicates the nature of this new science than John Dewey in a short essay titled "The Influence of Darwinism on Philosophy."[9] Writing in 1909, he effectively summarized the intellectual tenor of his times. Dewey here gives an account of the origins of an already regnant pattern of American social and political thought.[10]

As Dewey avers, the publication of *The Origin of Species* marked a revolution not only in the natural sciences, but in the human sciences as well, which can continue in their old form only because of habit and prejudice. To speak of an "origin" of species is itself a revolution in thought, implying that the organic sciences as well as the inorganic are defined by change rather than stasis. "The influence of Darwin upon philosophy resides in his having conquered the phenomena of life for the principle of transition, and thereby freed the new logic for application to mind and morals and life." Darwin, more than anyone else, allows us to move from old questions that have lost their vital appeal to our perceived interests and needs. We do not solve old questions, according to Dewey,

> we get over them. Old questions are solved by disappearing, evaporating, while new questions corresponding to the changed attitude of endeavor and preference take

their place. Doubtless the greatest dissolvent in contemporary thought of old questions, the greatest precipitant
of new methods, new intentions, new problems, is the one
effected by the scientific revolution that found its climax
in the "Origin of Species."

Dewey's Darwin lays hands "upon the sacred ark of perma-
nency" that had governed our understanding of human beings.
Darwin challenges the most sacred cow in the Western tradition, one that had been handed down from the Greeks: the belief
in the "superiority of the fixed and final," including "the forms
that had been regarded as types of fixity and perfection." The
Greeks dilated on the characteristic traits of creatures, attaching
the word species to them. As they manifested themselves in a
completed form or final cause, these species repeatedly exhibited uniform structure and function, to the point where they were
viewed as unchanging in their essential being. All changes were
therefore held "within the metes and bounds of fixed truth."[11]
Nature as a whole came to be viewed as "a progressive realization of purpose." The Greeks then propounded ethical systems
based on purposiveness.

Henceforth, however, "genetic" and "experimental" processes and methods can guide our inquiries into the human
things. In fact, on Darwinian terms, change is of the essence of
the good, which is identified with organic adaptation, survival, and growth. With maximally experimental social arrangements, change in useless directions can quickly be converted
into change in useful directions. The goal of philosophy is no
longer to search after absolute origins or ends, but rather to find
the processes that generate them.[12] What materially is becomes
more important than what ought to be because only the former
can be an object of the new empirical science. In the absence of
fixity, morals, politics, and religion are subject to radical rene-
gotiation and transformation. Essences are no longer the highest

object of inquiry, or indeed an object of inquiry at all. Rather, science concentrates on particular changes and their relationship to particular salutary purposes, which depend on "intelligent administration of existent conditions."[13] Philosophy is reduced from the "wholesale" to the retail level.[14] Through this emphasis on the administration of concrete conditions, Dewey claims that responsibility is introduced into philosophy. Instead of concentrating on metaphysics, or even politics in the full Aristotelian sense, we are in effect freed to concentrate on policy—or, in Dewey's language, "the things that specifically concern us." The implications of this understanding proved to be sweeping:

> Dewey's equation of philosophical absolutism with political authoritarianism proved the linchpin of the developing relativist theory of democracy because it provided the one basis on which most American intellectuals could unite. It was grounded on a thorough naturalism; it required acceptance of no specific ethical theory or philosophical system; and, best of all, it claimed that rational and religious absolutism was the real enemy of democracy. In short the absolutist-authoritarian equation appealed to all of the intellectual and emotional convictions of a great number of American scholars and at the same time allowed them to defend both naturalism and democracy by aligning their absolutist critics with European totalitarianism.[15]

Darwin broke down the last barriers between the scientific method and reconstruction in philosophy—and the human sciences generally—by overcoming the view that the human sciences are different from the physical sciences and therefore require a different approach. This is contrary to Aristotle's understanding that different methods of inquiry are required for

different kinds of beings—there is no single scientific or philosophic mode of inquiry that applies across the board. For Aristotle, philosophy or science is the human striving after wisdom
or knowledge. It seeks an understanding of the *highest* things
through an examination of *all* things, according to methods appropriate to each.

One way to understand Dewey's enterprise is to view it as
an attempt to reintegrate science and philosophy, which had
been torn asunder by modernity. While Dewey seeks their re-
integration, he does so on uniquely modern terms—philosophy
is *reduced* to empirical, naturalistic science—the process without the ends, or essences, or highest things.[16] We can therefore
reduce human sciences, including politics, to relatively simple
principles, contrary to the Aristotelian or ancient view, which
held that politics is much *harder* than physics precisely because
one must take into account unpredictable behavior, and choice-
worthy, purposive behavior toward *complex* ends—rather than
more predictable motions and processes toward simple ends.
The human sciences, which at the highest level involve statesmanship, are, for Aristotle, more complex than the physical and
rely on practical experiential wisdom as well as theoretical wisdom.[17] By contrast, for Dewey and his generation, Darwinism
seemed to break down the barriers between the human and the
nonhuman.

Dewey's elucidation of the utility of Darwinism for social
science and the new philosophy of man abstracts from the
thought of a number of the major social Darwinist thinkers,
including William Graham Sumner, Lester Frank Ward, and
W. E. B. DuBois. Together with Dewey, these men provided
many of the intellectual categories of their age. And these categories continue to exert a powerful control over political and
jurisprudential discourse to the present day. Collectively, they
point to a view of society as an organism that, constantly in the
throes of change, must grow or die. For the social Darwinists, to

look backward—whether to founding principles or to any other fixed or otherwise obsolete standard of political right—inevitably reflects a death wish. While to some degree borrowing Hegelian historical categories, American social Darwinism shares no rational end point with Hegelianism. Change in itself becomes the end, and it is always preferable to its opposite.

Darwinisms Right and Left

Of the American "right" social Darwinists, the most influential was Yale sociologist William Graham Sumner. His staunch defense of laissez-faire economic policies is often seen as the intellectual backdrop to the era of substantive due process and the vigorous defense, politically and judicially, of property rights. In fact, as I have mentioned, the Supreme Court justices most closely associated with what has become known as "*Lochner* era" jurisprudence were not, in any meaningful sense, Sumnerians or social Darwinists. Ironically, it was the Court's greatest critic of the *Lochner* case—Oliver Wendell Holmes—who was. The influence of Herbert Spencer and Charles Darwin on Holmes commenced while he was an undergraduate and strengthened over time.[18] However, intellectual influences are sometimes hard to spot, even by those they affect the most. The relationship between Holmes and Sumnerian social Darwinism (and between other progressive justices and other strains of Darwinism) becomes apparent when we recognize that Sumner's economic prescriptions were never divorced from his overall conceptions of science and philosophy. It is these conceptions which were shared by progressive justices such as Holmes, as well as by Brandeis and other "left" social Darwinists whose preferences, at the policy level, merged with movement progressivism.

In some ways, Sumner was the great synthesizer of three lines of thought: the idea of Protestant ethic, classical economics, and Darwinian natural selection.[19] In Richard Hofstadter's words, "we may wonder whether, in the entire history of thought, there was ever a conservatism so utterly progressive as this."[20] Following Darwin back through Herbert Spencer to Malthus, Sumner saw human beings competing for control of a finite amount of land resources. A particular conception of nature and natural right was at the heart of Spencer's thinking, albeit a conception that would have been alien to natural rights thinkers of the previous century. Spencer's insight, stimulated by Malthus's *Essay on the Principle of Population* and published well prior to *The Origin of Species,* was that human progress derives from the competition for survival. As the best of each generation rise to the top, and the weakest fall by the wayside, civilization itself moves forward. Population dynamics are such that not all are cut out for survival, but in this seeming cruelty is the motor of development and progress—"the survival of the fittest." Spencer's 1850 book *Social Statics* made the case for laissez-faire capitalism in the service of survival and growth. Contrary to the view of Jeremy Bentham, Spencer's claim was that legislative and social reforms designed to aid the poor would only stand in the way of maximizing social utility.

In a manner somewhat similar to Edmund Burke, Sumner comes across as a cautious organicist, skeptical of revolutionary change and egalitarianism. However, as Hofstadter notes, where

> Burke is religious, and relies upon an intuitive approach to politics and upon instinctive wisdom, Sumner is secularist and proudly rationalist. Where Burke relies upon the collective, long-range intelligence, the wisdom of the community, Sumner expects that individual self-assertion will be the only satisfactory expression of the wisdom of nature. . . . Where Burke reveres custom . . . Sumner is favorably impressed by the break made with the past when contract supplanted status."[21]

In a series of essays written from the 1870s through the first decade of the twentieth century, Sumner articulated a set of related arguments that defined the contours of American social Darwinism. Perhaps most significantly, he assimilated the modern view of science to a thoroughgoing philosophical historicism. He argued that science deals in facts, not values—or, in his language, in "consequences" rather than "purposes."[22] Social science is only concerned with the facts, or consequences, of human action, and therefore must be separated from religion, ethics, or any philosophy that does not accept the fact/value distinction. Purposes are the province of theologians and ethicists, but such individuals are not scientists in Sumner's typology.

Key social phenomena that lend themselves to empirical observation and categorization include the "folkways" and "mores" of a society.[23] The anthropologist in Sumner comes to the fore when he claims that groups exhibit widely shared concurrence on certain folkways that evolve from the basic motives of human action—including hunger, love, vanity, and fear. Only when a folkway acquires moral significance does it become a more. Each more, or morally weighted practice, is a function of its times. "Abortion and infanticide are folkways which simply satisfy the desire to avoid work and toil. . . . Religion sanctifies the acts. . . . In time, however, conditions change. If, for example, warriors are needed, then abortion and infanticide do not seem wise beyond question."[24] The preponderance of forces acting on a society at any given time precipitates moral categories. Echoing Thrasymachus in Plato's *Republic*, Sumner holds that all right is conventional in that it is dictated by might.

For Sumner, as for Dewey, religion is a fundamentally conservative force that reifies a status quo—one that always grows up from human needs, rather than one that is handed down from a creator. Sumner claims that "no dogmatic propositions of political philosophy"[25] are always and everywhere true. The principles of the Declaration of Independence are mere eigh-

teenth-century notions of equal natural rights, which carried
with them certain humanitarian, democratic implications stem-
ming from the need for manpower. We should have no faith in
"abstract propositions,"[26] but rather in institutions that respond
to clashing interests. The "organic life" of the nation must be
allowed to flourish, which cannot happen if traditions "become
petrified" and "form a prisonhouse."[27]

These themes are echoed in Sumner's book *What Social
Classes Owe to Each Other*.[28] In a word, social classes owe nothing
to each other, and state programs that rob Peter to pay Paul will
necessarily interfere with the "struggle with Nature"[29] in which
man, by nature, is engaged. Peter becomes the "forgotten man"
who is exploited, when people choose, through the mechanism
of state power, to appropriate the resources of another for the
alleviation of alleged social problems and economic disparities.
Such alleviation, by interfering with the processes of natural selection, only weakens the state and the race. Reformers inevitably create pet classes that are the recipients of redistributed
capital but who cannot use it productively.[30] Unlike other ruth-
lessly historicist schools of thought, from Marxism to Nazism,
Sumner and the "right" social Darwinists were not in favor of
eliminating those who would stand in the way of the organic
growth of the state. American social Darwinism never took on
the extremist character of its European variants. Instead, it advocated moving away from the tribal instinct for war toward
(relatively) softer forms of commercial society, which could be
developed through the accumulation of capital.[31]

Sumner adopts natural law *sub silentio*. The adoption comes
in the guise of his embrace of the relentless struggle for existence, which is nature's law. It is this law that individuals and nations must obey lest they steadily weaken to the point of death.
Sumner's natural law, in turn, points to natural right: We must
acquiesce fully in the struggle for survival, for to war against
ever-unfolding natural processes is fundamentally quixotic,

leading to inefficiency and, eventually, extinction. Yet, there is more to his understanding of natural law and natural right than an amoral and relentless struggle for existence. In counseling us to step back from the abyss, Sumner's work raises the underlying tensions in all accounts of the human condition informed by a strong historicism and materialism. He purports to describe a scientific process and to explain social phenomena in light of this process. This leads to his stark justification of laissez-faire economics. But this justification is undertaken on consequentialist grounds. He prefers material wealth to poverty, and smuggles in other social goods such as "respect, courtesy, and good-will."[32] And in his discussions of the forgotten man, the tenor of his argument does not suggest that he is simply describing a process whereby the forgotten man is in fact exploited, but that it is *wrong* to exploit him.

Yet the ends of his social science, and the human virtues associated with it, do not—and, on his terms, cannot—have an objective status. The apparent authoritativeness of nature and its consequences do not solve this problem because, if Darwin is right, nature dictates nothing—it is simply a process. In order for Sumner's argument to cohere, he would have to make the case that nature dictates the end of a comfortable life—or even bare survival—*and* that this end is good. In fact, nature does not dictate this end unequivocally, for the very reason of the bad policy choices—human choices—Sumner is at pains to condemn. Sumnerian man is both inside, and outside, the natural order.

Sumner himself must, at one level, be an organic part of the overall social process. As he argues, "in any true philosophy, it must be held that in the economic forces which control the material prosperity of a population lie the real causes of its political institutions . . . its moral code, and its world-philosophy."[33] But it is therefore difficult for him to justify or account for his own intellectual activity and moral preferences, which manifest themselves in terms of policy recommendations. His determinism is at odds with his own intellectualism and materialism, which lead him to claim that mind and capital together can in fact dominate nature. Man, being an "intelligent animal" who "knows something of the laws of Nature," can narrow "the sphere of accident" through the intelligent deployment of capital.[34] Confronting a problem similar in kind to that of Jean-Jacques Rousseau in his *Second Discourse*, Sumner wishes to explain how creatures seemingly beholden to nature can transcend it (for better in the case of Sumner, generally for worse in the case of Rousseau). Only in the writings of Karl Marx does capitalist materialism play such a central role in defining the human prospect. Sumner would have us respect the forces of nature by a policy of noninterference, while we simultaneously flee, through human ingenuity, the harsh and undesirable ends of nature. We must at once obey the dictates of nature to promote economic growth—in order to do "good"—and escape nature through capital and wealth creation. Progress thus requires a simultaneous embrace and rejection of nature.

The host of philosophical complexities and contradictions raised by Sumner can be further clarified by considering his system in relation to the thought of other philosophers, from whom he borrows liberally, if not coherently. Sumner's ethics share something with Aristotle, though they are not Aristotelian. Aristotle's prudential ethical system does, of course, involve consideration of consequences, but it does so in light of purposes, or ultimate ends. Sumnerian science, by contrast, limits itself by definition to the empirical, phenomenological world: That which is scientific is that which can be observed and quantified. Sumner powerfully restates the fact–value or is–ought distinction by asserting that the realms of knowledge and rationality are the realms of science, while opinion, ideology, and ethical purposiveness stand on the other side of an epistemological chasm. Yet, paradoxically, we are obligated to act for the sake of better ethical outcomes.

Sumnerian ethics also has a Kantian cast, insofar as Kant, too, claims that the ethical realm must be divorced from the empirical. The main difference, however, is that for Kant, this separation of the purposiveness of the ethical realm from the consequentialism of the empirical makes the ethical realm *more* scientific than the empirical for the simple reason that we can know our intentions far better than we can know the "facts," which are, at the highest level, fundamentally opaque. Sumner offers moral-political recommendations with an absolutist cast—advice on what we as a society *must* do, what our purposes ought to be—on the basis of a very non-Kantian account of consequences. Put another way, while Kant denies the moral reality of the world of consequences, Sumner denies the moral reality of the world of purposes. Unlike Kant, he cannot bring himself to leave fully behind the world he denies.

Meanwhile, Sumner's materialist economism shares much with Marxism in its dynamic historicism, insofar as it asserts that "the ideal for mankind would be to have material supplies without limit and without labor."[35] But paradoxically, Sumner, like Marx, claims to stand outside the "dogmatic ideals"[36] he excoriates. He conceives of the need for a supervening rationality or directing intelligence to ensure that History unfolds as it should. However, unlike Marx, the purpose of Sumner's intelligence is to minimize state intervention into the natural workings of the marketplace.

In the end—from his assertion that mind is rooted in folkways to his argument that to stop competing is to die—Sumner tells us we can never fully escape nature. He therefore looks backward just long enough to remind us how vigorously we must continue to move forward. By contrast, his critics from the left wished to be entirely forward-looking. In many ways, however, their critiques fell victim to the same tensions implicit in Sumner.

Sumner's great intellectual antagonist, the "left" social Darwinist Lester Frank Ward, attempted to grapple with some of the conundrums Sumner brings to light by openly asserting that we are no longer condemned to obey nature, but can begin to direct its course. Instead of Sumner's merely implicit embrace of human intelligence as a guiding light for the ever-unfolding political economy, Ward and those who followed in his footsteps brought social planning to the surface of their arguments. Schemes of "social reform" need not be unscientific.[37] The laissez-faire "gospel of inaction" can be combated while allowing that competition has been the cause of our progress so far.[38] Science can, once again, be made vital after a long period of sterility.[39]

According to Ward, we are now in a position to dictate to nature, including even human nature. Mind can no longer be seen as a mechanical force but as a "new power" in the world.[40] Through this power, we can embrace the organic character of all political phenomena and mold them to suit our ever-changing purposes. We can posit our own ends—centered on egalitarian social growth—and then use the new scientific method to achieve what we posit. Evolution to this point has been brutish, but from here on, mind can take charge of evolution, superintending it and protecting the weak. We can, and must, move away from our "natural" competitiveness.

Ward was in many ways the original American social engineer, enamored of both natural science and his own capacities, embracing the new scientific methodologies while always assuming that the sufficiently wise stand outside the "infinite series of antecedents and consequences" in whose midst modern science places all other objects. For Ward, we move ever forward with our evolving standards of compassion and altruism. Our "art" overcomes the "science" of natural processes; evolution can be guided by our ingenuity so that the weak as well as the strong can continue to grow. Paradoxically, nature is deterministic until it produces mind, which can then determine itself:

> When a well-clothed philosopher on a bitter winter's
> night sits in a warm room well lighted for his purpose and
> writes on paper with pen and ink in the arbitrary char-
> acters of a highly developed language the statement that
> civilization is the result of natural laws, and that man's
> duty is to let nature alone so that untrammeled it may
> work out a higher civilisation, he simply ignores every
> circumstance of his existence and deliberately closes his
> eyes to every fact within the range of his faculties. If man
> had acted upon his theory there would have been no ci-
> vilisation, and our philosopher would have remained a
> troglodyte.[41]

While a critic of Sumner, Ward shared Sumner's premises and single-minded commitment to natural processes. In Richard Hofstadter's formulation, "like many other youths who came of age in the early 1860s, Ward flavored his educational diet with liberal dashes of Spencer and admired Spencer's version of universal evolution."[42] But his dualism of animal versus human evolution led the new discipline of sociology in a particular direction, toward the study of human phenomena as exhibiting a real independence from teleological principles of motion (but not from motion itself). A democratic age sets the ideal conditions for growth by being open to the popular will in the guise of administrative rationality. It becomes the task of this age to ameliorate the condition of ordinary men. In fact, Ward's "advocacy of state management was prompted by a lower-class bias. He seems to have considered himself a lobbyist for the people in academic forums. His opposition to the biological argument for individualism stemmed from his democratic faith."[43] At the most abstract level, an equalization of opportunities for the exercise of freedom and the harmonization of individual striving with social purpose seem to have been his goal. From the time Herbert Croly penned *The Promise of American Life* in 1909, through the 1930s, the "managed society which Ward had anticipated and which Sumner had so stoutly opposed was becoming a reality. . . . the ideals of a cohesive and centralized society became increasingly triumphant over those of the heyday of individualism."[44]

With the full embrace of mind, or a scientific method of intelligence, as the solution to the problems plaguing the human condition, the number of points on the political spectrum occupied by social Darwinism becomes virtually complete. For example, W. E. B. DuBois embraced its essential tenets as he confronted the race problem in America. In a striking speech given at the National Negro Conference of 1909,[45] DuBois asserted that up to the death of John Brown, the doctrine that all men were created free and equal was winning out. However, the year of Brown's martyrdom was also the year of publication of *The Origin of Species,* which, temporarily at least, silenced voices of reform because of its appropriation by those who willfully misconstrued its teachings. In DuBois's analysis, the "splendid scientific work of Darwin" and others "has been widely and popularly interpreted as meaning that there is such essential and inevitable inequality among men and races of men as no philanthropy can or ought to eliminate. . . . [W]ith this interpretation has gone the silent assumption that the white European stock represents the strong surviving peoples."[46] It is this assumption—not the Darwinist premises themselves—that DuBois attacks. "Degenerate individuals and families" are to be found everywhere. The privileging of the white race threatens to force an artificial survival of "some of the worst stocks of mankind."[47]

Despite being a social reformer of the left, DuBois adopts right social Darwinist language to condemn interventions into the marketplace—in this case, the genetic marketplace. In language that has much in common with that deployed, for different purposes, by Theodore Roosevelt, DuBois laments the "signs of degeneracy" of the white races in falling birthrates and lack of physical and moral stamina.[48] This degeneracy is encouraged by barriers between the races that hold down the "efficient Negroes" and, with them, the social organism itself. The barriers must be eliminated to secure "the boundlessness and endlessness of possible human achievement" and the "social self-realization in an endless chain of selves" that Darwin promised. Our task is to create the political conditions for "the survival of the fittest by peaceful personal and social selection."[49] And this task can be justified only by relying on "scientific answers" that appeal to "one arbitrament and one alone and that is: *the truth*."[50]

Mind's Mastery of Nature

Despite the disparate uses to which social Darwinism was put, we should not lose sight of the fact that the "right" and "left" social Darwinists shared much common ground, beginning with the status of human nature itself. Taking their bearings from Rousseau as well as Darwin, they denied that it is fixed, emphasizing instead its constant evolutionary flux. Intelligent guidance and endless sociopolitical reform are always possible because no problem is understood to be an inherent facet of human nature. This understanding alone is sufficient to distinguish social Darwinism from the political science of *The Federalist*.

But the social Darwinists were themselves human beings writing to other human beings in an effort to get them to change their folkways, their mores, and their minds. They therefore assumed what a purer Darwinism might deny: that there is an intelligence and a "truth" that exists independent of the body and its reproductive processes, which are the last simulacra of nature in the social Darwinist dispensation. This intelligence, while formally scientific and therefore instrumental, in practice seems to rely on moral ideas or sentiments. Ward, by putting mind effectively outside nature, is simply more open in his acknowledgment of this than is Sumner. In keeping with their reliance on scientific rationality, the "right" social Darwinists called for human actions that allow existent nature to work. The "left" social Darwinists, by contrast, called for actions based on altruism and care for fellow humans, which actions would allow a new world to be born. Neither of these positions is reducible to mere evolutionary processes. If mind is reducible to nature as evolutionary process, it cannot superintend it. If it floats above it, it must be as malleable as the material, evolutionary outcomes it seeks to superintend, always aiding the inexorable movement of the species.

Mind and morality are made respectable to modern consciousness only by being *separated* from nature. The alternative of a moral reason rooted in our particular nature as eternal or created beings is deeply problematic in light of the new science. Indeed, we can say that in the separation of mind and moral sentiment from human nature, the intellectual groundwork is laid for a form of contemporary progressivism that sees as an obstacle to desirable social engineering any constitutional framework that recognizes human nature and natural standards. It is the separation of mind and morals from nature, first evident in America in social Darwinist thought, that provides the intellectual basis for modern progressivism and its institutional prop, the administrative state.[51]

There is thus a great chasm between the older human sciences and Darwinism and its offshoots. Whereas the former point to the struggle for a good existence according to nature, the latter are concerned with the struggle for existence in and against an ever-evolving nature. For the ancient philosophers as for the social Darwinists, human beings must improve on raw nature. But for the former, they do so through the self-conscious activation of their own natural capacities. Indeed, even the title of Darwin's great work, *The Origin of Species,* is a rebuke to Aristotelian ontology and biology, in which species were conceived of apart from questions of origin. For Aristotle, when we speak in terms of what a species *is*, we are really speaking of its formal and final causes. The primary questions for Aristotle do not revolve around where things come from, or how, mechanistically, they work, but what they *are*. The most reliable guide to answering this question is bound up with their form in relation to their perceived purpose or function. For Aristotle, all things have ends, especially animate things, and we understand things only through knowing their ends. It is in light of these ends that the "whys" and "hows" of the thing can be grasped. The parts are understood in relation to this whole. In other words, instrumental questions are secondary to ontological questions, and efficient and material causes are secondary to formal and final causes.

After Darwin, the primary and secondary questions are reversed, and even moral-political inquiry comes to concentrate on instrumental questions. The point of Darwinian science is not to look for repose or final truth, but for how things develop. Everything is in motion, but it is *relative* motion, or motion divorced from ends. There is no final or fixed position by which to judge the adequacy or propriety of the motion. Change always equals "progress" for Darwinists if survival results; it does not imply decline or decay, as it might for Plato. Change is ever an ally rather than an enemy to be feared.

Put another way, ancient science tended more to investigate with a view to understanding things, where modern science investigates more with a view to controlling the processes of nature, and in effect to be a lawgiver to nature, forcing or encouraging it to be what it otherwise would not. For the modern Darwinist scientist, continuing a project stretching back to Francis Bacon and beyond, the "why" question is collapsed into the "how" question. This collapsing is also, not coincidentally, characteristic of American pragmatism.

The ambivalent relationship of social Darwinism to nature is a consequence of a fundamental tension inherent in Darwinian theory. Darwin argues that, as "Natural Selection acts solely by accumulating slight, successive, favorable variations, it can produce no great or sudden modifications; it can act only by short and slow steps."[52] For Darwin, the end is survival and growth, the birthing of "new and dominant forms,"[53] and change is the means to this end. But while the lower animals have no choice but to compete for survival, to engage in what Darwin calls "the war of nature,"[54] human beings do face an array of choices, which are linked to their ability to reason over ends. Social Darwinism cannot explain the nature of the human organism. This lacuna is recognized by the best of the social Darwinists, who never fail to remind us to act politically. In effect, they advise us to act, whether through capital accumulation or humanitarian relief, against natural selection or at least against the vicissitudes or natural outcomes of evolutionary processes. By so choosing, humans do not simply follow nature. They refuse to be passive responders to natural or instinctive inputs, or flotsam on a sea of antecedents and consequences. They even prefer on occasion to spoil reductionist accounts of themselves by giving, in Lincoln's words, "the last full measure of devotion."

Pragmatism and Programmatic Liberalism

Despite the fact that it defined many of the terms of intellectual discourse in late nineteenth-century America, social Darwinism would not become known as the quintessential American philosophy. This honor belongs to pragmatism. In fact, it has recently been suggested that, by the 1890s, social Darwinism was a "fading ideology."[55] However, the links between pragmatism and social Darwinism are many and strong. It is impossible to understand the "American philosophy" of pragmatism without understanding its relationship to social Darwinism. It is also impossible to dismiss social Darwinism's enduring influence on American political thought. The pragmatic tradition worked "with the basic Darwinian concepts—organism, environment, adaptation," and spoke "the language of naturalism."[56] It is possible to draw a sharp distinction between social Darwinism and pragmatism, according to Hofstadter: "Spencerianism had been the philosophy of inevitability; pragmatism became the philosophy of possibility."[57] But the disjunction was never that clear-cut, as even Sumnerian social Darwinism called for "environmental" manipulation. In other ways, it is easy to see the convergence of the two philosophical systems. "Pragmatism was an application of evolutionary biology to human ideas, in the sense that it emphasized the study of ideas as instruments of the organism."[58] From one point of view, pragmatism "breathed the spirit of the Progressive era"[59] in the two decades after 1900. But in reality, the spirit was already willing long before 1900.

William James's reflections on "What Pragmatism Means"[60] elucidate the connections between the two schools of thought. James recognizes himself as the popularizer of Charles Peirce's argument that the only meaning of a thought or idea is what conduct or consequences it is fitted to produce.[61] Peirce argued that, under an evolutionary understanding, natural "laws" must be products rather than the driving force of evolution. A Spencerian early in his life, James moved toward pragmatism under the strength of Peirce's critique.[62] "With Walter Bagehot . . . James believed the changes [in communities] were the result of innovations by unusual or outstanding individuals, playing the same role in social change as variations in Darwin's theory of evolution; such persons are selected by society and elevated into positions of influence because of their adaptability to the social situation into which they happened to be born."[63] With pragmatism, the human factor was fully out of the closet.

Even though James rejected the Hegelian-Darwinian historical categories that were never far from the thinking of his fellow pragmatist and younger contemporary John Dewey, the two shared a thoroughgoing skepticism of the tradition of absolutes, a faith in progress, and an emphasis on the process, rather than essence, of human life and activity. With Darwinism, pragmatism rejects the "rationalist temper" that is ossifying rather than instrumental, and it accepts the displacement of design from scientific consciousness.[64] According to James, all ideas must be interpreted in light of practical consequences, rather than purposes or metaphysical underpinnings. If no practical difference in the realm of consequences can be found, the debate over competing notions is idle.[65] There are no important differences in abstract truth that do not express themselves in concrete fact—no principles, absolutes, or a prioris can govern the pragmatic method, which is an attitude of casting one's glance away from first things toward last things, meaning the "fruits, consequences, facts" of life.[66]

While pragmatism has much in common with earlier empiricism, it is purer in its rejection of finality and its concentration on action and power. And it does so without the materialist or anti-ideological bias that characterized empiricism, according to James.[67] Ideas "become true just in so far as they help us to get into satisfactory relation with other parts of our experience."[68] James's pragmatism therefore contains within it a theory of truth, not just meaning. New ideas are "true" if they gratify "the individual's desire to assimilate the novel in his experience."[69] The test of the truth of a proposition is its ability to marry what we know to new facts. Pragmatism thus becomes a method and means to bind old belief to a new set of facts when new beliefs are inchoate, providing a kind of psychic tranquility that prevents cognitive dissonance. "The reason why we call things true is the reason why they *are* true."[70] In short, what works for us is true, and the pragmatist understanding of what works is linked to the inevitability of change and growth. At the very end of his essay "The Will to Believe," James quotes approvingly Fitzjames Stephen: "We stand on a mountain pass in the midst of whirling snow and blinding mist. . . . If we stand still we shall be frozen to death. If we take the wrong road we shall be dashed to pieces. We do not certainly know whether there is any right one."[71]

It is hardly clear that these two understandings of pragmatism—as a theory of method to arrive at objective reality, and as a theory of subjective satisfaction that might affect the questions we choose to ask—are entirely compatible. Nonetheless, James runs with them, going so far as to argue that even mystical experiences are true if they have practical consequences. If "God" works for us—if religious belief is effective in guiding our actions or giving us comfort—then pragmatism can't deny it.[72] Religion—the will to believe—can have its place. For James personally, belief in the Absolute might clash with other truths whose benefits he would hate to sacrifice,[73] but for others it might not. If belief in the Absolute could be restricted "to its bare holiday-giving value," it would not clash with James's other truths,[74] for such a belief would understand religious symbols in purely secular terms. Alas, James cannot allow it, for underlying the belief is a logic and metaphysics of which he is the enemy.[75]

Of course, this opens James, and pragmatism, to the same lines of criticism that can be directed toward utilitarianism or laissez-faire economics: There can be different truths or goods for different people, depending on what is expedient for them. James's pragmatism here comes perilously close to reducing all human beings to atomized individuals seeking the greatest good not even for the greatest number, but for themselves. It has no fixed ends beyond growth and practicality, but the direction of this growth is not rationally intelligible in a way that transcends a consequentialist analysis. As James argues,

> Rationalism sticks to logic and the empyrean. Empiricism sticks to the external senses. Pragmatism is willing to take anything, to follow either logic or the senses and to count the humblest and most personal experiences. She will count mystical experiences if they have practical

consequences. She will take a God who lives in the very dirt of private fact—if that should seem a likely place to find him.

Her only test of probable truth is what works best in the way of leading us, what fits every part of life best and combines with the collectivity of experience's demands, nothing being omitted. . . .

But you see already how democratic she is. Her manners are as various and flexible, her resources as rich and endless, and her conclusions as friendly as those of mother nature.[76]

It is indeed the very protean nature of pragmatism—its willingness to absorb *anything*—combined with its democratic ethos and faith in scientific intelligence, that has made it an enduringly popular doctrine for Americans—politicians and jurists no less than private-sector entrepreneurs. Indeed, in the pragmatic understanding, it seems that any idea or pursuit can be justified if it serves this ethos and faith. The fact that versions of pragmatism are today espoused in all branches of American government—though they were not at the time of the founding—is telling with respect to the development of our constitutional understandings. Many have noted the movement in twentieth-century political rhetoric away from discussions of the Constitution or constitutionalism and toward discussions of policy.[77] This move is at least partly a reflection of the hold of pragmatism on the American political imagination.

Dewey, by showing their mutually reinforcing character, brought pragmatism and social Darwinism together cogently as a compact set of political ideas. Dewey's pragmatism in some respects follows James, but it remains reliant on the intellectual categories of "left" social Darwinism. James's purer pragmatism all but did away with the categories of nature and natural law that were still central, albeit only in a materialist sense, to the Darwinists. Dewey's pragmatism, by contrast, re-injects into pragmatism natural forces and a strong sense of historical idealism, with which any method of intelligence must comport itself. Like many other critics of classical economics, Dewey, as we have seen, celebrated the influence of Darwinism on philosophy—hence, a responsibility to History and its proper unfolding informs Dewey's thought as much as does experimentalism. It is in Dewey that social Darwinism and pragmatism together become an intellectual and political force to be reckoned with: a modern liberalism whose goal is to help History along its democratic path, relying on the intellectual inputs of an elite vanguard that need not directly consult the people or ask for their consent.

In fact, the psychologies of James and Ward help account for the emphasis that Dewey places on the roles of individual intelligence and passion for social reform, which Dewey's more holistic Hegelianism tended to diminish. History and progress always remained central concepts in Dewey's thought, but his pragmatic experimentalism also militated strongly against any theory of the individual or state that was bound by inexorable laws. In Hofstadter's apt phrasing, "The beginnings of the Progressive era . . . coincided with the growth and spread of Dewey's ideas. . . . [I]t is easy to see Dewey's faith in knowledge, experimentalism, activity, and control as the counterpart in abstract philosophy of the Progressive faith in democracy and political action. It is not far from Croly's appeal to his countrymen to think in terms of purpose rather than inevitable destiny . . . to Dewey's appeal for an experimental approach to social theory."[78]

While still a graduate student at Johns Hopkins, Dewey had fortuitously heard Lester Frank Ward give his "Mind as a Social Factor" paper.[79] But more fundamentally, Dewey was deeply antagonistic—as was an increasing proportion of the intellectual class of his day—toward classical economics and philosophical individualism. Like Ward, Dewey conceived of human beings as having the capacity and responsibility for choices aimed at directing organic social and individual growth otherwise stifled by outmoded notions of competition and individual rights. Such choices and the policies that flow from them are always provisional responses to the flux of life, but their ultimate end is a more democratic society. Ideas grow and survive not because they are true or transcend human experience, but because they respond to it most effectively. "Social action" is called for once we understand that scientific intelligence can in fact superintend the unfolding of History.[80]

In his short book *Liberalism and Social Action*, based on a series of lectures, Dewey offers a history of liberalism, an analysis of the crisis it faces, and its prospects for a renaissance that will cement it as the guiding force of social life. As reason became purely instrumental, no longer concerned with ultimate truths but only "concrete situations,"[81] liberalism would come into its own. According to Dewey, the Western understanding of liberalism had moved from Locke's natural rights, to Adam Smith's dynamic economism, to Bentham's psychology of pleasure and pain which sought the greatest happiness for the greatest number. Bentham's theory argued for judging law by its consequences and for the supremacy of the national over the local. Furthermore, Bentham picked up on Hume's denial of natural rights—which exist only in "the kingdom of mythological social zoology"[82]—and thereby set the stage for the final move from individualist to collectivist liberalism.[83] Interestingly, Dewey notes that the source of factory laws and other reforms in England was not Benthamite liberalism alone. Rather, liberalism has been informed by evangelical piety, humanitarianism, literary romanticism, and Tory hostility to industry. Also, German idealism had played a role, emphasizing the organic connection of individuals to the collective and the creation of the conditions for positive freedom.[84] Together, all these strains formed a collectivism concerned with the organic whole of state and individual.

Still, there was nothing fundamental to Bentham's doctrine "that stood in the way of using the power of government to create, constructively and positively, new institutions if and when it should appear that the latter would contribute more effectively to the well-being of individuals."[85] Liberalism accommodated and assimilated a wide range of doctrines but never lost its historicism, consequentialism, or scientism. The result is that "the majority who call themselves liberals today are committed to the principle that organized society must use its powers to establish the conditions under which the mass of individuals can possess actual as distinct from merely legal liberty."[86] The challenge for this modern liberalism is to make itself a "compact, aggressive force."[87]

This new liberalism is superior to its outmoded earlier version because it makes itself relevant to the problems of social organization and the integration of various historically situated forces. In fact, the lack of a historical sense on the part of earlier liberals blinded them to the fact that their own interpretations of liberty were historically conditioned rather than immutable truths. Historical relativity finally frees liberalism to recognize that economic relations are the "dominantly controlling" forces of modernity and that they require social control for the benefit of the many.[88] Free competition and the removal of artificial barriers are no longer enough. Instead, the individual's powers must be "fed, sustained, and directed"[89] through cooperative control of the forces of production.[90] Individuality itself does not simply exist but is attained through continuous growth.[91]

> The demand for a form of social organization that should include economic activities but yet should convert them into servants of the development of the higher capacities of individuals, is one that earlier liberalism did not meet. If we strip its creed from adventitious elements, there are, however, enduring values for which liberalism stood.

> These values are liberty, the development of the inherent
> capacities of individuals made possible through liberty,
> and the central role of free intelligence in inquiry, discus-
> sion, and expression.[92]

In Dewey we see a dominant theme of American progressivism
and twentieth-century liberalism: the belief that there is an
intelligence, or "method of intelligence," that can be applied to
solve social problems, which are themselves primarily economic
in nature. It is this intelligence, which makes no pretense to
knowledge except as a result of a pragmatic experimentation,[93]
that captures the spirit of democracy rather than any
philosophical or institutional analysis. While all social relations
are historically situated and in flux, there is one constant: the
application of intelligence as a progressive ideal and method.[94] It
is the only simulacrum of God in an otherwise desiccated world
of process, evolution, and growth.

Dewey rounds out his discussion by giving us insight into
the nature of a "renascent liberalism." Growth must be physical, intellectual, and moral, and all classes and individuals must
benefit. This, of course, means that a vast state mechanism must
be constructed that is confidently dedicated to ensuring growth
by means of progressive education, the welfare state, and the redistribution of capital. The older political science of the founding era, including that of *The Federalist,* is easily swept aside by
Dewey. While the exact contours of public power and policy are
not necessarily the same for him as they are for progressive political actors such as Theodore Roosevelt and Woodrow Wilson,
all agree that there are no inherent limits on state power. Like
Roosevelt and Wilson, Dewey's political theory is impatient with
constitutional restraints and institutional forms. Separation of
powers is a doctrine rooted in stasis and therefore political death.
Meanwhile, to concern oneself with constitutional forms and
formalities is to give to institutions an abiding character they do

not deserve. Certainly, Dewey did not concern himself with the possibility that many publics are formed by complex industrial societies and that a theory of representation and stable institutions to support it are needed to integrate them. Such considerations are subsumed under the newly political categories of change and growth. Long before "the courage to change" became an effective presidential campaign slogan, Dewey helped ensure that "change" would have a central position in American political rhetoric.

As constitutional restraints are seen to be counterproductive and even dangerous, the restraints of character take their place in a decent political order. Education becomes a check on the power of the state, by creating citizens capable of fully participating in the republic of experimentation.[95] But the old virtues— whether they be of Aristotle's *Ethics,* or Plato's *Republic,* or the Judeo-Christian Bible—are out. In their stead are the new virtues inculcated by a democratic education, including noncompetitive striving, cooperation, and self-actualization. Growth peculiarly seems to exclude certain *individual* strivings, such as those for honor, money, or power. Dewey is concerned about the exercise of arbitrary power, but he has little anxiety about the aggregate power of the state. The cure for a powerful democratic state seems to be constant evolution in the direction of more democracy. The key to the perpetuation of our political institutions is far removed from either the constitutionalism of the Founders or the statesmanship of Lincoln.

In a beautiful encapsulation of social Darwinism, progressivism, and contemporary liberalism, Dewey claims, "[Flux] has to be controlled that it will move to some end in accordance with the principles of life, since life itself is development. Liberalism is committed to an end that is at once enduring and flexible: the liberation of individuals so that realization of their capacities may be the law of their life."[96] Human life, therefore, *is* nothing in particular beyond a continual unfolding and advancement, and liberalism is dedicated to its liberation through social policy. When the economic necessities are provided, individuals may pursue the higher life according to their spiritual needs, whatever they might be, and however they might change. And change they will. Dewey's vision of liberalism posits an individual free of the various constraints previously thought by so many to be necessitated by a dangerous, and fixed, nature. This vision of liberalism is a version of Marx's utopianism: that truly free men may fish in the afternoon and philosophize after dinner. Although today's constraints happen to be, for Dewey, largely economic in nature, it is not materialism but growth toward unfettered freedom that is at the heart of modern liberalism.

4

Progressive Political Leadership

Progressivism as an intellectual and political movement amounted to the *politicization* of the twin doctrines of social Darwinism and pragmatism, supplemented by occasional dashes of German thought in the form of Hegel and Weber.[1] By harnessing these doctrines for political ends—as Dewey hoped—progressives were able to usher in a new order in American politics. Commencing in the early years of the twentieth century, political and judicial actors borrowed freely from pragmatic and Darwinist accounts of politics, constitutionalism, and human life. The age-old question of "what works," politically, was increasingly divorced from a sense of constitutional restraint. Instead it was informed by an organic conception of a state unlimited in principle and whose only end was growth and development according to certain contemporary understandings of democracy. The initial dissenters from "right" social Darwinism, including the pragmatists, were, after all, as Richard Hofstadter has argued, "thinkers who did not quarrel with the fundamental assumption that the new ideas had profound import for the theory of man and of society. They simply attempted to wrest Darwinism from the [right] social Darwinists by showing that its psychological and social consequences could be read in totally different terms from those assumed by the more conservative thinkers who had preceded them in the field."[2]

This democratic bias was supplemented by the progressive belief in the desirability, and perhaps necessity, of a coterie of administrative experts, versed in the new scientific methods, who were in the best position to apply the new understandings of politics to the ever-changing political organism.[3] Weber's theory of bureaucracy and elite administration entered American political thought just in time to flesh out Darwinian categories. The political and judicial actors under the spell of these doctrines of necessity became enemies of the earlier Madisonian constitutionalism of first principles and limited government.

In this chapter, we examine two key players in the evolution of American constitutional politics in the early twentieth century: Theodore Roosevelt and Woodrow Wilson. Roosevelt was, in many ways, the great transitional president of American history, with one foot in the traditional world of American politics, and the other firmly striding toward the progressive future. Wilson remains perhaps the most intellectual of all American presidents; he possessed a fully worked-out philosophy of History that marks a complete break with the older categories of American political science.

Theodore Roosevelt's Bridge to the Twentieth Century

Theodore Roosevelt stands at the tipping point of American political development. He in many ways began to put progressive theory into practice on a national scale. While one can still hear echoes of the traditional language of politics in his rhetoric, they are faint in comparison to his progressivism. He notoriously lived the most active of lives, one that can be compared to no other in the twentieth century, save Winston Churchill's, in the range of its energy, ambition, and accomplishments. In America's first progressive president we see an emphasis on strife and the inevitability of growth that is not to be found in the rhetoric of prior presidents. In living as well as theorizing the social Darwinist ethos of forward motion to stave off decay and death, TR was truly *sui generis.*

America's new imperial responsibilities at the dawn of the twentieth century provide a possible rationale for TR's view that citizens must ever live a national life of toil and striving. Yet this rationale is radically insufficient. TR's theoretical emphasis was more on domestic than international politics. He confronted the problem of maintaining the civic and manly virtues in an increasingly complex industrial world where material wants could routinely be satisfied. His efforts were largely directed at putting the moral status of industrialism and luxurious living in doubt. In his view, ease of life was corrosive of republican government. As a result, he overlaid his discussions of classical or traditional virtues with a progressive desire to *act* politically; in other words, to bring the administrative state into the service of the manly virtues. In order for the nation to remain successful and wealthy, TR believed that there had to be a continuing campaign to keep the nation in a fighting spirit. Shameful inferiority and, eventually, national death are the natural results of lack of competitive striving. Unlike Lincoln, for whom the task of America was to live up to its ideals, TR saw America's task as being a great power, for only in continual growth toward dominance is there evidence of national success.

TR's life and ideas formed a coherent whole built around a cult of masculinity and striving. This coherence can be difficult to discern when one considers his early fascination with the seemingly humdrum task of civil-service reform. But such a concern was in keeping with TR's belief in "efficiency," with which the spoils system, he argued, was fundamentally incompatible. In an 1889 address to the Civil Service Reform Association, he claimed that the spoils system reflected "a grasping and ignorant oligarchy" that led to an enormous waste of public resources. And no nation or organism can afford to squander the resources it needs in order to grow. But beyond the concern for material resources, the lack of openness, accountability, and democracy in the spoils system made it an ossified relic of a bygone era. It operated without the vital support of the life-giving forces unleashed in an open, accountable system. And it tended to favor special, political interests as opposed to national, popular interests. As TR wrote just a year later in an essay on the merit system,[4] the whole public must benefit from the civil service, which can only happen under a legalized, systematized regime of appointment and tenure. Only then might we have a "new nationalism" of regulatory bureaucracies dedicated to justice and governmental control over large-scale capital.[5]

The messiness of American politics was an enduring concern of TR's. By 1910, he was presaging a new era in American constitutionalism by advocating a substantial delegation of congressional powers to commissions of experts.[6] These experts would make recommendations to Congress, which Congress would then accept or reject but not change. His claim was that "[a]s soon as business becomes at all complex—and nothing can be more complex than the business of a nation of a hundred million people—it can only be performed by delegating to experts the duty of dealing with all that can properly be delegated." His intent was to find a way to overcome the influence of special interests on Congress; his assumptions were that there exists an apolitical expertise on complex matters of state, and that republican institutions are incapable of doing the job assigned them by the Constitution. We can thus see in TR an early statement of a characteristic disposition of contemporary liberalism: In the name of democracy, we need the rule of experts, for they alone can sense the direction the nation should be going and act preemptively to help it get there, regardless of public opinion as registered in the constitutionally defined legislative branch.

In TR's thought and actions we can discern three leitmotifs of American politics in the twentieth century. First, he betrays the characteristic progressive desire to replace politics with law, and a confidence that this can be done throughout the political system. In the progressive dispensation, law comes to be seen as something that can pave the way to an ever more democratic future by making politics "safe" and "efficient" through the neutering of mere politicians. The era of progressive thought and practice led by TR heralds the "criminalization" of what had previously been considered to be normal political activity. Second, he largely defines the era in which concern with the national, as opposed to the sectional or local, comes to the fore of American political life. TR claimed that there was a difference between his nationalism and an undesirable overcentralization,[7] but in practice it is hard to discern it. Third, TR's presidency marks the practical origin of the centralized, rational state that has as its raison d'être the ideal of a meritocratic bureaucracy. In theory, experts who are beyond political control will administer government for the sake of national growth.

Despite all this TR emphatically spoke the old language of politics when it suited his overall purposes. For example, his discussion of the traditional political virtue of patriotism was directed at purported solutions to modern problems, including those related to health, safety, social welfare, and control of big business. In meditating on the theme of "True Americanism"[8] in an 1894 essay, he dilated on the meaning of patriotism, which he linked to the willingness to discard any "prejudice" that might stand in the way of a "reform movement." True Americans were those strong souls with the ability and will to fight the problems of the day, who were "broadly American and national, as opposed to being local or sectional." Parochialism is the enemy of Americanism. In TR's view, the question of American nationality "has been settled once and for all," and we can now attach our loyalties to the whole rather than the "village or belfry." To be Americanized—whether one is a native-born citizen or immigrant—is to put aside all foreign or parochial attachments.

Unlike Lincoln's attempt to evoke the deepest meaning of the American creed, TR is less concerned with the *principles* of America than he is with the *fact* of the American nation. He rails against "cosmopolitanism" and those things which are not American—including especially European things—but never gives Americans a reason to love their nation beyond the organic attachments one has to one's fatherland and the strength that a nation and its people exhibit with the support of such attachments. National power is in itself a good, and national life always involves a "keen struggle" requiring the support of the vast majority, lest the organism perish. The struggle is for the sake of survival—for the sake of life, rather than the good life. For only by struggling for survival can a nation define its conception of the good or the just:

> It is always better to be an original than an imitation, even when the imitation is something better than the original; but what shall we say of the fool who is content to be an imitation of something worse? Even if the weaklings who seek to be other than Americans were right in deeming other nations to be better than their own, the fact yet remains that to be a first-class American is fifty-fold better than to be a second-class imitation of a Frenchman or Englishman. As a matter of fact, however, those of our countrymen who do believe in American inferiority are always individuals who, however cultivated, have some organic weakness in their moral or mental makeup; and the great mass of our people, who are robustly patriotic, and who have sound, healthy minds, are justified in regarding these feeble renegades with a half-impatient and half-amused scorn.

Rarely does TR's "traditional" language of patriotism disclose what makes America *worthy* of love, unless the Hobbesian imperative of survival exhausts the worthy goals of politics. The social Darwinist fixation on survival and growth—and the inexorable link between the two—seems to exhaust TR's conception of the natural moral order. The conventions of the nation with respect to its definitions of the good and just are worthy by definition because they reflect the survived fittest. For TR, might ultimately makes right.

In a definitive 1899 address on "The Strenuous Life,"[9] TR weaves together a discussion of foreign policy with an account of the manly virtues. The great theme of the address is the need for constant striving and "bitter toil," and the concomitant dangers of slothfulness, "easy peace," and "scrambling commercialism." Successful national life is bound up with virility, as well as with certain feminine virtues. A "healthy state can exist only when men and women lead clean, vigorous, healthy lives. . . . The man must be glad to do a man's work, to dare and endure and labor. . . . The woman must be. . . . the wise and fearless mother of many healthy children." The ruthless, Darwinian struggle for survival is very much on the surface of TR's thinking:

> When men fear work or fear righteous war, when women fear motherhood, they tremble on the brink of doom; and well it is that they should vanish from the earth, where they are fit subjects for the scorn of all men and women who are themselves strong and brave and high-minded.
>
> As it is with the individual, so it is with the nation. . . . Thrice happy is the nation that has a glorious history. Far better it is to dare mighty things, to win glorious triumphs, even though checkered by failure, than to take rank with those poor spirits who neither enjoy much nor suffer much, because they live in the gray twilight that knows not victory nor defeat.

In a fleeting moment in the speech, TR refers to the wisdom of Lincoln, but even this is in the context of the manly pursuit of the Civil War, whose purpose, more than the restoration of America's constitutional order, was to place "the mighty American Republic . . . as a helmeted queen among nations." There is barely a hint of what Lincoln understood the war to be about. The "years of strife endured" seem as great as the peace that ensued. One cannot help but see a kinship between TR's social Darwinism and the dark nihilism of Friedrich Nietzsche, who claimed:

> You should have eyes that always seek an enemy—your enemy. . . . Your enemy shall you seek, your war you shall wage—for your thoughts. And if your thought be vanquished, then your honesty should still find cause for triumph in that. You should love peace as a means to new wars—and the short peace more than the long. To you I do not recommend work but struggle. To you I do not recommend peace but victory. Let your work be a struggle. . . .
>
> You say that it is the good cause that hallows even war? I say unto you: it is the good war that hallows any cause.[10]

Woodrow Wilson and the New Constitutionalism

Woodrow Wilson unquestionably stands as one of the most influential presidents in American history. Of all progressive thinkers, he was the most conscious of the constitutional implications of the new organic theory of the state, and he in fact worked out his own comprehensive theory, or theories, which argued for the need to move the United States away from the Madisonian constitutionalism of the framers. He understood government to have a different nature and radically different purposes from those set out in the Declaration, the Constitution, and *The Federalist*. And he was no mere theorist. As president, he was in a unique position to help define the purpose of presidential leadership in the twentieth century.

Wilson was a member of the earliest generation of American political scientists. As such, he was deeply influenced by the Hegelian science of the state that permeated his academic training at Johns Hopkins University. For Wilson, the collective, rather than the individual, is the centerpiece of serious political thought, and the collective that is the state exists only in History, moving inexorably to a working-out of the democratic principle. The state, in Wilson's Americanized Hegelianism, is not a set of institutions, nor is it the sum of its citizens. Indeed, it is not the citizens' to alter. Governments are not founded on a law of nature, or social contract, or the dictates of a lawgiver; political systems are developed, not made.[11] There are no Founders or foundings to be revered or looked to for guidance. Evolution, rather than revolution, drives political change. The state is an organic expression of national character and will which are very much products of particular historical, cultural, and ethnic conditions, as well as physical causes. History is not a mere record of events, but a providential working-out of rational ends.

For Hegelians, it makes little sense in politics to speak of better or worse, good or evil, right or wrong. Rather, informed political analysis concentrates on distinguishing the more advanced from the less advanced. In this sense, Hegelianism and social Darwinism were natural bedfellows, except insofar as Hegelianism posited motion toward an increasingly rational bureaucratic state wherein the great constitutional and moral questions that had plagued previous generations were solved. Wilson merges Hegelianism and social Darwinism in a triumphal narrative of evolution toward democratic purposes:

In order to trace the lineage of the European and American governments which have constituted the order of social life for those stronger and nobler races which have made the most notable progress in civilization, it is essential to know the political history of the Greeks, the Latins, the Teutons, and the Celts principally, if not only, and the original political habits and ideas of the Aryan and Semitic races alone. The existing governments of Europe and America furnish the dominating types of to-day. To know other systems that are defeated or dead would aid only indirectly towards an understanding of those which are alive and triumphant, as the survived fittest.[12]

For the Hegelian mind, the only real political questions that remain have to do with the most effective instrumentalities for scientific advance. In positing such directional motion, rather than motion simply, American Hegelianism was reliably compatible with modern liberal purposes. In fact, by the height of the Wilsonian era, American Hegelianism, "left" social Darwinism, and Deweyan pragmatism had effectively become indistinguishable.

Because of his voluminous theoretical writings, Wilson, unlike most presidents, is entirely scrutable. As a young man, he argued vigorously for reconfiguring American government along parliamentary lines. For him, "Parliaments are forces for freedom; for 'talk is persuasion, persuasion is force, the one force which can sway freemen to deeds such as those which have made England what she is,' or our English stock what it is."[13] Cabinet government—where heads of executive departments chosen from the legislative branch take the lead in introducing legislation—is marked by "breathing the bracing air of thorough, exhaustive, and open discussion."[14] Under such a system, real debate by skilled debaters, and a real formation of public opinion, would become routine in America. Cabinet members would be forced to resign their seats if faced with defeat of their plans in Congress. In short, responsible leadership would be introduced into the American system.

According to Wilson, this is most unlike the actual U.S. system of government, which relies on select and secretive congressional committees with no organic ties to the will of the nation.[15] Legislation becomes essentially a private matter, impervious to the scrutiny or spirit of the whole. Wilson launches a direct attack on the wisdom of the Founders by suggesting that the constitutional Fathers made the grave mistake of taking the principle of separation of powers to the extreme of *isolating* the powers of government. They created a system in which there is no "one" to speak for the nation, which therefore lacks a "guiding or harmonizing power."[16] Even the president cannot effectively make himself a leader, since he merely responds to legislative initiative. Policy leadership is vital if America is to deal with modern challenges. In a reversal of the Founders' and Lincoln's model of statesmanship, Wilson proclaims, "*No leaders, no principles.* . . ."[17]

Throughout most of his public life, Wilson meditated on the problem of making American government more efficient. In doing this, he argued for a new political science for a new age. In an 1886 essay on administration, he quotes Hegel to the effect that philosophy always reflects the spirit of its time[18]—and the complexity of the present time calls for administration. With the great questions of American politics, from slavery to federalism, essentially settled by the Civil War, leaders must direct their attention to helping the new American democracy run fairly and smoothly. Instead of concentrating on high constitutionalism, we must redirect our attention to administering what we have. History has replaced the great question "Who shall make the law, and what shall that law be?" with the question "How should law be administered with enlightenment, with equity, with speed, and without friction?"[19] Society is to be "perfected through the instrumentality of government. . . . individual rights. . . . fitly adjusted and harmonized with public duties. . . . individual self-development. . . . made at once to serve and to supplement social development."[20]

For Wilson, civil-service reform is a prelude to broader administrative reform. Only a purified civil service can take on its most important task of ministering to the nation. In a system wherein public opinion reigns, that opinion must be instructed and persuaded and made coherent. Public administration therefore always faces the challenge of balancing democratic accountability against efficiency. In a stunning reversal of the teaching of *The Federalist*, Wilson writes:

> large powers and unhampered discretion seem to me the indispensable conditions of responsibility. Public attention must be easily directed. . . . to just the man deserving of praise or blame. There is no danger in power, if only it be not irresponsible. If it be divided, dealt out in shares to many, it is obscured; and if it be obscured, it is made irresponsible. But if it be centered in heads of service and in heads of branches of the service, it is easily watched and brought to book. If to keep his office a man must achieve open and honest success, and if at the same time he feels himself intrusted with large freedom of discretion, the greater his power the less likely is he to abuse it. . . .[21]

In the administration of a modern democratic government, the problem is to prevent public opinion from becoming "meddlesome [like] a rustic handling delicate machinery."[22] Public opinion plays a superintending role at the most abstract level of policy formulation, but otherwise it must be shut out. Wilson was not here speaking of the contemporary judicial function, but he might well have been. For the progressives, as for so many members of the contemporary Supreme Court, more expertise is almost always synonymous with more democracy. The soft despotism of the administrative state, of which Tocqueville so eloquently warned, is a matter of scant concern to the progressive mind.

Wilson, unlike the Founders or Tocqueville, was unwilling to sacrifice efficiency for the sake of self-government. In Tocqueville's analysis, American liberty is linked to the fact that the acts of the federal government are "important but rare." For Wilson, they must be commonplace, as must the acts of all levels of government. In Wilson's view, the spirit of liberty prevails not in local republican institutions and practices, but in a civil service in whom there will be no taint of "officialism." This is because the service will be "thoroughly trained." Indeed, "arbitrariness of class spirit" is a problem that has largely been overcome by a "cultured" civil service in touch with the popular sentiments of the age.[23]

For Wilson, there is no danger of an autocratic bureaucracy. History has moved us, through stages, from autocracy to democracy to perfected democracy via the administrative apparatus; regression is not possible. The work of government is to adjust continuously, through regulation and education, its efforts to deal with changing social and industrial conditions. The ultimate aim is to equalize conditions throughout society in order to ensure the free play of individual forces and self-development.[24] Government power is effectively unlimited as long as it is aimed at such equalization. There is thus no *summum bonum* at which politics aims, or at least provides the conditions for the achievement of; human happiness is defined by change in the form of self-development. This concentration on self-development is linked to Wilson's evolutionary framework; his notion of equality of competition is borrowed from "left" social Darwinism. A marketplace of forces, ideas, and experiments is the best means to ensure that the organic whole continues to grow and is not artificially frozen in time.

Of course, the work of modern government cannot be handled by the professional civil service alone. The administrative sector must in decisive ways be beholden to democratic leadership. Aiding in the formulation, transmission, and implementation of public opinion are "leaders of men." In one of Wilson's major addresses, first given in 1889, he comes close to inventing the modern concept of presidential leadership, and indeed American political leadership more generally. The leader is one who has insight into mass psychology. The leader can persuade by "creeping into the confidence" of those he leads, which confidence is gained "by things that find easy entrance into their minds and are easily transmitted to the palms of their hands or the ends of their walking-sticks in the shape of applause."[25] Wilson's emphasis is on persuasion as a *force* to commence motion in the direction that the times require. "If you would be a good leader of men, you must lead your own generation, not the next."[26] The audience is not conscious of the direction that History requires, but the leader is. In its emphasis on approval and forward motion, Wilson's is not the persuasion of Lincolnian statesmanship, which emphasized the formation of characters that would be compatible with the repose required of good citizens.

As in his discussions of administration, Wilson posits an easy reconciliation of public opinion with political leadership. Public opinion in the modern age must be "truckled to," but there is no danger of demagoguery.[27] If everything other than democracy has been overtaken by the democratic principle, no aristocratic, oligarchic, monarchic, or tyrannic forms of statesmanship remain *possible*. They have been doomed by History, and it becomes theoretically defensible to cast them aside as threats to the democratic, administrative state. Only the rational is real, and only the real rational. In a further seamless blending of Darwinism and Hegelianism, Wilson asserts that society is an organic whole that moves in a particular direction, depending on the spirit of the age, thus making demagoguery literally unthinkable:

> This organic whole, Society, is made up, obviously, for the most part, of the majority. It grows by the development of its aptitudes and desires, and under their guidance. The evolution of its institutions must take place by slow modification and nice all-around adjustment. And all this is but a careful and abstract way of saying that no reform may succeed for which the major thought of the nation is not prepared: that the instructed few may not be safe leaders, except in so far as they have . . . transmuted their thought into a common, a popular thought.
>
> Let us fairly distinguish, therefore, the peculiar and delicate duties of the popular leader from the not very peculiar or delicate misdemeanors of the demagogue. Leadership, for the statesman, is *interpretation*. He must read the common thought: he must test and calculate very circumspectly the *preparation* of the nation for the next move in the progress of politics. If he fairly hit the popular thought, when we have missed it, are we to say that he is a demagogue? The nice point is to distinguish the firm and progressive popular *thought* from the momentary and whimsical popular *mood.* . . .[28]

If the leader's task is simply one of "interpretation," or preparation of the people to move where History wishes them to be, Wilson stands at an opposite pole from Plato and other classical philosophers. He claims that there can be no unbridgeable difference between the understanding of statesmen, or leaders, and the mass of the people. Truth is not interpreted *down to* the many, but *up from* the many to prepare for the future. Leadership is a fundamentally historical enterprise, oriented always toward progress rather than return, movement and growth rather than stasis and decay. Wilson sees statesmanship, or the rational component of it, as requiring accommodation with passion, or the habits and customs of the multitude, from which the leader cannot deviate. As the leader must always hear the voices of the people, so legislation—even legislation that "advances and modifies habit"—must remain very close to the thought of the people, drawing out what is latent in it. The leader is like a centaur, half man and half beast, his head ever aware of the needs of his lower, animal parts. As mind is never free of body, so the leader is never free of the greater body of society.[29] In the cautious, prudential calculus of the leader, principle is not an end, but merely a reflection of where a society has been, and a very rough guide to where it is now. The goal is always incremental forward motion. Politics cannot follow the stars, because the ship of state is on the river of History. "Politics must follow the actual windings of the channel of the river: if it steer by the stars it will run aground."[30] Nothing above—neither faith nor reason—can be the leader's guide, only what is ahead or behind on the river of time.

In tandem with his theory of leadership, Wilson reflects on what becomes of Hegel's world-historical men—the men whose passions are the unconscious driving force of History—when History has in essence come to an end. With all great questions resolved, world-historical men become self-conscious and take up leadership, which involves understanding their place in History and superintending the low-level working out of problems best tackled administratively. This is linked to the organic nature of politics. The "aspiring soul" seeks to be set free from the body, in this case the body of society, but it cannot be. The leader can do no more than arouse, formulate, or make explicit the general sense of the community. He can make public opinion aware of its permanent purposes, but not create it or fundamentally alter or correct its course.[31] Even "great reformers" are nothing more than "early vehicles of the Spirit of the Age."[32]

In this Wilsonian-Hegelian analysis, Lincoln simply possessed the most sensitive receptors for the faint signals of his era. The elimination of slavery came not from the highly prudential choice of means for principled ends, but because this elimination reflected History's movement. The criterion for judging a statesman such as Lincoln is his success, i.e., that his chosen means and ends were *timely*. Success on a large scale is the true measure of human greatness. There is no room for tragedy in politics. For Wilson it would indeed be intellectually bankrupt to oppose a social movement that is successful or appears to be winning, for one would be on the wrong side of History. And indeed, this is the central reason why "conservatism" is seen by progressives, then and now, to be bankrupt. For Wilson, statesmanship is democratized and historicized, and so becomes leadership, for there is nothing else for the statesman to do.

Leadership is central to Wilson's mature constitutional thought. By the early twentieth century, he was beating a retreat from his desire to reform the Constitution in the direction of a parliamentary system. But the retreat was only tactical. His fundamental view of the Founders' errors did not change. As he wrote in 1908, *The Federalist* amounted to an effort to apply Montesquieu's mechanical theory of checks and balances to America:

> The trouble with the theory is that government is not a machine, but a living organism. It falls, not under the theory of the universe, but under the theory of organic life. It is accountable to Darwin, not to Newton. . . . No living thing can have its organs offset against each other as checks, and live. . . . Government is not a body of blind forces; it is a body of men. . . . Their cooperation is indispensable, their warfare fatal. There can be no successful government without leadership or without the intimate,

almost instinctive, coordination of the organs of life and
action. . . . Living political constitutions must be Darwinian in structure and practice.[33]

Wilson's desire to throw off "Newtonian" constitutionalism
ran head-on into the reality that the Newtonian Constitution
in question could not easily be amended, precisely because of
its rejection of the desirability of a "ready response to the needs
of instinct or intelligence."[34] He therefore began to argue for a
strong president to speak over the heads of members of Congress, thereby consolidating public opinion and legislative support in such a way that a president might occupy a position of
concentrated governmental leadership in much the same manner as a successful prime minister. The president's role is to be
the "unifying force" of the nation rather than merely a legal executive.[35] "If he lead the nation, his party can hardly resist him.
His office is anything he has the sagacity and force to make it."[36]
Wilson claims that the Constitution is a document that contains
no theories. The movement of History toward the democratic
prospect coincides, constitutionally, with the move from a legal executive to a political presidency; from a deliberative Congress to an administrative state, wherein Congress acts more as a
committee of detail and overseer rather than as an initiating or
deliberating body with respect to the broad directions of policy;
from a limited administration to a vast bureaucracy of experts
who take on executive responsibilities previously assigned to the
constitutional presidency.

As Wilson claimed in his presidential campaign, we are in
need of "new freedom"[37] rather than, in Lincoln's words, "a new
birth of freedom." For Wilson, there can be no rededication to
old principles for the very reason that they are old—and principles. The collective achievements of the founding era can be
nothing more than curiosity pieces in the museum of political
history. The new freedom for a new age, by contrast, involves the

assertion of political leadership in order to control the captains of industry, and thereby achieve the fairness that a largely developed nation requires. Innovation in politics is always to be embraced, rather than feared. Wilson's explicit goal is "to make the young gentlemen of the rising generation as unlike their fathers as possible."[38] To favor the status quo, much less the past, is to be intellectually corrupt:

> Progress! Did you ever reflect that that word is almost a new one? No word comes to the lips of modern man, as if the thing it stands for were almost synonymous with life itself, and yet men through many thousand years never talked or thought of progress. They thought in the other direction. Their stories of heroisms and glory were tales of the past. The ancestor wore the heavier armor and carried the larger spear. "There were giants in those days." Now all has altered. We think of the future, not the past, as the more glorious time in comparison with which the present is nothing. Progress, development,—those are modern words. The modern idea is to leave the past and press onward to something new.[39]

History makes redundant the reflections of classical philosophy and *The Federalist* and Lincoln on human nature, memory, and reverence. These older views suggested that man was subject to so many passions that politics needed to rely not only on reason but also on prejudice, habit, and custom—themselves irrational—to preserve rational forms of government. In this understanding, one of the disciplines required, especially of a free people, is the belief that those who went before were greater, and that present accomplishments occur in a spirit of emulation.

Progressivism as Programmatic Liberalism

The growth of Wilsonian progressivism into programmatic liberalism was logical enough. The ideology of progressivism needed to transform itself into a concrete and permanent part of the American political landscape. For Herbert Croly, Wilson was not going far enough fast enough. While Theodore Roosevelt had, through the force of his personality, moved mountains to rally public opinion behind a combination of political and social reform, Wilson's studied ambiguities were not up to the task of maintaining adequate forward motion.[40] According to Croly, the Constitution was designed to preserve oligarchy rather than to lay the groundwork for democracy. The forces of conservatism that affirmed the "traditional constitutional system" remained so wedded to a "final political philosophy" that the currents of the age could not, without significant aid, move History forward.[41] History must be taken by the hand. A Wilsonian theory of leadership might be a necessary condition for History's unfolding, but it is ultimately an insufficient one. Leaders need to be connected with the currents of their age, but ultimately an *apparatus* of public works is required to help clear the obstacles in the path of forward movement.

Treating disparagingly any reference to "natural and fundamental rights," Croly argues for ways to institutionalize the pursuit of progressive goals. He allows that courts, and especially the Supreme Court, "are continually broadening the scope of the valid exercise of administrative discretion."[42] However, he also anticipates the coming scope and power of commissions of experts acting in a quasi-judicial capacity, the glory of which is to dispense with "rules" in the traditional sense—that is, rules as binding norms, rooted in principle, to be changed only infrequently. Administrators of social programs would be entitled to the same kind of respect and independence as common-law judges, on the condition that they share the "faith upon which the program depends for its impulse" and practice the "scientific method" upon which it relies for its realization.[43] The legislature would confine itself to setting goals only at the highest level of abstraction, such as factory health and safety. The experts would handle the rest. "The community will be united not by any specific formulation of the law, but by the sincerity and the extent of its devotion to a liberal and humane purpose."[44] Thus will true democracy be born.

With the rise of the New Deal, the progressive quest for the Croly Grail came nearer to fruition. FDR, partly under the influence of Croly's thinking, institutionalized presidential leadership not only of party and people, but of administrative agencies with far broader mandates than even Wilson had contemplated. The modern welfare state began with the New Deal. It was New Dealers who began in a comprehensive way to permanently reorient public opinion and political institutions behind the progressive vision of society. They did this through a multipronged attack on traditional American beliefs and practices. Underlying this attack was the understanding, expressed by FDR on the campaign trail in 1932, that the government accords rights to the people—and the goal of statesmanship is to redefine those rights to suit the times.

There were five essential elements to the New Dealers' strategy of reorientation. First, they denied that private interest translated into public benefit. The invisible hand of the marketplace only ensured injustice and an unequal division of the existing economic pie. Second, they asserted "positive" freedoms—such as freedom from fear and want—that implied the need for an active, all-encompassing state for their attainment and protection. Third, they argued for, and began implementing, the managed state, with the goal of wealth redistribution always in mind. This would be managed partly through fiscal policy, including the government establishment of macro-level goals for the economy, and partly through regulatory mechanisms, including semi-autonomous administrative commissions. Fourth, aided by World War II, they fully realized the goal of presidential leadership and the new theory of representative democracy that went along with it. The president would be a leader of men, overcoming the inefficiencies of the separation of powers and the federal system. He would channel the great currents of popular national sentiment and thereby concentrate power for national purposes. Finally, they secured a compliant Supreme Court, thereby laying the groundwork for an activist Court in the decades that followed. At first, pliancy was all that was required, as the New Dealers concentrated on economic problems that were approached legislatively and through presidential leadership. However, the ultimate progressive goals of unencumbered and all-around growth, experimentation, and self-development would not be ignored for long.

The consequence of the development of the progressive model of politics is that, today, citizens are more influenced by the federal government than by state or local governments, and they are increasingly governed by judicial and quasi-judicial decrees rather than by statutes. The citizen is less a vigorous member of a self-governing republic, and more a constituent of various federal programs—or a beneficiary or victim of various decrees. Voting becomes a less important act, because representation is reduced to dealing with administrative agencies, and other promulgators and interpreters of decrees. As the progressives desired, government today is less political, and more administrative.

Whether in support of the manly virtues of vigorous and fair competitive striving championed by Teddy Roosevelt, or the virtues of administrative efficiency championed by Woodrow Wilson, or the virtues of equal opportunity and economic control championed by Franklin Roosevelt, progressives carved out a significant place for the rule of nondemocratic expertise. For later progressives, the challenge would be to maintain the virtues of openness and experimentalism in the service of personal autonomy. But even this was foreshadowed in the progressive era by the judicial branch of government. In a manner that is little understood, the Supreme Court in that era positioned itself as the vehicle par excellence for the imposition, in the name of democracy, of the rule of experts, for experts are best able to understand the direction in which History must move—and what is required to guarantee this movement.

5

The New Science of Jurisprudence

Let us examine the thought and jurisprudence of Louis Brandeis, Oliver Wendell Holmes, and Benjamin Cardozo in an inductive effort to elucidate the legal theory implied by progressive thought. Of all the thinkers and actors of the progressive era, these three jurists encapsulate the essence of progressivism as legal theory in the most comprehensive and telling manner. Yet none was essentially, or even substantially, a theorist. Rather, each represents progressivism in juridical action. Our task, therefore, is to cull from many individual arguments and assertions a cohesive characterization of progressivism as a legal—as opposed to a philosophical or political—movement. In the course of so doing, we will sketch the implications of this movement for our own time.

These jurists, along with Harlan F. Stone, tended to be dissenters in what is commonly understood to be the era of substantive due process (or the "*Lochner* era"), which lasted roughly from the turn of the twentieth century until 1937. A common interpretation of them is that they championed deference to legislative judgments.[1] This is at best a partial truth, though it can be said that they shared the view that legislation was the best means of advancing not just particular policy objectives, but new understandings of constitutionalism itself.

111

This view goes beyond the notion that many constitutional meanings are far from fully articulated, and can therefore be defined by legislative actions and interpretations of legitimate constitutional powers. Instead, the new constitutionalism understands all constitutional meanings to be *nothing more than* interpretations that exist only in History. Dewey identified the problem that progressive jurists had to solve when he lamented the "unusually inflexible" nature of our political institutions "because of the interpretations made by courts of a written constitution."[2] Such institutions must be directed toward "further development" in aid of "constructive social application."[3] For this to happen, a new legal logic would be required, one that is far from syllogism, fixed forms, and the mechanical application of antecedent principles; one that looks instead to concrete consequences.[4] For Dewey, the "great practical evil of the doctrine of immutable and necessary antecedent rules" is that it "sanctifies the old" and "widens the gap between current social conditions" and legal principles.[5]

The moral realism of philosophers and statesmen stretching from Socrates to the American Founders to Lincoln suggests that justice consists in something in particular. The new constitutionalism would change all this. "In American law, the beginning of the final third of the nineteenth century marks a surprisingly bright divide" between the earlier legal theorists and commentators—including Locke, Blackstone, Jefferson, Wilson, Madison, Tucker, Marshall, Kent, Story, and Lincoln—who credited natural law, and the later ones who did not.[6] The age of Holmes, Brandeis and Cardozo, among others, was the age of skepticism and the rejection of moral realism.

Progressivism as legal theory now comes to sight as a handmaiden to progressivism more generally. The judiciary of the *Lochner* era, dissenters excepted, was perceived (and to some extent is still perceived) as an enemy of progressive reform. This perception is not borne out by the historical record. As Richard

Epstein has noted, the "Old Court" did not engage in "anything like a dogmatic or reflexive protection of either state interests or individual rights. The full picture of the traditional view is far more complex than the Progressive caricature of it."[7] The Old Court was more than willing, when the situation demanded it, to "introduce the nontextual element" into constitutional interpretation, showing "sensitivity to structure and function as well as text."[8] Most progressive legislation that came before the Supreme Court in this era was in fact upheld.

> In their published writings and in case after case, the justices revealed not a reactionary conservatism based upon a purely materialistic view of laissez-faire constitutionalism or upon an implicitly Social Darwinist social and economic agenda, but a reasoned conservatism based upon an unshakeable belief in an individualistic, voluntaristic, and moral social order resting upon eternal metaphysical truths expressed by American Protestantism and academic moral philosophy.[9]

In Christopher Wolfe's analysis, the "traditional" era of constitutional interpretation—from 1789 to 1890—was premised on the assumption that the Constitution was intelligible and substantive, and it evinced concrete legal rules "rather than merely proclaiming vague generalities."[10] Constitutional interpretation from the Founders' point of view owed much to Blackstone,[11] who argued for interpreting law according to "signs the most natural and probable," including "the words, the context, the subject-matter, the effects and consequences, or the spirit and reason of the law." Rules of interpretation cannot solve all constitutional problems, but words—and documents—have meanings that are fixed by the documents themselves, or considerations that grow naturally out of the documents. Such considerations never float freely above the document, to be defined by History. Even if meaning is difficult to discern, good-faith efforts rooted in the documents themselves must be made.

During the traditional era, the Supreme Court made these good-faith efforts. After the Civil War, this era slowly started to give way to the era of a new natural-rights jurisprudence—particularly property rights.[12] This transitional era occurred under the rubric of the due-process clauses of the Fifth and Fourteenth Amendments, and under the rubric of the commerce clause. The shift was obscured, according to Wolfe, because of the basic conservatism—political and rhetorical—of the late nineteenth-century justices.

The third or "modern era"—post-1937—has been defined by the shift from economic activism to activism in the realm of civil rights and liberties. This shift occurred under the rubrics of the First Amendment, the Bill of Rights provisions dealing with criminal defendants, and the equal-protection clause of the Fourteenth Amendment.[13] In the modern era, judging became fully legislative in character, though the rhetoric of the common law was maintained, so that this transition, too, was partly obscured. Contrary to the dominant practice of the common-law tradition, judicial legislation was increasingly viewed as legitimate "not only in the absence of statutes but even when overriding them."[14] And we should add another divergence from the common law: the absence, practically speaking, of a doctrine equivalent to parliamentary supremacy, whereby courts are kept in check constantly and directly by the will of the people speaking through Parliament. This still defines jurisprudence in England and other common-law countries, or did until very recently. The U.S. has been the only country in the common-law world with a relatively long-standing tradition of "judicial activism." Far from being typical, it is a mark of American exceptionalism.

A "new theoretical understanding" of judicial legislation marked the modern era as compared to the transitional era.[15]

The transitional-era judges still understood themselves to be interpreting a constitutional document according to established, and fixed, principles. Per Blackstone, they did not believe that judges made law, but rather discovered it in the authoritative documentary records and customs of the community. Justice Brewer and other economic substantive due-process justices understood themselves to be enforcing the natural law, which was embodied in the Constitution.[16] The modern era justices, by contrast, deny in principle the existence of natural standards, or the authority of the Constitution as it was written. The earlier justices looked back; the modern justices look forward. The transitional-era justices of the Old Court might have been mistaken, but they were not motivated by a sense of the need to keep abreast of History. Being less prone to open-textured analysis, they were far less dangerous: "Modern constitutional law invokes the text at such a high level of generality that it ceases to function as an effective constraint on the interpreter," according to Wolfe. "The text is reduced to a delegation of power to the judiciary to make public policy. . . ."[17]

By contrast, Richard Hofstadter alludes to the convergence of social Darwinist philosophy and Old Court jurisprudence when he remarks that "Spencer was advancing within a cosmic framework the same general political philosophy which under the Supreme Court's exegesis of the Fourteenth Amendment served so brilliantly to turn back the tide of state reform."[18] This statement vastly understates the revolutionary character of that which Spencer and the social Darwinists wrought. Their thought was well outside the mainstream of American life until it was adopted by the progressives themselves. Hofstadter instead presents a view of history, itself sympathetic to left social Darwinism and progressivism, that tends to read back into American political thought Spencerian arguments and worldviews that scarcely existed prior to the late nineteenth century. Hofstadter suggests, unpersuasively, that "Spencer's doctrines were imported into the Republic long after individualism had become a national tradition. Yet in the expansive age of our industrial culture he became the spokesman of that tradition, and his contribution materially swelled the stream of individualism if it did not change its course. If Spencer's abiding impact on American thought seems impalpable to later generations, it is perhaps only because it has been so thoroughly absorbed."[19] Ironically, it is Hofstadter who is under the impalpable influence of Spencer, and who shows a fundamental misunderstanding of the nature of individualism and natural rights as understood by the Founders and by Lincoln. The judges, like virtually all Americans save for the progressive elites, were ignorant of the strong progressive historicism that Hofstadter is at pains to demonstrate.

In their reactions to the new regulatory state promoted by the progressives, the members of the Old Court, right or wrong, were not revolutionaries. That title belonged to the left social Darwinists and pragmatists who would eventually replace them on the Court. It was only the progressives who "saw in constitutional interpretation the opportunity to rewrite a Constitution that showed at every turn the influence of John Locke and James Madison into a different Constitution, which reflected the wisdom of the leading intellectual reformers of their own time."[20]

The progressive understanding of the Constitution began in fits and starts, both legislatively and judicially, but it bore much fruit. As Clement Vose has argued,

> Through the half century from the 1890s to 1940 the Populists, Progressives and Liberals were insurgents on the make, gradually persuading the majority of the rightfulness of government intervention to protect both unions and unorganized workers. They argued that the police power afforded correct constitutional grounds to support these assertions of governmental power. . . . [T]hey became engaged in constitutional warfare at just

about every conceivable level: winning federal and state legislation, working for amendments to the Constitution, criticizing the judicial function as practiced by conservative activists, attacking the right-wing bar and its associations, being concerned with judicial appointments and—in that connection—fighting off the conservative attack on president Wilson's nomination of Louis D. Brandeis in 1916 and joining the successful assault on President Hoover's nomination of John J. Parker to the Supreme Court in 1930.[21]

Most fundamentally from a jurisprudential point of view, the progressives "attacked the twin doctrines that most limited government power—federalism, on the one hand, and the protection of individual liberty and private property, on the other. . . . However grandly their rhetoric spoke about the need for sensible government intervention in response to changed conditions, the bottom line, sadly, was always the same: replace competitive processes, by hook or by crook, with state-run cartels."[22]

During this time period, the federal government, with Court acquiescence, vastly expanded its power to control monopolies and regulate interstate commerce. One need only mention the Court's upholding of the Hepburn Act of 1906, under which the Interstate Commerce Commission was given teeth and administrative regulation was thereby sustained. Under the impetus of progressive thinking, the Sherman Antitrust Act of 1890 was also reinvigorated in *Northern Securities v. United States* (1904)[23] and *Swift and Co. v. United States* (1905).[24] In the latter case, Justice Holmes, writing for the Court, asserted the "stream of commerce" doctrine, which held that manufacturing could not in fact be separated from commerce and was thus subject to Congress's regulatory power. This marks the nascence of the apparently plenary commerce power exercised by Congress for most of the twentieth century. Sometimes, moral disapprobation of a particular practice was combined with a growing sympathy for federal regulatory authority, as in *Champion v. Ames* (1903),[25] where the Court upheld a broad congressional police power over the interstate transportation of lottery tickets. *McCray v. U.S.*[26] (1904) affirmed the right of Congress to base federal police power on its taxing authority. In other words, taxation could be used as a regulatory device. In the wake of cases such as these, the exercise of both the federal commerce and taxation powers came to be almost beyond judicial reproach.

This is not to say that the Court was a bastion of progressive utopianism, or that it was as committed to radical reform as were some of the progressive intellectuals and social critics. In *Standard Oil Co. v. United States* (1911),[27] the antitrust "rule of reason" was applied whereby the Court indicated that it would break up only those companies that unreasonably restrained trade. This rule required a case-by-case analysis that eventually came to mean that the courts would consider various factors, including the nature of the business in question, the effect on the business of an alleged restraint of trade, and the type of restraint.[28] And the Court did occasionally find that Congress had overstepped its constitutional bounds. For example, in *Howard v. Illinois Cent. R.R.* (1908),[29] the Court invalidated a federal liability regulation on the basis that it did not regulate workers who were, strictly speaking, engaged in interstate commerce.

In *Adair v. United States* (1908),[30] the Court ruled that the Erdman Act, which banned yellow-dog contracts and the firing of employees for union activity, violated the liberty of contract guaranteed by the due-process clause of the Fifth Amendment. Dissenting in this case, Holmes restated the commitment to legislative supremacy that he had expressed (also in dissent) in the celebrated *Lochner v. New York* (1905) case,[31] wherein the 5–4 majority of the Court invalidated New York State's law purporting to limit working hours in bakeries as an unconstitutional violation of liberty to contract protected by the due-process clause of the Fourteenth Amendment. In *Hammer v. Dagenhart* (1918),[32] the Court held (in a 5–4 decision, with Holmes and Brandeis dissenting) that the Keating-Owen Child Labor Act prohibiting interstate traffic in articles manufactured by children did not disclose a legitimate power of Congress, but was rather an act that impinged on the police power of the states. The Court in this case reverted to a distinction it had drawn at the end of the nineteenth century between manufacturing and commerce. To some extent, this case was symptomatic of a larger, albeit temporary, postwar reversion to a pre-progressive understanding of federalism and laissez-faire economics (though not necessarily of judicial power).[33]

In short, the Court in the progressive era alternated between a narrow and broad conception of judicial review, but it by no means proved a consistent opponent of the progressive legislation emanating from Congress. The Court's reputation as a reactionary institution is largely founded on its substantive due-process review of state legislation. At the state level, as at the national level, legislative interpretations of legitimate police power were broadened during the progressive era to include regulation aimed at child labor, hours and wages, safety, employer liability, and worker's compensation. The symbolic, though not temporal, high point of substantive due process was almost certainly *Lochner*, but just three years later the Court, whose membership had changed little since *Lochner*, adopted a noninterventionist position in *Muller v. Oregon* (1908).[34] Here, the Court upheld Oregon's expanded interpretation of police power in a 9–0 vote, effectively overruling the *Lochner* case, albeit without explicitly saying so. *Lochner* was quickly revealed for what it was: an aberration rather than a conclusive statement of the Court's antagonism to progressive reform.[35]

The late-nineteenth-century Court's decisions on the police power generally show a deference both to state morals regulation and to economic regulation as long as it "did not appear to threaten either the moral principles of individual free will and accountability" or the federal system.[36] In *Muller v. Oregon*, Justice Brewer was willing to recognize the long-recognized special status of women, based on their different natural attributes. The Oregon statute operated equally on all members of the same class—i.e., men and women, respectively, and was therefore constitutional.[37]

Furthermore, whatever the majority decision in *Lochner* and other substantive due-process cases represented, it was not, as we have seen, a reflection of a particular ideology such as "right" social Darwinism, as Justice Holmes famously claimed in his dissent. The justices of the time did not understand themselves as relying on a historicist account of human affairs that was deeply hostile to America's founding principles, and it is hard to impute such views to them. In fact, whatever their errors of application, they understood their mission in light of deeply held religious and ethical principles largely shared by the Founders.[38] As Epstein has noted, the *Lochner* decision

> asked only whether a state law limiting bakers to a ten-hour workday was a genuine health measure or was instead a disguised "labor" regulation. The opinion contains many references to the dangers of legislative paternalism, but a second, if tacit, dimension of the case concerns the competitive positions of small, immigrant-owned bakers against their larger, unionized rivals. Justice Peckham held that the safety issues were in fact a pretext for hobbling those workers, and it surely counts as a clear point in his favor that the case arose from a state criminal prosecution, and not from any private suit by Lochner's bakers.[39]

Ironically, the only social Darwinist on the Court at the time of *Lochner* was Oliver Wendell Holmes.

Louis Brandeis and Sociological Jurisprudence

The *Muller* decision was based largely on the so-called Brandeis Brief drafted by then counsel Louis Brandeis. The brief supported the constitutionality of the Oregon statute governing women's working hours. The brief was a model—indeed, it remains the model—of sociological jurisprudence, notoriously devoting a mere two of its more than one hundred pages to legal analysis strictly speaking, and the rest to analyses of the effects of working conditions on women, from medical and psychological points of view, supported by reams of empirical observations. It also gave great weight to such considerations as they appeared in the legislative record. It was nothing if not an argument for judicial restraint, understood not as a theory of jurisprudence or constitutionalism, but as a default disposition for jurists that would allow the furtherance of progressive legislative ambitions. In fact, "Brandeis's advocacy of judicial restraint was seldom far removed from his Progressive goals."[40]

The brief emphasized the importance of social research and empirical evidence to the solution of social problems and made it clear that the legislative branch could best undertake such investigation, utilizing social scientific expertise to guide it and to craft original and experimental legislative solutions. The legislature itself, in Brandeis's later writings, becomes a fully rational, coherent organism dedicated to the use of social facts and is uniquely attuned to their logic.[41] The Court's majority explicitly commended the brief as showing the reasonableness of the legislature's actions.

Brandeis's influence was wide and deep, affecting both the Supreme Court and the legal academy. The organization driving the litigation in *Muller* and subsequent cases (the National Consumers' League) raised money specifically to make its briefs available to a wider public, including college and law-school libraries.[42] Even by the first decade of the twentieth century, the importance of litigation—based on a new understanding of what counts as a constitutional argument—was clearly recognized by progressive leaders.

This quick move away from *Lochner* therefore foreshadowed an alternative form of substantive due process, rather than an attempt to limit substantive due process by questioning its constitutional basis. It was a form that encouraged the Court to take judicial cognizance of information traditionally only available to, and appropriately considered by, the legislative branch. Even Brandeis's ideological enemies were quickly co-opted, using their own versions of the Brandeis Brief to oppose progressive legislation. The manner of approaching legal questions suggested by the Brandeis Brief reached its apotheosis in *Brown v. Board of Education* (1954),[43] in which sociological and psychological analyses came to replace, all but completely, pre-progressive legal reasoning.

Woodrow Wilson nominated Brandeis for the Supreme Court in 1916, just eight years after his counsel work in *Muller,* and amid heated opposition to his appointment by business and conservative interests. When he was nominated, he told Wilson's attorney general that his "views in regard to the Constitution are as you know very much those of Mr. Justice Holmes."[44] But his influence on Holmes was probably greater than this acknowledgment suggests. Then as now, many have argued that he came to push Holmes's more inchoate pragmatism in a reliably progressive direction, so that Holmes himself became known as the progressive era's "great dissenter."[45]

Brandeis carried the basic approach exhibited in the original Brandeis Brief with him throughout his twenty-three-year tenure on the Court. For example, dissenting with Holmes in *Burns Baking Co. v. Bryan* (1924),[46] he adduced evidence to show why the Nebraska legislature ought, in fact, to be able to regulate the weight of a loaf of bread. His reasoning was characteristically progressive in style, substance, and tone, citing a variety of governmental, congressional, and expert findings to support the reasonableness of the impugned statute, and criticizing the Court as a "super-legislature" far exceeding its constitutional power of judicial review. It is significant that he relied on such reasoning when there were other paths he might have taken to reach the same result. For instance, a compelling case might have been made for allowing such a law to stand on the basis that the Court does not deal in trifles, or that the Constitution is simply, and obviously, silent on such matters. Alternatively, it could have been said that the Court ought not to put itself in the position of schoolmaster to the nation, finding substantive due process grounds to inject itself—by way of either opposition or support—into the minutiae of the exercise of state police powers.

The manner in which the new sociological approach to jurisprudence cut, politically, can be seen in Brandeis's commendable ability to put his personal, progressive *economic* views aside. This is demonstrated, for example, by his *support* for a Depression-era Oklahoma statute granting ice companies local monopolies.[47] He most often did not find it constitutionally necessary for sociological analysis to trump deference to legislative judgments in the economic sphere. He in fact largely restricted sociological analysis, in the economic realm, to supporting such legislative judgments, as in the *Burns Baking* case. In Brandeis's view, economic man ultimately does not prove important enough to warrant protection from the larger will of the community expressed through law. This emphasis was not unrelated to the basic democratic, anti-elitist tendency of progressivism viewed as a social movement, as opposed to an intellectual and political one. Brandeis's view was that "[i]t was not informed statesmanship to try to freeze privilege or to thwart change indiscriminately; neither was it desirable or safe to stand aloof from the struggle. The reformer's role was to guide the forces of social experimentation and thus to direct change along the lines of evolution rather than revolution."[48]

But if Brandeis's bias was against second-guessing legislative judgments in certain areas, how consistent was this bias? Does the bias disclose a theory? Some scholars claim that Brandeis "challenged all the new truths" that social Darwinism purportedly visited on American jurisprudence in the last decades of the nineteenth century.[49] Others come closer to the truth in noting that "Brandeis (and, to a much lesser extent, Holmes) was convinced that their jurisprudence was fundamentally anti-Darwinist [but this] is simply a testament to the centrifugal pull of ideas as powerful as social Darwinism."[50] While Brandeis outwardly scorned social Darwinism, he was greatly influenced by Holmes, including especially his belief that law must evolve to suit social necessities and that the judiciary must be adept at ensuring that the Constitution keeps up with social growth.[51]

There was, however, a difference of emphasis between Brandeis and Holmes: The former was willing to admit that morality made a difference and that it helped define the spirit and necessities of the age.[52] Holmes was much less willing to allow that morality—excepting his own—made much of a difference to social or legal outcomes. As was the case with "left" social Darwinists, Brandeis had reformist tendencies that relied on, without necessarily accounting for, explicitly moral language. For Holmes, law conforms to social conditions, with occasional prods from the judicial branch. For Brandeis, the prods—in the form of sociological jurisprudence—could be a regular and more openly acknowledged mechanism for social growth. Holmes wrote to Brandeis about the view they shared—that social experiments should be tried. But he expressed reservations as to their ultimate effect—implying a belief in laws that were beyond human control.[53] Some would suggest that these kinds of experiments or their outcomes were therefore unimportant to Holmes.[54] As we shall soon see when we examine Holmes's First Amendment jurisprudence, this is at best a partial truth. It is, however, accurate to say that there was more fatalism in Holmes.

As Philippa Strum puts it, "like Holmes, Brandeis put his faith in the marketplace of ideas; unlike Holmes, he believed that the choices made in it mattered and ultimately would be the correct ones."[55] Put another way, "Brandeis's goal was harmony of individual and community. He frequently spoke of the citizen's right to speech as if the right flowed from the need of the community for an informed electorate rather than from any individual need."[56]

In this fashion, and as was typical of progressive legal thinkers, Brandeis was much less sympathetic to legislative discretion in matters of "civil," rather than "economic," rights.[57] In *Schenck v. U.S.* (1919),[58] Brandeis concurred with Holmes's introduction of the "clear and present danger" test for restrictions on free speech. Subsequent to this case, Holmes and Brandeis together began using this test. Initially they had to use it in dissent, as a sword against suspect laws; after *Schenck,* the Court briefly reverted to the "bad tendency"[59] test, which made it clear that the First Amendment is designed to promote the public good, so that speech that has good effects is protected, whereas speech that seeks to undermine the basis of the public good—including the Constitution itself—is not. And whether speech will promote good or bad effects is primarily a legislative question. The common law of England allowed prosecutions for abuses of freedom of speech and press, and so had American law since the founding. But this reversion to "bad tendency" would prove to be short-lived, quickly succumbing to a version of the Holmes-Brandeis test.

Brandeis and Holmes indeed saw freedom of speech as a central constitutional freedom worthy of special judicial solicitude. This belief was not unrelated to the dangers that each perceived in the political, social, and biological stagnation that would result if speech were stifled. The interests and aspirations of the time, to which law must conform, are set in the marketplace of ideas, which, in turn, influences truly democratic outcomes on policy questions. Historicism itself dictates the special privileging of speech. Later in the century, this privileging would extend beyond speech to expression, sentiment, passion, and relatively unconstrained individual autonomy, whose protection can therefore be seen as a conclusion not of principled rights-based liberalism, but of historicized liberalism, or progressivism.

In Brandeis's separate opinion concurring in the judgment in *Whitney v. California* (1927), joined by Holmes, he made the following argument:

> Freedom to think as you will and to speak as you think are means indispensable to the discovery and spread of political truth; that without free speech and assembly, discussion would be futile; that with them, discussion affords ordinarily adequate protection against the dissemination of noxious doctrine; that the greatest menace to freedom is an inert people, that public discussion is a political duty; and that this should be a fundamental principle of the American government.[60]

For at least one latter-day interpreter, the very "idealism" of this reasoning "makes it arguably the most important essay ever written, on or off the bench, on the meaning of the First Amendment."[61] Dewey also concurred with this reasoning, citing approvingly Justice Brandeis's claim in this case that "those who won our independence believed that the final end of the State was to make men free to develop their faculties."[62] For Dewey, as for Brandeis, "liberation of the capacities of individuals for free, self-initiated expression is an essential part of the creed of liberalism."[63]

Although Brandeis "could not speak of 'tyranny of the majority' in the manner of his lifelong political opponents, those who exalted the rights of private property and entrepreneurial capital," he did acknowledge the problem of "occasional tyrannies of governing majorities."[64] The very notion of inherent human tendencies, so central to the Founders' Constitution, was alien to Brandeis. His ad hoc doctrine, by its very nature, called for the implementation of selective, as opposed to institutional, constraints on majority tyranny. This is the beginning of an explanation of how Brandeis reconciled his majoritarianism in most areas with his defense of minority rights in speech cases.[65] But of course it does not account for why Brandeis saw restrictions on speech as tyrannical rather than as a mark of good government, as they were under the "bad tendency" test. They were tyrannical for Brandeis insofar as they suppressed free-flowing developments that were good for both the individual and society, in joint motion. And this motion must, by its very nature, be away from an earlier starting point, which the bad-tendency test was designed to preserve. Stasis is the enemy for Brandeis; unfettered freedom of speech and association are the key tools of dynamism and growth. In pursuit of these ends, he lays the groundwork for an all-encompassing intellectual and moral reformation and emancipation.

> To Brandeis, the measure of courage in the civic realm is the capacity to experience or anticipate change—even rapid and fundamental change—without losing perspective or confidence. Assessments of the benefits and risks of unregulated discussion are certain to be affected by what general disposition the decisionmaker has toward the phenomenon of change. And while speech no doubt contributes directly to change by ventilating grievances and reform proposals, the freedom of speech may be most valuable for its indirect effect, salutary even if subtle, on public attitudes toward change. Those attitudes largely determine how the political economy responds to the grievances and reforms that are ventilated. Not just judges

but all of us need to be emancipated from "the bondage of irrational fears" as we encounter unsettling proposals for political change. The essence of civic courage is a healthy mentality regarding change.[66]

There is thus a deep communitarianism in Brandeis's thought; a sense of the desirability and possibility of reconciling individual and community. This communitarianism opposes those natural, pre-political rights which are regarded as isolating individuals from society, and it seeks to replace them and the legalistic formalism they imply with a mechanism aimed at an organic, noninstitutional harmonization of interests.[67]

We see the sense in which progressivism as legal theory reaches down to homogenize and nationalize in *Gilbert v. Minnesota* (1920),[68] in which Brandeis, in dissent, argued that state powers to prohibit antiwar propaganda were preempted by the federal war power. He also became the first on the Court to suggest that the liberty protected by the Fourteenth Amendment might well be interpreted to apply the provisions of the First Amendment to the states. The seed of incorporation having been planted in *Gilbert*, by 1925 it grew into a majority opinion in *Gitlow v. New York*,[69] where the Court held that the Fourteenth Amendment applied the protections of the First Amendment to the actions of state and local governments. In time, of course, incorporation would result in the application of most of the protections of the Bill of Rights—a document initially understood, ironically, as a shield for the people and states against the encroachments of the federal government—against the states themselves. The final result seems to be directly contrary to the Founders' understanding: state lawmaking has itself become nationalized through the power of the federal courts.

In a meditation on the uses of substantive due process, Brandeis made the following argument, preserved in the handwritten memorandum of his protégé Felix Frankfurter:

1) d.p. [due process] should be restricted to procedural regularity or

2) in favor of repeal but

3) while it is, must be applied to substantive laws and
so as to things that are fundamental.

Right to Speech

Right to Education

Right to choice of profession

Right to locomotion[70]

Brandeis would provide the ideal vocabulary for the con-
solidation of national power and the overcoming of Madisonian
constitutionalism. Growth, in the progressive dispensation—
following in the grand tradition of Theodore Roosevelt, among
others—would be equated with *national* growth, *national* standards, and *national* superintendence of traditionally local matters. Despite his belief in judicial restraint, Brandeis, in pursuit
of a doctrine of fundamental, noneconomic individual rights,
would at various points in his judicial career assert the desirability of judicial lawmaking where legislatures had failed to act.
Those rights which in his view were necessary for individual and
social flourishing deserved judicial protection.

In this regard, the significance of Brandeis's articulation of
the "right to be let alone"—which time would transmogrify into
a broad right to privacy—cannot be underestimated. Brandeis's
emphasis on this purported right, first in a law-review article in
1890 and later in dissent in *Olmstead v. U.S.* (1928),[71] along with
his expansive view of substantive due process for ends appealing
to him, illustrate the extent to which he was, in fact, a progressive legal visionary. Brandeis would, significantly, confess his
great "faith in time" to Frankfurter.

In sum, we may say that Brandeis's success as a judicial actor
was to marshal the Court's older activism in defense of property
rights, individual freedom, and federalism into an activism in

support of social rights, social change, and nationalism as manifested by the progressive legislative agenda. In this fundamental sense, he spearheaded the Court's move from a reactionary to a full-blown progressive posture.

Oliver Wendell Holmes and the Rise of Legal Realism

Brandeis's comrade-in-arms on the Court was Oliver Wendell Holmes. Appointed by Theodore Roosevelt, Holmes served from 1902 to 1932 and remains one of the few figures in Supreme Court history whose name is more of a household word than Brandeis's. He was also the more theoretical of the two. As an intellectual founder of sociological and realist jurisprudence in his great work *The Common Law,* Holmes was a natural for his role as the greatest progressive thinker on the Court.

In his great essay titled "The Path of the Law," Holmes revealed that he was a devotee of legal realism, a doctrine that had an important impact on contract and tort law in the United States and Britain at the time. Legal realism is a variety of legal positivism, which is the view that law is that which is promulgated by the sovereign (in this case, the courts). Law, like society, is always in flux, and one adjudicates and promulgates based on law's practical effects. Positivism, along with sociological jurisprudence and realism, are best understood as disciplinary offshoots of the new "scientific" attitudes toward politics and human affairs.

According to Holmes and the legal realists, morals have nothing to do with the law—they are only internal states of mind. Only what one *does* counts, and the measure of what one does is utility. There is no single just or constitutional answer to a legal problem; there is no natural, or even constitutional, basis for law—legal adjudication comes down to weighing questions of social advantage. In Holmes's view, the jurist should have an evolutionist's modesty with respect to law, taking into account the needs of an ever-changing social order.[72] Holmes thus raises squarely a fundamental question: If the Constitution does not dictate anything in particular—if it is neutral on moral matters as well as legal forms—is there any ground for faith in the Constitution or liberal constitutionalism itself? As Edward Purcell notes,

> Although the realists were firm believers in democratic government, the empirical naturalism they embraced and attempted to apply to legal theory raised both practical and theoretical questions about the nature of democratic government. The most important practical point of their argument was questioning and in many cases rejecting the idea of a government of laws rather than men. Most democratic legal theories—and many state constitutions—held that established and known laws alone should be binding on free citizens; the realists maintained that such laws were nonexistent and impossible to attain.[73]

Or, as Albert Alschuler has succinctly put it, "Champions of both the mild brand of skepticism (utilitarian pragmatism) and the piquant (law as power) are the heirs to Holmes."[74]

It is at least true that most contemporary scholars and practitioners of the science of jurisprudence are heirs to the ideas to which Holmes himself was heir. Certainly, instrumentalism, accompanied by a studied vagueness about ends, defines much contemporary American pragmatism.[75] The inventors of pragmatism were influenced by the Darwinists, insofar as they saw pragmatic thought as a means of adaptation to the environment. Pragmatism's test was not truth, but adaptive success; furthermore, even without clear ends or purposes, experimentation could generate progress.[76] Some form of utilitarianism thereby becomes the standard test of an experiment's success.

Although conventionally placed with Brandeis as an advocate of judicial restraint, Holmes saw clearly the need for courts, when necessary, to provide the creative responses dictated by the times. For Holmes, the Constitution can indeed be what the Supreme Court says it is. One irony in all of this for the "great dissenter" is that if "law is simply a matter of what the courts do in fact, dissenting opinions always have the law wrong."[77] In the wake of Holmes, it is not so much formalism that is rejected as objective concepts of right and wrong. Holmes is a candidate for many labels—pragmatist, utilitarian, Nietzschean, social Darwinist, nihilist.[78] As Holmes dismisses natural law, his jurisprudence as the science of positive law becomes merely a predictive tool. Well-trained lawyers, according to Holmes, become the oracles of the new legalism and, indeed, new constitutionalism. It is beyond their ability—as it is beyond the ability of anyone—to point to the constitutional truth of things. To know legal dogma is to be able to make predictions: "People want to know under what circumstances and how far they will run the risk of coming against what is so much stronger than themselves, and hence it becomes a business to find out when this danger is to be feared. The object of our study, then, is prediction, the prediction of the incidence of public force through the instrumentality of the courts."[79] This is far from Plato's notion that law seeks to be a discovery of *what is,* or Aquinas's assertion that proper human law must not conflict with the natural law, which is accessible to unaided human reason, or the Founders' written constitutionalism. In fact, the Platonic character Thrasymachus—who famously claims that justice is the advantage of the stronger— anticipates Holmes.[80]

Holmes's conception of law's predictive nature shows law to be distinctively modern in a scientific sense. In the manner that modern science predicts the motions of bodies, so modern law predicts the motions of actors within the legal system. It thus provides a kind of order, but it is an order derivative from instrumental concerns rather than fixed philosophic, moral, or constitutional principles. Alas, as Alschuler writes, "One cannot revere predictions of what the courts will do in fact; patriots have never pledged their lives, their property, or their sacred honor to the prediction of judicial decisions. . . . Holmesian positivism falsifies Lincoln's experience. . . . What Lincoln said of Douglas might better have been said of Holmes: '[H]e is blowing out the moral lights around us.'"[81]

Not coincidentally, this view of law and its study has grown in tandem with the case method, invented in and by the law schools. One might argue that this view of law is still largely confined to law schools, which rely overwhelmingly on a teaching methodology dedicated to perpetuating it. Court decisions and legislation, as Holmes avers, are found in the "sibylline leaves" that gather the "scattered prophecies of the past" and form "the oracles of the law."[82] The case method, as it has come down to us, is preeminently a historical and historicized pedagogy, not a statement of fundamental principles. Reliance on it to the exclusion of other approaches has the tendency to transform law's character. To the citizen, law continues to be defined and delimited by questions of justice and injustice; to the law student, it is defined and delimited by consultation with the oracles.

In what terms are we to understand what law's instrumentality—the courts—will actually *do?* Holmes claims that law reflects not logic but experience. Law cannot be understood to be syllogistic with the major premise of sound legal analysis being found in the law itself, and the minor premise in the facts of the case. Such analysis implies that judges can decide particular cases on the basis of right reason. Rather, judges look to history and incorporate science—especially economic science—into their jurisprudence. Holmes's social Darwinism is exhibited in his view that judges express the wishes of their class at a particular historical point, albeit this view is in clear tension with his view that judges must decide cases fairly. The content and growth of law are determined as much by organic "forces" as by men.[83]

In this sense, there is some truth to the claim that "Holmes's social Darwinism lay in his belief that progress or the lack of it was as much a matter of chance as was evolution." That is why "he scorned Spencer's and Sumner's attempt to transform Darwinism into a moral justification of domination by supposedly superior races."[84] But this claim is not without difficulty. As we have seen, there is more fatalism in Holmes than in Brandeis— less confidence that the competition of ideas will allow the best to triumph—but Holmes was hardly consistent on this point. Indeed, at various times, he was capable of displaying considerable comity with both "right" and "left" social Darwinism.

The actual grounds of decision, according to Holmes, are based on the "felt necessities" of the time; judges decide questions first, and find reasons for them *ex post facto.* There can thus be no logical necessity or reasoning about law apart from calculations dictated by answers to questions of advantage, especially material advantage. Holmes maintains that one of the problems of the common law prior to legal realism was that it had not been, in a certain sense, theoretical enough—that is, it had not been reliant enough on utilitarian social and economic theory, as opposed to insight into eternal questions of justice. In fact, the judge gives his conclusions

> because of some belief as to the practice of the community or of a class, or because of some opinion as to policy. . . . Such matters really are battle grounds where the means do not exist for determinations that shall be good for all time, and where the decision can do no more than embody the preference of a given body in a given time and place. . . . [O]ur law is open to reconsideration upon a slight change in the habit of the public mind. No concrete proposition is self-evident. . . .[85]

Does all this make Holmes nothing more than a garden-variety "pragmatist" in the loosest sense—a man without broad theoretical consistency beyond an indeterminate utilitarianism? According to the contemporary legal theorist Richard Posner, it does. For Posner, Holmes exhibited a quintessential form of legal pragmatism—law based on a balancing approach calibrated by judges' evaluation of consequences.[86] But the Posnerian account misses something vital: the deep-seated historicism at the heart of Holmes's thought.

> For economically minded scholars and others, the function of law, the market, and other social institutions is to achieve the maximum satisfaction of human wants regardless of their content (or, if you prefer Posner's variation, to achieve maximum satisfaction of desires backed by wealth). This viewpoint elides a distinctive and persistent characterization of human thought—the evaluation of desires on scales other than intensity.[87]

The core of Holmes's legal realism—its pragmatism along with a confidence in, or grim acceptance of, the progress of History—is brought into relief when one examines its insistence on the notion that courts must interpret and balance rights in light of questions of social advantage and progress. Such a notion was largely alien to American law prior to Holmes and his fellow travelers (including Cardozo and Roscoe Pound). The importance of a weighted judicial balancing for Holmes is nowhere more evident than in his free-speech jurisprudence. In *Schenck*, Holmes had stated the famous "clear and present danger" test as a pragmatic doctrine that avoided inquiry into the content of speech and concentrated only on its likely effects. Prior to the articulation of this doctrine, the content of speech was considered of vital constitutional import.

For example, in *Abrams v. United States* (1919)[88]—decided just months after *Schenck*—a majority of the Court had used the "bad tendency" test to uphold the convictions of antigovernment, antiwar radicals who had advocated violence. Holmes dissented in *Abrams,* interpreting his own clear-and-present-danger standard more liberally than he had in *Schenck,* where he and Brandeis, notwithstanding the test, had in fact voted with the majority to uphold the conviction of antiwar radicals distributing literature to draftees. According to Holmes in *Abrams,* free speech fosters free trade in ideas, and the test of truth is its ability to get itself accepted in the marketplace of ideas, which will happen when the market assesses its needs. Holmes's reasoning—quite circular—implies that truth will triumph because that is what truth does, and society need not fear what triumphs, for it is true and useful.[89] Implicit here is a genuine Darwinian confidence that the strongest thing—truth—will win out.[90] Though Holmes's clear-and-present-danger test has, in language at least, been subsequently modified, it still in practice defines much First Amendment jurisprudence. For Holmes, writes Wolfe, "the intellectual marketplace was more sacred than the economic marketplace."[91] His language is "radically modern,"[92] in a distinctly Darwinian and historical sense. The beliefs that will triumph in the long run are key, not the constitutional or regime beliefs that have existed up to the present.

According to Posner, all of this reduces to pragmatic consequentialism—the "greater the probability of harm, the greater the *expected* harm and therefore the greater the pragmatic justification for preventing or punishing speech that creates the danger."[93] For Posner, Holmes's different approach in *Abrams* was a result of his pragmatic emphasis on the benefits as opposed to harms of free speech, which was necessary to justify his acceptance of the First Amendment claim in *Abrams* that he had rejected in *Schenck*. The acceptance of the First Amendment claim in *Abrams* was, in turn, linked to a consequential difference between the two cases—in *Schenck,* leaflets were being distributed to draftees in an attempt to obstruct the draft; in *Abrams,* they were being distributed at large, so any actual obstruction of the war effort was destined to be minimal.[94] In a breathtaking paragraph, Posner suggests that the First Amendment, Holmes, Dewey, Darwinism, and the rule of law itself can be reduced to a pragmatic calculus:

> These two opinions of Holmes's, though imperfect like all legal innovations, are the germ of modern free-speech law. Their prestige and influence suggest that pragmatic balancing is part of the First Amendment interpretive tradition, and this is reassuring because . . . one of the systemic consequences of legal decisionmaking to which a good pragmatist judge will attend is the unsettling effect on people's legal rights and duties, and the stimulus to cynicism about the judicial process, produced by judges who make scant effort to maintain continuity with established understandings of the law and to observe correlative limits on judicial creativity. Not . . . that the judge has a duty to abide by constitutional or statutory text, or by precedent. That would be the idea rejected by John Dewey that law is entirely a matter of applying rules laid down in the past. . . . My point is that continuity and restraint in the performance of the judicial function are important social goods, the goods summarized in the term "rule of law," and any judge proposing to innovate must consider not only the benefits of the innovation in making the law better adapted to its social environment (the Darwinian analogue) but also the costs in injury to those goods.[95]

Posner's attempt to reduce Holmes's reasoning to a nonphilosophical "recusant" pragmatism is clever but unconvincing, for two reasons. First, the very discussion of benefits and harms is a way of smuggling in, without acknowledgment, moral categories. Posner's admission that pragmatic adjudication is a form of cost-benefit analysis[96] does little to help his case unless law is directly analogous to economics, wherein there are essentially universal, noncontroversial definitions of costs and benefits that are reducible to monetary gains and losses. Or, as Alschuler puts it, "The skepticism of welfare economists, pragmatists, and utilitarians is only partial. These thinkers attempt, without much success, to put on the brakes halfway down. Their beliefs are vulnerable to the same 'sez who?' skepticism that leads them to reject the creeds of others. They are unable to justify even the minimal values they retain."[97] The commensurability of desires, and their commensurability with monetary value, is at the heart of this analysis.[98] Posner attempts to reduce the political to the economic, which is not fully possible for the social Darwinists or progressives. Holmes, at least, is willing to acknowledge a political good of sorts—the survival of the organic whole of state and society—*this* organic whole, as opposed to *that*—which is vitally threatened in wartime.

Second, Posner ignores Holmes's own clearly Darwinian concerns, in *Abrams*, with experiment, conflict, and triumph—which Holmes understands as forms of exercise good for the body of the living organism, of which it may be said, what doesn't kill it makes it stronger. The marketplace metaphor of *Abrams* brings to mind struggle, which, by the time the case was decided, had been a central feature of Holmes's thought for decades. H. L. Mencken's quip about Holmes—that at the age of seventy-eight a strange amiability overcame him—is not quite apt. If our analysis is right, there is no need to impute a shifting worldview, a new jurisprudential outlook, or a newfound personal amiability to Holmes.[99]

For Holmes, rights are nothing more than what certain groups will.[100] Whatever prevails is right, and therefore all political developments are good until they are no longer in ascendancy, and every regime is worthy until it is overthrown or crumbles. Judges themselves, as well as legislators, must to some large degree reflect dominant forces according to the state's position in History. Holmes was therefore a progressive in this historical sense, rather than in his individual judgments, which could favor repressive law as well as progressive law. Some people, warns Alschuler, "mistook his reverence for struggle with sympathy for progressive causes."[101]

Another way to view the matter is to note that an interpretation of Holmes's free-speech doctrine that reduces it to some version of utilitarianism obscures the key premises that support it. If a society protects all or most kinds of potentially destructive speech, one of three propositions must be true of that society: 1. It is indifferent to the result of the contest between truth and falsity, or, more properly, wholesome and destructive speech, and therefore to itself as an order worthy of preservation; 2. It is powerless to distinguish between truth and falsity, wholesomeness and destructiveness; or 3. It is confident that unwholesome speech is essentially impotent in the face of truth.

Of these three hidden premises, Holmes's reasoning relies most obviously on the third. He seems to understand freedom of speech as a social policy preferred—at least in his common-law world—above other potentially conflicting policies. But why should he prefer this if law does not reflect a natural or providential order? The best account of Holmes's thought is his belief in a "new" natural law—a Darwinian process of triumph over lesser forms, or, in other words, progressivism as legal theory.

However, by the time of his judgment in *Gitlow* (1925), Holmes was claiming, again in dissent, that it matters not which view wins. In his words, "If in the long run the beliefs expressed in proletarian dictatorship are destined to be accepted by the dominant forces of the community, the only meaning of free speech is that they should be given their chance and have their way."[102] Holmes therefore appears to be relying here on the first premise, i.e., that society is indifferent to the outcome. But one might then ask, if the Constitution—or the presently established constitutional order—is itself neutral or indifferent on this question, what is the basis for a constitutional ruling in favor of a First Amendment claim? Again, we are led to Darwinian experimentalism, albeit of a more foreboding, fatalistic kind.

Like Brandeis, Holmes in general was willing to show great deference to legislative judgments as the sovereign expressions of popular will. As we have seen, in *Lochner* Holmes dissented (on the grounds of constitutional neutrality) from a majority that held that state economic regulations limiting work hours were unconstitutional. He famously claimed, "I strongly believe that my agreement or disagreement has nothing to do with the right of a majority to embody their opinions in law. . . . I think the word liberty in the Fourteenth Amendment is perverted when it is held to prevent the natural outcome of a dominant opinion. . . ." But his often-modest conception of the judicial function in a democracy was hardly consistent. His jurisprudence, like that of Brandeis, suggests that the Supreme Court is to intervene when Congress limits free speech, but not when Congress limits economic freedom. In one leading interpretation, "the jurisprudential postures of certain justices have aided in the creation of a double standard. . . . [Holmes] was willing to go so far as 'to help my country go to hell if that's what it wants.' Yet he nevertheless drew the line and called a firm halt to legislative experimentation when it came to basic '*non*economic' rights."[103] In another recent interpretation, the progressives "were determined that their vision of the managed economy should take precedence in all areas of life."[104]

But there is more to the story than the distinction between the economic and noneconomic realms. Holmes's activism can be fully meshed with his restraint only if we understand his relationship to the dominant political and sociological theories of his day. Holmes seems open either to activism or restraint, depending on how, pragmatically, either will work itself out—but he seems always to have organic entities and their laws in mind; his pragmatism is tethered to a deeper organic historicism. Holmes, like Brandeis, thinks along recognizably progressive lines: Regulation of the economy can generally be considered good, but the regulation of free speech is bad. Such a Darwinian pragmatism in conjunction with a set of preferred ends quickly culminates in the notion that the Constitution is what judges say it is (which notion is a species of common law, as Holmes understands the common law).

For Holmes, survival or progress might require activism or restraint, and reliance on either is purely an instrumental—or experimental—question. Indeed, there is the enduring sense that "truth" itself is a pragmatic question. Holmes notably claims, "When I say that a thing is true, I mean that I cannot help believing it. . . . But as there are many things that I cannot help doing that the universe can, I do not venture to assume that my inabilities in the way of thought are inabilities of the universe. I therefore define the truth as the system of my limitations. . . ."[105] Even more dramatically, Holmes's efforts to debunk the philosopher's quest for "absolute" truth or the jurist's for "natural law" leads him to suggest that the morality of even the greatest human struggles depends entirely on the outcome:

> I used to say, when I was young, that truth was the majority vote of that nation that could lick all others. Certainly we may expect that the received opinion about [the First World] war will depend a good deal upon which side wins (I hope with all my soul it will be mine), and I think that the statement was correct in so far as it implied that our test of truth is a reference to either a present or an imagined future majority in favor of our view.[106]

This account of natural law—or, more properly, an inexorable law of historical unfolding—paints it as nothing more than a dominant opinion. Holmes thereby lays the foundation for a judicial seeking-out and support of such dominant opinions, and, concomitantly, judicial search-and-destroy missions for "weaker" opinions or entities that appear not to support the strength and growth of the social organism.

Racial improvement through eugenics was one outgrowth of this early-twentieth-century progressivism, possessing as it did considerable faith in the ability of science and purportedly scientific administration to solve social problems. Sir Francis Galton, Darwin's cousin and the father of eugenics, aimed to improve the human race through the containment of defective genes.[107] So great was the passion for eugenics in the early decades of the twentieth century that one influential lobby and litigation group even developed a "Model Eugenical Sterilization Law."[108] By the late 1920s, compulsory sterilization operations were proceeding in many state mental hospitals. The early eugenicists were "in large part responsible for the emphasis upon preserving the 'racial stock' as a means of national salvation—an emphasis so congenial to militant nationalists like Theodore Roosevelt. They differed, however, from earlier social Darwinists in that they failed to draw sweeping laissez-faire conclusions; indeed a part of their own program depended upon state action."[109] Paradoxically, eugenics can be understood as a manifestation of the turn toward social reform and social consciousness in the early twentieth century, albeit under the influence of social Darwinism. The collective good and empiricism replaced "ancestor worship"[110]—in Hofstadter's rather unfortunate phrasing—as dominant motifs of American society. "Perpetuation" of the existent society and its political institutions took on a whole new meaning.

In *Buck v. Bell* (1927),[111] plaintiff Carrie Buck challenged the sterilization order entered against her under a Virginia law allowing sterilization for the mentally handicapped (on the recommendation of "experts," after an appeals process). In one of his most notorious judgments, Holmes wrote the 8–1 majority opinion that upheld the Virginia law. Counsel for the state of Virginia argued for the law on the basis of general state police powers to protect the public good—as well as the good of the handicapped. Counsel for Buck put forth, among other arguments, an equal-protection claim. Holmes upheld the law on the grounds that those within the specified class were treated with scrupulous procedural fairness. Decrying those who "sap the strength" of society, and contending, in reference to the affected litigant and her family, that "three generations of imbeciles are enough," Holmes seemed to accept the eugenic arguments to the point of endorsing them on public policy grounds. Holmes reasoned by analogy. He compared the hardships of sterilization with the sacrifices of soldiers in battle. Referring to the Civil War, he argued that if "the public welfare may call upon the best citizens for their lives," surely those who "sap the strength of the state" could be called upon for a lesser sacrifice. "It is better for all the world, if instead of waiting to execute degenerate offspring for crime, or to let them starve for their imbecility, society can prevent those who are manifestly unfit from continuing their kind."

Buck illustrates the fact that Holmes's judicial "restraint" betrayed a moral and political tendentiousness. The influence of extra-judicial ideas was so great in *Buck* that one commentator has suggested that "with the eugenics movement at its height in 1927 the Court was its prisoner."[112] Although Holmes personally disdained much that he voted in favor of, when it came to *Buck v. Bell* he expressed in personal letters positive pleasure in the outcome.[113] The belief that "good" and "bad" genes could and should be isolated by the state lost respectability in the decade after *Buck*, because of attacks from both theologians and scientists. But *Buck* has never been explicitly overruled.

What can be made of a case like *Buck* in the overall context of Holmes's jurisprudence? The conventional view is that Holmes's reasoning was shallow and epigrammatic, rather than deep or truly reflective. But this is unfair. Although he was poetic—expressing ideas with brevity and often wit—he was coherent and logical. He rejected the notion that natural law or natural rights were embedded in the Constitution, as he rejected even the need to *interpret* the Constitution. Indeed, in the wake of Holmes, we have introduced new terms into our constitutional vocabulary: interpretivism versus non-interpretivism have come to replace strict versus loose constructionism.[114]

Holmes did not invent the notion that law evolved and adapted; in this sense, he added little to what had gone before him. He and the other progressives did, however, take something away: moral realism itself, or the belief that law is something beyond syllogism or interest or tastes.[115] The formalism against which they railed never reduced to a purely mechanical jurisprudence or to a straightforward discovery of legal rules.[116] Sensitivity to experience, rather than universal or mechanical abstractions, has, in fact, been a hallmark of American political and jurisprudential thinking from the founding onward, as it is of all common-law jurisprudence. Alschuler reminds us that those who would regard Holmes as revolutionary simply for declaring that the life of the law is not logic but experience would do well to hearken to "John Dickinson's admonition to his fellow delegates: 'Experience must be our only guide. Reason may mislead us.'"[117] Or to Matthew Hale, or Publius in *The Federalist*, or St. George Tucker, or Blackstone, or Joseph Story; or to the line of common-law and constitutional decisions pronounced by state and federal courts from the dawn of the republic, decisions that were sensitive to experience and the exigencies of the time.[118] As Alschuler writes, "Possibly some now-obscure German legal theorist fit Holmes's description of the deductive formalist bogeyman, but I know of no American who did,"

It was in their rejection of natural law that Holmes and other historicist judges broke not only with the founding and Lin-

coln, but with the very notion that human beings are creatures
of a certain type, with transcendent purposes and ends that do
not change with time. The new jurisprudence was suspicious of
the very idea of justice itself. With this change, judges came to
look to the future more than to the past, and thus to take on a
new role.

This contrasts sharply with the old view of the nature of common-law jurisprudence, which Alschuler captures succinctly:

> In essence, the traditional division of labor between legis-
> latures and courts has been a division between the future
> and the past. Although the boundary between legislative
> and judicial tasks was never fixed and always permeable,
> legislators specialized in governing the future and judges
> in rectifying past wrongs. The Constitution recognized
> this allocation of responsibility by forbidding Congress
> from enacting *ex post facto* laws, bills of attainder, and
> other retrospective measures while limiting federal courts
> to the resolution of disputes about past events—"cases of
> actual controversy."[122]

The retrospective conception of the common law still exists
in a few places, notably in the birthplace of the common law,
England.[123] By contrast, it has largely fallen by the wayside in
America under the influence of social Darwinism and pragmatism, each of which focuses on the future. As we observe these
forms of consequentialism, we can also observe that "over the
course of the twentieth century, courts (the U.S. Supreme Court
in particular) increasingly came to see litigants as trimmings for
their rulings. They focused less on corrective justice and more
on concerns like efficiency, deterrence, cost-benefit analysis,
the systemic reform of defective institutions, and shaping 'the
law.'"[124] Courts began to feel themselves independent of heaven
itself.

The sources of Holmes's peculiar organicism are apparent in the work of his intellectual contemporaries, who together defined the dominant strains of social and political thought at the turn of the century. Holmes's thinking is reminiscent, for example, of Wilson's, which held the state to be an organic association limited only by the needs of society, not by the "rights" of individuals. The goal for Wilson, as for Holmes, was always the equalization of conditions for the sake of development—individual and social. Impersonal forces must be allowed free reign to interact with one another (with an occasional helping hand from governmental institutions to ensure that no "artificial" barriers stand between them). A marketplace of such forces—including ideas—will best ensure the evolutionary growth of the organism; it will be strengthened by the natural selection of the strongest, and therefore best, voices. The importance of *equality* in grounding this competition derives in large measure from Dewey's "left" social Darwinism and his quasi-Marxist interpretation of the American condition.[125]

Holmes was largely consistent, but no human being perfectly comports himself with a theory, however powerful. Alschuler goes so far as to claim, "Nearly all of the statements that Holmes's admirers treat as proof of his idealism, romanticism, utilitarianism, and moral vision prove compatible on examination with a Nietzschean-Darwinian worldview."[126] Furthermore, when "one abandons efforts to transform Holmes into a utilitarian or pragmatist and sees him as an existentialist, social Darwinist, Thrasymachian, and Nietzschean, he no longer appears complex, contradictory, or dualistic."[127] Each of these adjectives tells us something important about Holmes—and about progressivism and the new science of jurisprudence. Yet, each also introduces its own layers of complexity and potential contradiction. In the end, Holmes's progressivism, rooted as it was in social Darwinism, led him to the view that the Court, beyond establishing procedural guarantees designed to ensure a competitive playing field, should only rarely intervene substantively on behalf of rights-bearing individuals, dissident voices, and minorities. Many have said that his view of civil rights was therefore narrow—but it was narrow only where ideology did not dictate that it be wide.

Benjamin Cardozo and the Growth of Progressive Jurisprudence

Benjamin Cardozo succeeded Holmes to the Supreme Court. President Hoover nominated him, and his tenure came at the end of what is understood to be the progressive era. In his Supreme Court decisions (following on those he wrote as a judge on the New York Court of Appeals from 1914 to 1932), we see the flowering of judicial progressivism during the New Deal period. Like Brandeis and Holmes, Cardozo confronted an increasingly emboldened regulatory state in the realms of both economic policy and civil liberties. His ambition, like theirs, was to confront the possibilities and limits of judicial review of the republican branches of government. Like Brandeis and Holmes, Cardozo leaned toward judicial deference in matters economic, but high scrutiny in certain civil-rights matters. In Christopher Wolfe's words, Cardozo was "part of a generation of lawyers trained in law schools in which Holmes's influence was profound. Thus Cardozo could say in 1921 that Holmes's opinions were 'the voice of a new dispensation.'"[129]

On the New York Court of Appeals, Cardozo displayed his progressive bona fides by manifesting a marked willingness to expand the common law to protect new classes of people and new interests in society. He wrote the majority opinion in *Macpherson v. Buick Motor Company* (1916),[130] which affirmed the broad reach of New York State tort law to protect victims of defective products—even in the absence of a contractual relationship between the victims and the manufacturer of those products.

Likewise, in *Ultramares Corporation v. Touche* (1931),[131] Cardozo moved the common law toward protecting third parties from fraud, rather than only those parties to the fraudulent transaction. In *Jacob and Youngs v. Kent* (1921),[132] Cardozo sought at once to strengthen and to rationalize the common-law of contract by presuming intent where it is unexpressed, and presuming cooperative, as opposed to competitive, behavior. Such presumptions serve to preserve contractual relationships in an increasingly complex commercial society and prevent an unsuspecting party from being unfairly taken advantage of by a too-rigorous adherence to the letter of an agreement whose overall purpose seems in some way to be at odds with its language.

Of course, such hallmarks of interpretation in the realm of private law can become—and indeed did become in Cardozo's usage—a broader form of sociological jurisprudence when applied to public law. Indeed, in explicitly arguing for sociological jurisprudence in his Storrs Lectures at Yale Law School,[133] Cardozo emphasized that law should be interpreted in light of social function rather than formalistic criteria. And this interpretation cannot be separated from the interpreter. According to Cardozo, all of us—judges included—possess a "resultant outlook on life, a conception of social needs, a sense in James's phrase of 'the total push and pressure of the cosmos,' which, when reasons are nicely balanced, must determine where choice will fall."[134] The judge must act as "the interpreter for the community of its sense of law and order" and "supply omissions," looking always for the "'light among the social elements of every kind that are the living force behind the facts.'"[135] In the face of the Heraclitean flux of life, the judge must prevent legal principles from withering and dying.[136]

In a passage that anticipates Justice William Douglas's infamous claim decades later, in *Griswold v. Connecticut* (1965),[137] that a keen judge can detect "penumbras, formed by emanations" from specific constitutional guarantees, Cardozo wrote,

"History or custom or social utility or some compelling sentiment of justice or sometimes perhaps a semi-intuitive apprehension of the pervading spirit of our law must come to the rescue of the anxious judge, and tell him where to go."[138]

Cardozo went on to argue that the "final cause of law is the welfare of society,"[139] properly understood. Such a concern for social justice "finds outlet and expression in the method of sociology."[140] Right standards derived from the method of sociology are to be found in the "accepted standards of the community, the *mores* of the times,"[141] unless "practices in opposition to the sentiments and standards of the age may grow up and threaten to entrench themselves if not dislodged."[142] In a reflection of the old tension within Darwinism, for Cardozo human affairs are organic, yet they also involve human choice. Distinguishing between the true *mores* of the times and corrupt imposters requires, of course, wise men—identifiable by their conformity with, and grasp of, the spirit of the age. They must by the very nature of their task be a guiding force of this spirit.

Cardozo thus openly admits that progressive legislating is the highest form of judging. However, as Christopher Wolfe argues,

> Such an understanding of judicial power marks a radical change in the role of the judge in American political thought. A traditional understanding of judicial power would raise serious questions about the very possibility of such judicial "objectivity" in legislation, since the framers' understanding of human nature recognized that power, while necessary, was always likely to be abused. There was little need to devise institutional mechanisms to check all but the grossest abuses of judicial power (by impeachment) because that power was so limited in its nature. Certainly the framers would have provided other institutional mechanisms to counteract the "ambition" of

judges, if they had conceived of judicial power as essentially legislative in nature, however "interstitial" it might be.[143]

The framers, confessed Cardozo, did not see the courts as protecting "the spirit of the age, but the principles—especially the rights of man—that transcended ages and had been embodied in the Constitution."[144]

Views such as Cardozo's are bound to have constitutional consequences. Cardozo, like his predecessor, became a great dissenter. In *Carter v. Carter Coal Company* (1936),[145] a majority of the Court rejected New Deal legislation that relied on the commerce power to regulate prices and labor relations in the coal industry. Drawing on the Court's traditional, limited reading of the federal commerce power, Justice George Sutherland held for the majority, that there was no direct effect on interstate commerce from the production of coal and that Congress had no power over items of production, as opposed to items in the flow of interstate commerce. The Tenth Amendment, together with a limited reading of the commerce clause, thus prohibited federal action. In dissent, Cardozo (joined by his fellow progressives Brandeis and Stone) famously maintained that a "great principle of constitutional law is not susceptible of comprehensive statement in an adjective." He rejected constitutional formalism in favor of open-ended interpretation based on perceived social needs, a stance that was to define the Court's approach to economic regulation for more than half a century.

Under the threat of Roosevelt's court-packing bill, sent to Congress in early 1937, the direction of the Court began to change in earnest toward a kind of permanent progressivism. In that year, Cardozo wrote the majority opinions in *Steward Machine Co. v. Davis*[146] and *Helvering v. Davis*.[147] In each of these cases, the Court reversed itself on its earlier vigorous defense of federalism and endorsed the constitutionality of the Social Security Act. In *Helvering*, Cardozo wrote, "The line must still be drawn between one welfare and another, between particular and general. Where this shall be placed cannot be known through a formula in advance of the event. There is a middle ground or certainly a penumbra in which discretion is at large. The discretion, however, is not confided to the courts. The discretion belongs to Congress, unless the choice is clearly wrong, a display of arbitrary power, not an exercise of judgment."[148]

Cardozo's judgment in *Palko v. Connecticut* (1937) shows the extent to which progressive thinking—hostile to substantive due process in the economic realm—remained creative and willful in its desire to create much the same type of judicial review for noneconomic or "civil" rights.[149] According to Cardozo's doctrine in *Palko*—which built both on *Gitlow* and on Brandeis's notion of "things that are fundamental"—those rights which are "fundamental" to "ordered liberty" are subject to incorporation. Substantive due process—scorned by earlier progressive jurists such as Holmes—was reborn in earnest. By incorporating various provisions of the Bill of Rights into the Fourteenth Amendment, they could be applied against the states in a manner that gave federal courts effective jurisdiction over state legislation. And this jurisdiction was gained on grounds more theoretically respectable (because under most provisions of the Bill of Rights, "civil" rights—not economic rights—were implied) than a simple invocation of the due-process clause. Such "selective incorporation" would be the constitutional peg on which generations of activist judges would hang their hats as they set the conditions under which Americans could live, work, pray, raise their children, and order their lives. It took the rabid incoherence of *Roe v. Wade* (which nominally relied on the Third, Fourth, Fifth, Ninth, and Fourteenth Amendments)[150] three and a half decades later for many observers to conclude that such substantive judicial entanglements raised more problems than the judiciary is capable of solving.

Judicial progressivism, from its organic rejection of formalism to its creation of the framework for selective incorporation—did not command a reliable majority of the Court until just before Cardozo's death in 1938. In a nationwide 1937 radio broadcast in support of his court-packing bill, Roosevelt said, "We must take action to save the Constitution from the Court."[151] History is full of ironies, and the reaction against Roosevelt's court bill is a great one. The bill failed after the bitterest domestic struggle of Roosevelt's presidency. But those who opposed Roosevelt ensured that the war against judicial supremacy was to be lost, while the judicial supremacy that triumphed was to serve very different ends from the economic ones that defined the *Lochner* era. As Edward Purcell notes, "Popular faith in the Court's special role defeated the dominant president of the twentieth century at the summit of his power. . . . [T]he extent to which the anti–New Deal forces succeeded in using Roosevelt's proposal to elevate the Court to a seemingly untouchable position would have a continuing impact in the radically altered world of the coming decades."[152] Roosevelt managed to win his battle through attrition rather than legislation. By 1941, he had made seven appointments to the Court, including Harlan Stone to the position of chief justice. FDR won by losing, while those skeptical of progressivism as a political outlook and jurisprudential theory lost by winning.

Progressivism as Legal Theory

A theory is an abstract proposition or set of propositions that both accounts well for existing facts and allows us to predict the future course of events, and which does each of these things in a parsimonious manner. Does progressivism disclose a legal theory? At first blush, perhaps not. The leading progressive jurists, in their deference to legislative judgments in the economic realm and activism in the realm of civil rights, are difficult to place on a scale conventionally recognized by analysts of the judiciary. They were neither consistently activists nor practitioners of judicial restraint. While it may be said that none was a textual formalist or scholar of original intent (indeed, the various schools of legal thought that have grown out of progressivism explicitly eschew such formalism), their informalism reliably favors neither liberalism nor conservatism, big government nor small, the little person nor the large conglomerate. Certainly their progressivism does not amount to a judicial doctrine expressible in one or a few lines.

Their progressivism rather is a judicial disposition in search of a theory. Like its overtly political counterpart, it is a disposition to step outside the bounds of Madisonian constitutionalism for the sake of a faith in the future rather than the past. It is theoretical in this more important sense. Its accepted model of man is not man *qua* man—and certainly not modern man, exemplified by *homo economicus*. Rather, postmodern man in the form of expressive individualism is a dominant motif of progressive jurisprudence, which first took its Darwinist, and to some extent Rousseauan, turn more than a century ago.

This jurisprudence sees America as having moved away from a purer, more elemental state toward a future that will be more corrupt in the absence of superintending economic and social regulation. At the same time, it is a future that cannot be avoided, any more than Rousseauan man can turn back the clock and reenter the state of nature. The progressive task—both political and jurisprudential—is to read the public mind and loosen the chains of large-scale industrial society enough to allow for social growth. Brandeis referred to the "curse of bigness"—large institutional arrangements or monopolistic players that stifled rather than developed the individual's capacities. Individual development was at the heart of even his economic concerns. And in this there is a deep, if ironic, kinship with Holmes. As Alschuler writes, "Perhaps the greatest paradox of

Holmes's thought was this: Although he described judging in terms of 'weighing considerations of social advantage,' Holmes valued personal action mostly for its expressive and not its instrumental qualities. Individual action was admirable to the extent that it was 'uneconomic.' The less functional an action, the more it became 'sublime.' Blind commitment alone gave meaning to life."[153] Progressive jurisprudence becomes deferential to the general will, albeit the general will acting in the guise of administrative rationality. At least, it is deferential to this will in areas that do not seek to stifle the free-flowing ideas, passions, and sentiments of the human animal that make up the zeitgeist of which courts must take notice.

There is a residual incoherence to progressivism as legal theory. It alternates between two poles. On the one hand, it expresses the desire to make decisions that are legitimate in the eyes of the community—ones that respond to something like the "felt necessities" of the age. On the other, it seeks to make decisions that counter what it claims is illegitimate majority will. Neither pole is rooted in constitutional text, tradition, logic, or structure, but rather in the judge's view of just what necessities are most deeply felt, most in accordance with social growth, and therefore most compatible with the dictates of History.

The practical result, in contemporary jurisprudence, is that art trumps economics, expression trumps the common good, subjectivity trumps morality, freedom trumps natural law, and will trumps deliberation. Such is the face of progressivism as legal theory, a face that now seems barnacle-encrusted from its triumphal march of a hundred years' duration. Having rooted itself so firmly in the thought that guides the Western world as a whole, and having gained so much strength and momentum on its virtually uninterrupted path, it will not be slowed down, or wiped clean, any time soon. Its success is marked by the fact that it no longer seeks victory, only legitimation in a constitutional system still at odds with it.

6

Academic Progressivism

Progressivism's relationship to the academy—and particularly to political and legal subjects—was destined from the outset to be intimate. Faith in science, including faith in a science of society, is deeply entrenched in the Western tradition. Its roots run from Greek rationalism through medieval realism through Francis Bacon and the Enlightenment. But in America it was Darwinism that served as "the great intellectual catalyst" for the production of the contemporary social sciences,[1] manifested as disciplines within the university. Nearly all the founders of the modern social sciences were Darwinians. From the founding of Johns Hopkins University in 1876 to the curricular reforms of Charles W. Eliot at Harvard University throughout the late nineteenth century to the influence of William Rainey Harper at the University of Chicago in the 1890s and through the early years of the twentieth century, the new scientific, empirical, fundamentally evolutionary understanding of things began to grip American higher education. By the dawn of the twentieth century, the American academy was increasingly marked by an intellectual movement away from teaching about, and belief in, unchanging principles of political life, and toward a faith in pragmatism, relativism, and never-ending growth.

One of the self-appointed tasks of educational reformers was to make the new naturalistic social-scientific inquiry "relevant" to actual social problems. For those schooled in the new methods, objectivity resided in the measurable rather than that which might be knowable to unaided human reason. A fascination with materialist consequentialism was central to the new social sciences. This eventually led to an emphasis on methodology over substantive moral or political understandings, although these understandings invariably lurked in the background of even the most cutting-edge inquiries.

It was into this environment that the modern discipline of political science was born. Because of the Darwinian influence on social thinking, "science" was joined at the hip with "progress" from the very beginning. The new political science, initially centered at Columbia and Johns Hopkins, was marked by the study of institutional forms and their evolution, often using comparative methodologies rooted in the observation of the particular characteristics and historical prospects of various peoples. The first person in America to be identified as a "political scientist" was Francis Lieber, appointed as such at Columbia in 1857. Lieber was a German immigrant deeply influenced by Hegelian historical categories and a notion of the state as an entity far more organic than formal.[2] For him, no standards of political judgment could exist outside the historically conditioned texts and traditions of actual nations, which reflect their character and will. As John S. Dryzek writes, "The concept of 'the state' was cemented into American political discourse by figures who were to become central to the new discipline of political science in the late nineteenth century. . . . From Francis Lieber . . . to Woodrow Wilson . . . the main practical task of political science was seen as the establishment of a unitary national state accompanied by a virtuous national citizenry."[3]

Lieber's successor at Columbia, John William Burgess, was one of the original importers of "German" political science into

America and the founder of Columbia's graduate program—the first in the nation—in political science. He was therefore responsible for training many members of the first generation of American political scientists. Burgess was himself trained at the great German universities of the day and was fascinated by the prospect of a science of peace that would be linked to the growth of the rational state along modern Germanic lines. Meanwhile, at Johns Hopkins, where American institutional history was a particular emphasis, the seminar room in which Woodrow Wilson took much of his training prominently displayed the motto "History is past Politics, and Politics present History."[4]

Prior to the explosive growth of "political science" and the university departments that went along with it, politics had been studied in America under the rubrics of history, law, philosophy, literature, and like fields. The goal was not research or "creation" of knowledge, but rather transmission of knowledge about the great institutions, ideas, and actors that had shaped America and the West. Almost all institutions of higher learning were therefore, in effect, liberal arts colleges—albeit liberal arts colleges with more serious core curricula than almost any to be found today. Contemporary university departments, political science among them, are largely artifacts of the move toward scientific specialization of the late nineteenth and early twentieth centuries, when the university came to think of itself as serving the state. The "newer type" of professor was profiled in a 1902 issue of The *Atlantic Monthly* as one who "instead of occupying himself solely with the dead languages and a little mathematics and philosophy, pursues studies and gives instruction that bring him into touch, at a thousand points of contact, with the material interests, the practical concerns, of the American public."[5]

It was into this environment that, in 1903, the American Political Science Association (APSA) was born, with Frank Goodnow, a protégé of Burgess's, as its first president. Woodrow Wilson would be its third. As we have seen, Wilson understood political scientists to be key actors in bringing to bear democratic expertise on society's new problems. Political scientists would form a kind of informal commission, playing a key intellectual role in synthesizing and coordinating the various organic parts of society into a coherent whole in the form of law.[6] This sense of the mission of political science was related to Wilson's concern about the practical and technical nature of legal education, divorced as it was at that time from larger theories of the state and History.[7] As we shall see, this technical and non-theoretical orientation of legal education would soon enough change radically, in keeping with trends in progressive social science.

The APSA was founded contemporaneously, and not coincidentally, with the peak of progressivism as a social and political movement. It was conceived from the outset as an organization dedicated not merely to studying politics, but to *doing* something.[8] The discipline was "founded not only to study politics but also to advance a political agenda" that grew out of a sense, shared by the discipline's leaders, of the inadequacy of the "Madisonian system."[9] The early years of political science were defined by faith in doctrines of progress, along with the quest for a disciplinary identity linked to scientific methodology that would bestow on political science the necessary respectability to influence policy-makers. In fact, the methodologies of the burgeoning social sciences, including behavioralism, were inextricably related to their commitment to relevance and consequentialism.[10]

The new social sciences would support historical progress, but they would do so indirectly, for direct support would contradict their purported objectivity and value neutrality. As John G. Gunnell observes, "Between the institution of the APSA and the appearance of the first issue of the *American Political Science Review,* Max Weber published his 1904 essay on 'The "Objectivity" of Knowledge in Social Science and Social Policy.' . . . in both theme and context there were a distinct family resemblance and mediated intellectual connections."[11] Goodnow's first presidential address to the APSA in 1904 noted that the disciplinary identity of the APSA revolved around the study of the state, and that political scientists could take on the role of "closet philosopher" by influencing men of action.[12] However, the "philosophy" of the political "scientist" would be grounded in the empirical realm and would thereby stave off the worst flights of fancy to which political philosophers of old had been prone. In Weberian terms, political scientists could ground practical politics in an ethic of responsibility rather than an ethic of ultimate ends. It would be a responsibility to the measured, all-around growth of the social organism and would be devoid of any traditional teleology. In Dennis J. Mahoney's account of the early years of American political science, "Human society was envisaged as capable of permanent and perpetual improvement, and the state was the chosen instrument for accomplishing that improvement. That ideology was never challenged within the discipline, and, in fact, continues to dominate the discipline even into its second century."[13]

The birth of American political science created a bastion within the academy for the view that perpetual societal improvement is possible and inevitable, partly because of evolutionary unfolding, but partly with the aid of the right kind of superintendence. The institutional and theoretical departures implied by this view would have made the new political science unrecognizable to the American Founders, whose "new science of politics" had almost nothing in common with it. It was certainly the case that the new political science, in its dismissive contempt for traditional political philosophy, unchanging principles of political right, and ideas and institutions from prior centuries, turned its back on the Founders. For the most part, it still does. American political science therefore remains almost genetically incapable of understanding the Constitution of the fathers.

Legal Education and the Progressive Mind

In the founding of the APSA, we see the merger of a philosophy of History, a faith in intelligence as a method, and a suspicion of existing institutional forms. This merger of ideas closely parallels that which occurred only slightly later within the corridors of American law schools. It was clear by the 1920s that legal scholars, in the name of a new science of jurisprudence, were increasingly rejecting traditional understandings and approaches, whether they were considered formalist or natural rights–based. There is some consensus across political lines that Oliver Wendell Holmes Jr. provided the inspiration and catalyst for this new disciplinary outlook and approach.[14] Holmes was clearly a more thorough-going expositor of the new jurisprudence and its theoretical underpinnings than any other jurist of his day.

Progressivism did much to set the boundaries and aspirations of sociological jurisprudence, and later an even more inherently skeptical form of academic legal realism. In the Darwinian age, the emphasis was destined to be on processes, functions, and change more than on principles, rules, and stasis. This new "functionalism" transcended political and legal theory and came to define the social sciences generally. Laura Kalman summarizes key developments in these terms:

> By the 1930s, John Dewey and James Rowland Angell had moved psychology away from structuralism, which stressed the elements of consciousness, to functionalism, which emphasized "how and why conscious processes are what they are." Rejecting all philosophy that employed the concept of consciousness, John Watson had begun to study the raw behavior of animals and humans; behaviorism, he boasted, was "the only consistent and logical functionalism." . . . Beard had examined the relationship between the Founding Fathers' constitutional aspirations

and their pocketbooks. Political Scientist Charles Mer-
riam . . . asked whether it was "not possible to go more
deeply into the basis of the city, scrutinize more accurately the social and political processes of which the political
is an integral part?"[15]

For the new generation of "realists" who would eventually
come to dominate the legal academy, jurisprudence must be understood not only in light of its practical social and economic
consequences, but also in terms of the psychological motivations
of judicial actors. All judicial acts, in other words, are designed
to perform a certain function in and for society, as that function is refracted through the sometimes idiosyncratic minds of
judges.[16] Legal principles are to legal functions as Platonic forms
are to empirical reality. Principles express an ideal world that
does not exist and cannot guide human behavior in practice.
For the realists, one had to understand the relationship between
law and society in the broadest sense and not pretend that principles, doctrines, or rules by themselves accounted for, or were
synonymous with, legal reasoning. Judicial decisions, purportedly reliant upon legal principles, were often rationalizations of
results arrived at for other reasons, often understood through
a psychological reductionism.[17] Process, rather than black-letter
law, became a central focus of inquiry. For the realists, the notion of law itself could not be taken seriously—at least it could
not be taken seriously as an independent science.

New legal theories were also required of progressive legal
thinkers in order to take account of the practical politics of the
progressive era. The promulgation of laws and regulations increased the need for well-trained lawyers and policy experts to
draft and interpret them. Weberian expertise applied to public
questions became the gold standard for effective participation in
a progressive republic, and increasingly this expertise had to be
of a legal nature. For progressive aspirations to be realized, law

professors and their students had themselves to become social reformers, policy experts, and, eventually, defenders of a new status quo.

Despite the inherent demands of progressivism, and the almost irresistible intellectual and political currents it introduced, the law schools initially proved resistant. Edward Purcell has noted that, with respect to the new social science, "law, with its basis in centuries-old custom, its traditionalist orientation, and its comparative intellectual isolation, proved a much less receptive field than did philosophy and the newer social sciences."[18] Theodore W. Dwight, one of the founders of modern American legal education and the first dean of what is now Columbia Law School, maintained a "principles before practice" approach during his long tenure there in the second half of the nineteenth century.[19] He therefore "stood squarely in the tradition of Blackstone and Kent."[20] Dwight proved very hostile to subjects outside the law school. While Lieber had gone to Columbia as America's first political scientist, Dwight effectively limited his influence in the law school, despite Lieber's joint appointment there.

The dam was breached when, in the late nineteenth century, Harvard Law School under Christopher Langdell adopted the now ubiquitous case method. This method requires that professors and students concentrate their attentions on a large number of appellate decisions, especially those of the Supreme Court, in order to familiarize themselves with the logic of judicial reasoning. Langdell's view was that legal principles, rules, and procedures are best discerned through the study of—and induction from—many individual cases. From one point of view, the "scientific" case method retained a formalist, logical façade that deemphasized the justice of current claims in favor of the wisdom of experience—the present and future were not everything. From another, the case method was from the outset distinctly historicist, rather than historical in the old sense. Each case—as an individual datum—can be assimilated to a new understanding of science that relies on empirical observation rather than metaphysics thereby allowing observers to see each incremental, evolutionary alteration in the forms of law. In this more fundamental sense, the spirit of positivism and Darwinian science undergirds the case method. Langdell and Harvard's president Eliot saw the case method as eminently practical, providing the clearest answers to legal questions.

Legal method—as one facet of the new "scientific" method—thus became central to legal education. This pedagogy, with the theoretical orientation that underlay it, had its early critics, both in the practicing bar and in the academy, who saw in it precisely the triumph of method over content. "The lasting influence of the case method was to transfer the basis of American legal education from substance to procedure and to make the focus of American legal scholarship—or at least legal theory—increasingly one of process rather than doctrine," states Robert Stevens. "'Science' and 'practicality' remained the watchwords of the case method."[21] This is somewhat ironic insofar as the method was, at its inception, conceived of as a means to see more clearly "black-letter law" without philosophical biases or anachronisms. Some, including many realists, claimed that a reinforcement of the late-nineteenth-century "logical orientation" toward the law—i.e., formalism—could be traced to the case method, which, according to Langdell, was a scientific method reinforcing "a rationalist and deductive theory of judicial decision."[22] And indeed, the case method did allow for extraction of quasi-independent legal principles or rules from the manifold of circumstances. The method separated legal principles from their roots in the natural law, common law, or American constitutionalism broadly conceived, but it did at least retain the suggestion—sometimes explicit, sometimes implicit—that there is an independent science of jurisprudence that can be consulted apart from intellectual and social movements and extra-legal social science. Legal principles, along with the cases in which they were found, could, to some degree, be understood on their own terms.

Despite these early hopes that jurisprudence might be reduced to an objective or exact science, the case method had an inherently nonformalist, and nonlegal, tendency in its atomism. The American court system, compared to other common-law countries, is so layered, vast, diffuse, and productive of reported opinions, that a large degree of atomism is inevitable. As Cardozo quipped in 1924, "the fecundity of our case law would make Malthus stand aghast."[23] To the extent the case method was in any way a friend to formalism, it was destined from the outset to collapse under its own weight. The method presented law in fragmentary form, without purpose or even existence beyond the distillation of principles from the transitory purposes of litigants and their appellate arguments. The case method served to undermine faith in the certainty of legal and constitutional principles that transcend particular factual circumstances. The belief that "facts" are determinative of legal principles is an almost irresistible conclusion when cases become the only lens through which the common law is viewed.

In addition, more integral to the case method than induction is the notion that the law is what courts say it is, and therefore is not nearly as formalistic, logical, or grounded as it might at first appear. The case method was therefore presented by many progressives as a breath of fresh air, compared to the stultifying attempts to systematize principles and present them in lecture format largely independent of empiricism or experience. Of course, it helped the reformers' case that they defined "experience" as goings-on in courts of law.

The case method spread like wildfire, due in no small part to the prestige of Harvard and the sense, especially at less elite schools, that emulation was necessary for academic respectability. By the first decade of the twentieth century, about a third of the law schools in the nation had adopted it.[24] Even Columbia, the dominant force in American legal education until the turn of the century, quickly succumbed. Its older method, in its concern for the transmission of established principles, seemed to the progressive mind to embrace stasis and even Aristotelian teleology in an era that believed only in pragmatism, progress, and History.

Holmes quickly embraced the new method, which he claimed imparted a precision to the thought of his students that had theretofore been lacking.[25] For Holmes, the case method was indeed a usable science of jurisprudence. In characteristic Holmesian language, he argued that "to make a general principle worth anything you must give it a body. . . . You must show how it gradually emerged as the felt reconciliation of concrete instances."[26] The facts themselves—reconciled in concrete cases—take precedence over, and indeed determine, the "principles." Holmes was no doubt quite conscious of the conformity of the case method to his ideas for a new science of jurisprudence. The absence of any fully worked-out theoretical underpinnings to the Langdellian innovation made it easy for him to translate the scientific search for rules into a scientific analysis of facts as *determining* principles or rules. There was, moreover, enough latitude in the Harvard model to justify Holmes's proto-realist interpretation of the intellectual purposes of the case method.[27]

It was decades after Holmes's early embrace of the case method that the independence of legal principles was fully challenged in the law schools on the basis that they were, in fact, subservient to, or products of, the requirements of social life—or, for that matter, to the preferences of individual judges. This challenge came with the growth of full-blown legal realism throughout the 1920s and 1930s, which borrowed from progressive political thought and sociological jurisprudence and melded them into a jurisprudential theory of law suited, exponents claimed, to the new demands of a twentieth-century nation that needed to throw off the shackles of its constitutional past. As sociological jurisprudence was the analogue to the progressive era, so realist theory was the analog to the New Deal.[28] In the words of Stevens,

> The Realists went a long way toward killing the idea of "the system" altogether. All legal logic came under suspicion. . . . Law became less valuable as an objective force binding together different elements in the community. It was one thing to agree that legal objectivity and neutrality were myths; it was another to destroy such myths, providing as they do vital elements of social control, without offering any alternatives. Such an undermining of legal sinews proved to be the Realists' lasting monument.[29]

Indeed, the "same assumptions made by the realists were made by the framers of the New Deal. The New Dealers were also demythologizers. They set out to eradicate the notions that private property was sacred and that self-help was the only way to deal with adversity."[30]

The vast and ad hoc nature of the American common-law system, with cases adduced to support the ever-shifting exigencies of litigation (what Richard Posner would call pragmatism), would seem to prevent the dominance of substantive trends or tendencies in law. At least one might expect this in the absence of a supervening ideology. But the extended republic of American jurisprudence has in fact proved quite tendentious on certain kinds of questions. This tendentiousness is best accounted for by the ideology that progressivism supplies. The assimilation of sociological jurisprudence and the case method to realism was a function not only of the logic of these methods themselves, but of the main currents of American political thought. The case method, at least in the late-nineteenth-century American context, could not long serve any kind of formalism or be limited to an inductive method for establishing guiding principles.

Herman Belz has argued that the age of constitutional realism began as a reaction to the rise of the kind of judicial supremacy that came about in the transitional period at the end
of the nineteenth century. But the realists refused to blame bad
men for corrupting theoretically sound institutions. Instead,
they criticized the very notion of stasis and legalism, employing
instead an evolutionary rather than mechanistic model.[31] As we
have seen, many of the early realists were vigorous critics of judicial power, for it was the judiciary that was most closely tied to
a dead past and opposition to democratic power. Conversely, the
legislative branches were most open to reform and democratic
growth.

What began as a critique of America's lack of efficient and
responsible government quickly morphed, under the influence
of Charles Austin Beard and others, into a broader criticism of
the Founders as having established an oligarchy of the prop-
ertied classes.[32] "The net effect of the writings of progressivist
writers such as Smith, Beard, and Parrington was to undermine
the profound (at times even exaggerated) respect for the Founders that was characteristic of nineteenth-century America,"
writes Christopher Wolfe. "How would it be possible to vener-
ate men whose devotion was not really to the common good,
but to their own class interest . . . ?"[33] Whatever the theoretical roots or disciplinary orientations of realist legal critiques,
all saw the Constitution as a fundamentally flawed document
and decried any efforts to interpret it on its own terms. Indeed,
the very definition of formalism for realists seems to have been
the effort to interpret and enforce the Founders' Constitution
in earnest. Law, and especially the Constitution, was seen as
an epiphenomenon of deep class biases and social forces, and
therefore unrelated to principles of right or justice.[34] The movement of the Court away from substantive economic due process
was therefore understood to be a movement of the Court away
from the Founders.[35]

Yet the best and brightest could extract themselves from the influence of the biases and forces that swept others along like tiny corks on a great river. With the help of a clear-eyed view of what law "really" is, along with sympathetic legislatures, the right kinds of sociological arguments, and, eventually, a less conservative judiciary, these intellectual elites could put themselves in the vanguard of History. Healthy evolution always lay just over the horizon for most of the realists, as it had for the earlier advocates of sociological jurisprudence.[36] The recognition that courts exercised not just judicial power, but also executive, legislative and administrative power—and that they could be a force for shaping law in accordance with social need—was explicit in the work of some scholars of constitutional realism.[37] As one legal historian noted in the 1960s, the new attitude toward law was and is linked to an overall spread of secular rationalism throughout the Western world. "No longer inhibited by the 'transcendental nonsense' which has from time immemorial blinded lawyers to the function of law, we are for the first time capable of using law to attain socially determined ends."[38]

Ideas and Institutions

In many ways, the legal academy of the early twentieth century was playing catch-up to progressivism as a social and political movement. Perhaps because of the practical conservatism of legal education, the owl of Minerva spread its wings rather belatedly. The political and jurisprudential ideas and characters that we sketched in earlier chapters had their intellectual doubles in the academic world, which they influenced in countless ways. In 1921, while a judge on the New York Court of Appeals, Benjamin Cardozo was arguing publicly and theoretically for the centrality of sociological jurisprudence to the law.[39] As Holmes was reducing law to a "practical question of social management,"[40] Harvard's John Chipman Gray was working out a theory of the idiosyncratic role of judges. As Brandeis was concentrating in practice on the role of social needs to the outcome of cases, so Roscoe Pound at Harvard was formulating the same ideas in theory.[41] According to Pound, "The sociological movement in jurisprudence is a movement for pragmatism as a philosophy of law" and a movement away from "assumed first principles."[42] For Pound, the question of "*whether* law is the product of evolution, had already been settled. The task that lay ahead was the reconstruction of jurisprudence, *given* the fact of evolution."[43] It is fair to say that by the time "the theory of evolutionary jurisprudence spilled onto institutionalized jurisprudence (that is, jurisprudence conducted in law schools rather than in social-science departments), the big issue was no longer *whether* the law evolved, but rather what useful conclusions should or might be drawn from that fact."[44]

As the New Deal years approached, within the academy the realists "formed a younger generation of scholars who had grown up with the triumph of scientific naturalism and the rapid proliferation of the social sciences."[45] This naturalism undermined any rationally determinable or absolute moral standards.[46] Indeed, the new professionalism of law teachers, symbolized by their creation of the Association of American Law Schools, only emphasized their desire to place their specialized expertise at the forefront of the new realist and sociological movements[47] and served to distinguish them from the old guard and mere "practitioners." Realism prided itself on its emphasis on consequentialism or functionalism, as against the case method's alleged emphasis on reducing law to principles or doctrines.[48] More profoundly, however, realism was rooted in the deep intellectual skepticism of Dewey and Holmes, as well as the impulse toward social engineering of the left social Darwinists such as Lester Frank Ward.

Significant institutional rivalries grew out of the realists' positioning of themselves as the archenemies of the "formalism" of the case method. By the late 1920s and 1930s, legal realism had become most closely associated with Columbia and Yale.[49] Notable proponents included Thurman Arnold at Yale, Karl Llewellyn at Columbia, and New Deal braintruster Jerome Frank.

Llewellyn emphasized that law was essentially behavioralism and thus reliant on the fact–value distinction. In this view, only behaviors or consequences are real and therefore proper objects of study. Purposiveness, formalism, and traditional jurisprudence are mere words to be distinguished from practical consequences not only in terms of form, but in terms of their very reality and appropriateness as objects of scientific inquiry. Frank went even further, arguing that all traditional features of common-law reasoning, including rules and precedents, were irrelevant. In his influential work *Law and the Modern Mind,* he "deplored the myth that legal rules made law predictable and blamed two eminent Harvardians, Joseph Beale and Roscoe Pound, for sustaining the illusion. Frank's indictment applied to trial and appellate courts alike. It was 'not the rules but the personalities of judges' that were 'of transcendent importance in the workings of the judicial process' at all levels" writes Kalman.[50]

For Frank, "law meant a particular judicial determination upon a particular and singular set of facts. Reducing law to what he considered an unequivocal empirical minimum, Frank equated it solely with the specific individual judicial decision."[51] Engaging in a blistering psychological reductionism, Frank in effect claimed that judges work backward from their "hunches" to their decisions. In this view, most common-law judges are hucksters, claiming formally to do what they cannot or will not—that is, to be bound by rules or precedents.

The intellectual assumptions of the academic realists, like so much thought of the progressive era, seemed utterly anchorless. At their extremity, they went too far even for Pound. In 1931, he accused many realists, and Frank in particular, of adhering in effect to a kind of "philosophical nominalism that denied the existence of legal rules, doctrines, principles, and concepts. They overemphasized irregularities and contradictions and ignored the uniformity and reasonableness of the law."[52]

By the 1920s, a plethora of disciplines seemed relevant to law in ways they had not before. The insights, real or alleged, of all the social sciences were increasingly brought to bear on the legal curriculum. As economic, sociological, psychological, or political circumstances changed, so must—and inevitably did—the law. Curricular revisions and new faculty followed, and Yale Law School in particular presented itself as an alternative to Harvard's vision of a more "pure" law,[53] though even at Harvard Pound conceived of lawyers as broadly trained social scientists prepared to assume roles as leaders of the people.[54] One prominent western school—Boalt Hall at Berkeley—was founded in 1911 with progressive aims in mind. It took quickly and naturally to realist theory under Dean O. K. McMurray, formerly of Columbia Law School.[55]

In the 1920s, social scientists started to appear on the faculty rosters at Yale and Columbia, and new casebooks moved away from titles such as *Cases on X* in favor of *Cases and Materials on X*.[56] Yale in the 1930s added social-science materials to its library holdings, appointed more social scientists to its teaching faculty, and created at least one joint institute with psychology.[57] The sheer number and specialized nature of course offerings and supporting materials increased markedly at the leading realist institutions, suggesting at once the inseparability of law from social problems—particularly those addressed by the administrative state—and the ever-increasing atomization of the field. Through the 1930s and 1940s, as a response to the thrusts of progressivism, courses in various public-law fields, including administrative law, burgeoned.[58] This growth continued throughout the postwar period.

With these courses grew the view of law as a problem-solving tool of the new age, rather than as a set of constraints on human conduct. Law tended to be seen as a means of social control and as a way to deal with corporate groups, whose interests were to be harmonized by elite mechanisms, as opposed to the free interplay of individuals and organizations in a large republic. The move from constitutional law to public law in the law schools followed and paralleled the move from constitutionalism to the administrative state in the progressive mind, and the move toward regulatory and entitlement politics in the American regime as a whole.

The opposition of Yale's faculty to anything smacking of formalism or dogma, and its emphasis on empiricism and social research, made government service attractive to many Yale faculty members, a number of whom defected to New Deal posts, thus showing the symbiosis between realism and New Deal politics.[59] "Democrats were in the majority on the Yale Law School faculty, and they made frequent trips to Washington. Of the ten men at Yale recruited for government service by 1936, eight were on the law school faculty," reports Kalman.[60] From Berkeley and other law schools, too, the professors moved into government service.[61] The pragmatic, functional understanding of law was a natural intellectual foundation for New Deal braintrusters, whose spirit was activist. When they returned to the law schools, ever more courses in specialized public-law topics were offered.

By the mid-1940s, Harvard was considered by the realists at Yale to be distinctly behind the times. For them, Supreme Court Justice Felix Frankfurter symbolized the anachronistic nature of Harvard's program. A product of Harvard Law School, Frankfurter understood himself to be in the "noninterventionist" mold of Holmes. Together with Justice Robert Jackson, he was cautious about extending the Supreme Court's reach into nonjusticiable civil-rights questions. In this regard, Frankfurter and Jackson opposed the William O. Douglas–Hugo Black wing of the Court. For Yale's Fred Rodell and Walton Hamilton, Frankfurter—and Harvard—represented the view that "judges should not treat law as an instrument of social policy" or that judges "should camouflage their activism with legalese."[62]

In fact, the extent to which legal realism could, on its own theoretical premises, support a vigorous policy agenda seemed to some doubtful. Early critics of some aspects of realism, such as Myres McDougal and Harold Lasswell, believed that legal theory should be more explicitly policy-oriented.[63] Law schools were to produce policy makers who would advance democratic values. Participatory democracy, freedom of information, and equal recognition of and respect for autonomous individuals were the lawyers' goals. It was not so much that McDougal and Lasswell doubted the premises of realism. Rather they wished to define the ends toward which realism could be put. For example, courses dealing with property-use questions, such as nuisance laws, could emphasize "the specific goal of implementing the definite, intelligible, and generally accepted norms of community planning experts for building stable and livable urban communities."[64] Under the influence of McDougal and Lasswell, legal theory more explicitly joined forces with progressive political thought and political activism. Their criticism of theories divorced from application or policy purposes paved the way for what was to come by the 1960s. Traditional legal concepts could be taught in new ways, all with the goal of showing the efficacy of social planning in one form or another.

As legal education through the twentieth century transformed itself from a system of rules to be learned, to principles or predictions to be gleaned from cases, to a vehicle for social change, so American lawyers—at least the ones concerned with public questions—saw themselves as the facilitators of change and the formulators of public policy made increasingly by judicial decree.[65] Policymaking is always and everywhere a normative endeavor. Early progressive efforts, from labor reform to eugenics, bear witness to this truth. It was a small step from a concern with policy to a concern with "values," which quickly made their way into the law-school curriculum, particularly at elite institutions. This occurred largely in what is regarded as the "postrealist" period which commenced in the 1960s. However, this period is better understood as an inevitable outgrowth of realism, or perhaps a realism that is simply clearer about its purposes.

Throughout this period and beyond, the case method persisted—though cases and "materials" now inevitably stood side by side—but its function came to be understood in an even more radicalized light. The inductive search for principles gave way to the search for strategies—rooted not only in law but in various social-science disciplines—for winning policy outcomes. Disciplines such as psychology, sociology, and economics increasingly provided the glue for legal theory and, to some extent, court doctrine. The "values" that guided the study and application of law came from outside the law, but in the hands of the new, socially conscious "postrealists," they were all for the good. Law, and constitutionalism itself, were not to be revered for their reflection of eternal truths or their embodiment of the insights of the wise, but for what they could deliver to a variety of constituencies hungry for a shortcut to policy victories.

A form of principled liberalism came to dominate the jurisprudence offerings of law schools by the 1970s. This period saw a rise in influence of "formalist" theorists such as Ronald Dworkin, who maintained an insistence that law sprang from rules or underlying principles. Dworkin's *Taking Rights Seriously* became the book most widely read in jurisprudence courses.[66] Because he relies on a concept of fundamental law that transcends calculations of social utility or policy goals, Dworkin is sometimes seen as an anti-realist. But the progressive inclination of Dworkin and other advocates of "liberal principles" suggests that there is a deep kinship between legal realism and liberal principles. "Insofar as a coherent theory of progressivism can be identified, the essential element of that theory is the doctrine of directed progress," in Mahoney's words.[67] And indeed, various versions of the liberal principles school seem bent on supplying principles precisely for the purpose of organic, directed progress. One can never escape the impression that liberal policy conclusions are front-loaded into liberal principles. The range of acceptable principles, and acceptable questions, grows out of democratic, egalitarian political biases, and the desire for judicial superintendence of progress. In criticizing various forms of unprincipled or pragmatic adjudication, the advocate of liberal principles doth protest too much.

Theory and Practice

However much the law schools initially played catch-up to political ideas and jurisprudential trends that were first manifested elsewhere, the progressive vision of the law schools has for many decades been very much an influence on constitutional jurisprudence. Many of those who litigate, and those who judge, are trained to conceive of constitutionalism in essentially historical terms. There has long been an interlocking network of ideas and policy goals shared by leading legal scholars, special-interest groups, lawyers, judges, and Supreme Court justices alike. The New Deal era simply provides the clearest snapshot of this network. For example, writes Clement E. Vose,

> [Felix] Frankfurter in 1915 was only thirty-three but, as a professor at Harvard Law School and converted to intense interest in public affairs by Brandeis himself ten years earlier, was an ardent believer in state protective labor legislation. . . . Frankfurter thus felt with Brandeis that . . . states were social laboratories in which to try out novel legislation that might overcome some of the deficiencies of modern

industrial life. Moreover, he agreed with . . . Holmes and with Roscoe Pound . . . that courts should give legislatures the benefit of the doubt and permit them considerable discretion in experimentation. Maximum hour and minimum wage laws were among the kinds of new regulations Frankfurter particularly endorsed.[70]

For the New Dealers, the intellectual rubber really met the road only in the late 1930s. The case of *West Coast Hotel v. Parrish* (1937) not only marked the "switch in time that saved nine" but also secured the victory of the new science of jurisprudence for the remainder of the twentieth century and into the twenty-first.[71] In *Parrish*, the majority upheld a Washington state minimum-wage law for women, overturning the Court's decision in *Adkins v. Children's Hospital* (1923) that it had relied on just a year earlier and with it the Old Court's liberty-of-contract doctrine.[72] More broadly, it also signaled a new and permanent deference to legislative judgments on matters of economic regulation. Whether or not the 5–4 decision was actually a response to external pressures on the Court, the case symbolized the coalescence of progressive political, intellectual, and jurisprudential forces into a new governing consensus. With *Parrish*, the progressive victory was nearly complete. There would be no more jurisprudential see-sawing as elite opinion closed around the case. According to Vose,

> If the test of an idea is its ability to get itself accepted in the market place then there is, in the rough way of continents, a great divide between legal ideas on government regulation of property before and after March 29, 1937. . . . [T]he rise of the legal realists was expressed in the law reviews. The brilliance of Roscoe Pound, Thomas Reed Powell, Felix Frankfurter, Karl Llewellyn and Charles Groves Haines leveled the arguments of liberty of contract. . . . Twelve articles

attacking the decision of the Supreme Court in *Adkins v. Children's Hospital* were put together in book form by the National Consumers' league and sold by the *New Republic* in 1924. The finality of the *Parrish* rule was sealed by the presence of this approval in the law schools as already registered in the law reviews.[73]

Another case from that time illustrates the convergence of intellectual forces around central progressive themes of constitutional interpretation. In *Erie Railroad v. Tompkins* (1938),[74] Justice Brandeis, for a unanimous Court, rejected the precedent of *Swift v. Tyson* (1842),[75] in which Justice Story, for a unanimous Court, affirmed the existence and preeminence of a general federal common law that could be followed by federal courts in commercial cases in which they had "diversity jurisdiction"— that is, cases concerning commercial transactions with an interstate or general, as opposed to local, component in the form of litigants from different states arguing a question of state law. This common law could be followed notwithstanding contrary state court decisions as to its content. The Judiciary Act of 1789 required federal courts to follow state "laws" as the rules of decision in such cases, but Story held that the decisions of state courts do not constitute "laws," being themselves nothing more than the courts' attempts to articulate the commercial law that itself had grown out of longstanding customary practices and that therefore had an existence outside the purely positive command of any sovereign.

National commercial rules, and the power of federal courts, arguably encouraged commercial growth by protecting it from local idiosyncrasies. But the nationalism of *Swift* was unacceptable to progressives. This was largely because of its application to economic matters, coupled with the ever expanding uses of a federal or "general" common law—beyond commercial transactions or instruments—in the hands of an increasingly activist federal judiciary. Beyond this, *Swift* contained within it a con-catenation of assumptions about common-law jurisprudence, including assumptions about the ontology of law and the pos-sibility of objectivity and rationality on the part of the jurist. Progressive jurists rejected these assumptions.

Holmes, for example, was hostile to *Swift*—"a very fishy principle started by Story"—because it violated the constitu-tional authority of the states and, more importantly, rested on what he saw as a false and outmoded jurisprudence. A decade before *Erie*, Holmes had written in dissent in *Black & White Taxicab Co. v. Brown & Yellow Taxicab Co.* (1928), in which the majority refused to overturn *Swift*. Holmes criticized the notion that the common law was a transcendental body of law and vig-orously attacked the federal courts' reliance on such a notion. Holmes's argument was conceptual, denying the authority of federal courts to determine common-law questions independent of state-court determinations. No common law could possibly exist independent of a sovereign entity with the power to enforce it. State sovereignty, and a purely positive theory of law, motivat-ed Holmes's opinion. In his view, *Swift* gave voice to the theory of preexistent law; it implied that judges reached their decisions through a deductive process; it rejected the idea that judicial de-cisions made law; and it denied that law was based on the au-thority of a sovereign. There could be no judgment on what the common law *is* independent of sovereign, positive power.

"Darwinian science suggested that legal rules and institu-tions responded to social changes, an emphasis that undermined faith in unchanging principles and directed analysis away from formal rules and toward their de facto social context," explains Edward Purcell. "By the beginning of the twentieth century the jurisprudential assumptions underlying the declaratory theory of law and attributed to *Swift* were subject to intense theoreti-cal criticism."[76] The forces of realism and sociological jurispru-dence together put the diversity jurisdiction implicated in *Swift* in their crosshairs. At Yale, a study directed by the progressive dean Charles Clark purported to show that corporate defendants, rather than individuals, overwhelmingly benefited from diversity jurisdiction, giving rise to equity considerations, quite apart from considerations of constitutional propriety.[77] Frankfurter, at Harvard, also launched a sustained scholarly call for jurisdictional reform.[78]

In *Erie*, Brandeis, like Holmes and the academic critics of *Swift*, sought to advance state power, including the power of state courts. The purpose, as he saw it, was to overcome the Supreme Court's favoring of powerful interests in its decisions concerning cases between citizens of different states. Brandeis argued that there is no such thing as federal general common law. He went so far as to hold the *Swift* decision itself to be unconstitutional, rather than simply in error. He thereby cemented his reputation as the Court's leading opponent (since Holmes had retired six years earlier) of federal common law and all that it implied. *Erie* served the progressive ends of constraining judicial power that had operated at the expense of legislative power, and federal power that had operated at the expense of the states. The corollary of Brandeis's theory of legislative primacy was that, absent explicit congressional action (except, notably, in the areas such as individual constitutional rights), the federal courts had no right to make or proclaim law. Indeed, on the facts of *Swift*, Congress had no power to act, and therefore neither should the federal courts. Law *is* nothing but sovereign command.

Loose Theories, Loose Ends

In place of the old common-law framework, the realists saw law as the product of decision-making that reflected the social circumstances of the day and the particular social and psychological makeup of the judges. However, given the combination of left social Darwinism and pragmatism that defined the era, realism was always tempered with the hope and confidence that social realities, translated into appropriate legal discourse, would win the day in courts. Eventually, they did.

The progressives laid the groundwork for a thorough reconfiguration of the Supreme Court's role in the constitutional order. That role shifted from the relatively modest one of impartial interpreter of unchanging constitutional principles to a much more hubristic one. As Robert H. Jackson put it in 1941, the Court must be seen as an arbiter

> between fundamental and ever-present rival forces in our organized society. . . . The student of our times will nowhere find the deeper conflicts of American political philosophy and economic policy more authentically and intelligently portrayed than in the opinions and dissents of members of the Supreme Court. . . . The Constitution, in making the balance between different parts of our government a legal rather than a political question, casts the Court as the most philosophical of our political departments.[79]

Or, to put it another way, "the Supreme Court Reports present a cinematograph of the movements of our society, revealing . . . the clash of forces. . . . Subtly the impregnating intellectual climate of an era also affects the Court."[80]

Legal realism opposed moral realism in favor of empiricism and behaviorism, which, in themselves, are morally neutral. In fact, they rely on the rigid distinction between facts and values. In severing the linkage between the two, values were understood to be unscientific and ultimately unknowable, as Sumner and Holmes and many other Darwinists maintained. Therefore, as legal realism undermined the possibility of moral knowledge, it also undermined the possibility of a rule of law:

Although the realists were firm believers in democratic government, the empirical naturalism they embraced and attempted to apply to legal theory raised both practical and theoretical questions about the nature of democratic government. The most important practical point of their argument was questioning and in many cases rejecting the idea of a government of laws rather than of men. Most democratic legal theories—and many state constitutions—held that established and known laws alone should be binding on free citizens; the realists maintained that such laws were nonexistent and impossible to attain.[81]

If judges do not decide according to law, they are despots rather than democrats. This is why judges today—even good "pragmatic" ones—carefully deny pure subjectivism. They almost invariably try to link broad principles of constitutional interpretation, rooted in one or another form of consequentialism, back to constitutional text or tradition. They usually fail. Even a cursory reflection on the legal theories many of them imbibed in law school reveals why. Edward Purcell asks, "First, how could the idea of the subjectivity of judicial decision be squared with the doctrine that free men should be subject only to known and established law, one of the hallmarks of republican as opposed to despotic government? Second, if the acts of government officials were the only real law, on what basis could anyone evaluate or criticize those acts?"[82]

Let us recall that political science, too, moved in the same direction as law: de jure value-free, but de facto value-laden. It therefore confronted the same theoretical problems.[83] The new "scientific" study of politics could not give a rational account of why one regime type is preferable to another. Only concepts such as "power" could officially occupy the attention of empiricists in the grip of the fact–value distinction. Even the notion of rational man, on which depends the possibility of a government by the people, was put into question.[84] Skepticism went hand in hand with empirical, statistical techniques.[85] Scholars Edward S. Corwin and William Y. Elliott notably reacted against the antidemocratic thrust of modern political science, with Elliott insisting that the "emphasis on power and factuality in the study of politics" undermined respect for law as something beyond power and interest-based politics.[86] Value-free pragmatism was the slippery slope to fascism.[87]

As a teacher at Yale Law School in the late 1920s, Robert Maynard Hutchins rode the legal realist wave, seeing law as that which courts chose to enforce rather than something with an ideal or independent existence.[88] For him, as for Holmes, the science of jurisprudence was predictive. But his rejection of metaphysical views of law was relatively short-lived and began to crumble rapidly when he left Yale for the University of Chicago in 1929. Partly triggered by his reflections on certain of Justice Brandeis's opinions, Hutchins realized that pragmatism must smuggle in personal values in order to provide a rule for decision-making. "In attempting to decide which rule worked better . . . we had to assume a social order and the aims thereof."[89] Another critic of realism was Lon Fuller, who argued in *The Law in Quest of Itself* that psychological reductionism destroyed the very identity of the law as a cognizable body of thought. There was no longer any possibility of distinguishing legal things from other human phenomena.

Unfortunately, second thoughts such as these seem very far indeed from the minds of many of today's judges, largely because of the seemingly unshakable confidence that History is still their guide. As Felix Frankfurter and Henry M. Hart put it in 1933,

> The Supreme Court is the vehicle of life latent in the letter of the Constitution. This implies the traditional process of extracting new meaning from old cases, of seeing beneath words to things. . . . To meet these issues with

the learning, wisdom, and largeness of vision appropriate
to their majesty, the Court must have that serenity and
spacious feeling of detachment which an effective control over its own business alone can afford. Only a Court
thus freed from undue external pressures will be equal
to those demands of judicial statesmanship to which the
times summon it.[90]

"Seeing beneath words to things." In one of the many ironies
of such hubris, contemporary courts, as we shall see in the next
chapter, have claimed that the times have summoned them to
de-link words from things entirely—to see no hell below them,
and above them only sky.

7

The Future Is Now

In George Orwell's great novel *1984*, a philologist—an expert in "Newspeak"—proclaims, "It's a beautiful thing, the destruction of words. In the end we shall make thoughtcrime literally impossible, because there will be no words in which to express it. In fact there will be no thought, as we understand it now. Orthodoxy means not thinking—not needing to think. Orthodoxy is unconsciousness." The philologist is explaining to the novel's hero, Winston Smith, the ultimate purpose behind the manipulation and command of language. Nowadays, American courts, under the continuing influence of progressive ideology, have taken the idea of manipulation of language to places heretofore unknown to the common-law world.[1]

The advocates of same-sex marriage, for example, have a political and linguistic purpose similar to that expressed by Orwell's philologist. They have advanced their agenda with stunning rapidity by finding sympathetic ears on a number of state benches. How much longer it will be before federal courts take up the challenge on a national level to lead History in the correct direction is anyone's guess. Suffice it to say that we are given a clue by Justice Kennedy's majority musings in *Lawrence v. Texas* (2003) on the "emerging recognition" of new rights in sexual matters, derivative from a Constitution that "persons in every generation" can invoke in their search for "greater freedom."

Laws that confer unique legal status and benefits on the union of a man and woman have come under attack only recently. In America, the first legal decision to challenge such laws successfully was *Baker v. State of Vermont* (1999),[2] in which the Vermont Supreme Court held, on the basis of indeterminate language in the state's 1777 constitution, that the state legislature must provide same-sex couples in "committed relationships" with identical benefits to married "opposite-sex couples." The Vermont legislature responded by creating "civil unions"— though not marriage—for same-sex couples. Under the *Baker* holding and subsequent legislation, civil unions were to be materially, and therefore legally, indistinguishable from marriage for all purposes of Vermont law and the benefits it conferred.

But much more was at stake than the right of same-sex partners to enjoy such mutually fulfilling experiences as filing a joint state tax return. In winning the right to "civil unions," same-sex partners and their lawyers slipped the camel's nose under the tent. Unsatisfied with the reservation of the word "marriage" to opposite-sex couples, lawyers before the Supreme Judicial Court of Massachusetts won (just five years after *Baker*) the right for their clients to be called "married."[3] In so doing, they forced the entire camel into the tent. They also effectively wrested control of the English language from popular usage and from the dictionaries in which that usage was enshrined.

Since all the benefits and incidents of "marriage" might have been conferred via civil-union status, the Massachusetts litigants effectively vindicated a quite different, indeed arresting, claim—the right to a noun. This is something unknown to the common law and American constitutional law. One is tempted to speculate, idly, on whether there has been an unequal pattern of noun distribution in American history. We have entered a brave new world in which major legal arguments are not so much about statutes, the constitutions of the various states, or the federal Constitution, but about the contents of the *Oxford English Dictionary*. As the Massachusetts court declared in a subsequent advisory opinion, invidious "labeling" by government is now impermissible. It is as though black citizens of the United States had won, by judicial decree, the "right" to be called African American, or, for that matter, white. This is truly a revolutionary development that can only breed unprecedented mischief.

The legal conscription of the English language has the effect of limiting our range of thought. Terms of such recent origin as "same-sex partnerships" or "domestic partnerships" are already obsolete in Massachusetts. The even more recent phrase "civil unions" became antique with head-snapping speed—redundant almost before it entered the lexicon. The result is that it has become increasingly difficult for anyone to view same-sex relationships as essentially, and therefore morally, distinguishable from heterosexual relationships.

Our lament, therefore, must not be for the loss of a word, for all words are in themselves purely conventional. Nor should we lament the redefinition of "marriage" merely because of the immediate moral, political, or policy consequences. As judicial review becomes literary deconstructionism, our lament must be for the loss of the possibility of a natural basis for human laws. The argument for same-sex "marriage" (and even much of the argument against it) elides the question of whether the noun "marriage" refers to anything in nature. Is the thing that marriage signifies a particular concept with an essence outside the mind and control of the observer—or is it a whim subject to infinite reinterpretation by lawyers and judges?

According to the Massachusetts court's majority, one must "have the right to marry—or more properly, the right to choose to marry" in order to be fully human. The language of the court is significant, for it reduces essence to action, or the right to choose certain actions or commitments over others—thereby denying essence. For the court, modern psychological reductionism—"I choose, therefore I am"—is the only philosophical position worth taking seriously. Even the dissenters in the case eschew essentialism. They appear reluctant to redefine marriage only because of the lack of scientific consensus that such redefinition "will not have unintended and undesirable social consequences." In either case, the essential natures of human beings, and therefore their relationships to each other, are reduced to choice and its consequences.

In the debate over same-sex "marriage," we see a partial and highly simplified replay of the medieval debate between realists and nominalists. According to the realists, we possess minds capable of transcending individual phenomena and seeing the objective truth or essences that link phenomena. Thus, we know that the phrase "man is a rational animal" is tautological. To this version of the Christian mind, the phenomenal world is a real reflection of God's creation and mind, and the permanent connections we perceive among the things that compose it are not illusions. The nominalists, by contrast, emphasized that words cannot express things-in-themselves, for these are unknown and unknowable to us. We intuit only individually existing things, and can perceive, through reason, no ineluctable relationships among them. Words cannot signify universals, only particulars, and to the extent they do point to universals, they are but sound and fury, signifying nothing. For the nominalists, to claim that we can know things in themselves, or a universal natural order, is to be impious and full of hubris—it is a claim to read the mind, and therefore constrain the actions, of God.

For the medieval nominalists, at least, revelation filled the gap that reason could no longer bridge. By faith and faith alone we might be aware of the order that the noun "marriage" signifies, being the order presently established (but changeable) through the free will of God. But in the absence of a guiding revelation, God's will itself disappears, and we are left only with the changeable. Modern-day nominalists, in the guise of progressive legal thinkers, lack the overwhelming faith of the medieval mind. And thus we are no longer permitted the *concept* of marriage as it has ever been. The best way to express and enforce this aversion to any knowledge of or faith in essence, as Orwell foresaw, is through control of language.

Marriage, across all religions and cultures, has had a similar, though not identical, meaning. It is a rite of passage signifying and reminding us of the divine or natural order's purposes with respect to procreation. (Love or "commitment" are, at best, incidental to this rite.) As Blackstone says, the relationship between husband and wife is founded in the natural desire to propagate the species—which is marriage's "principal end and design." "The most universal relation in nature"—that between parent and child—proceeds directly from marriage. The "natural obligation" of the father to provide for his children is, in turn, cemented by the marriage tie. The law has the right, even duty, to recognize those "civil disabilities," quite apart from ecclesiastical ones, which render a union, in Blackstone's words, meretricious rather than matrimonial.

Civil marriage is therefore not what the Massachusetts court called an "evolving paradigm" (dedicated, for now at least, to fostering "stable adult relationships"). Neither can the ban on same-sex marriage be compared to those long-discredited ones on interracial marriage. The distinction between the two, rooted in nature, was invisible to the court. From the point of view of civil authorities, the institution of marriage exists for the purpose of propagating and civilizing the species. It binds and benefits natural couples whose obligation is to use, and inculcate, the characteristically male and female virtues and abilities for the benefit of those whom they propagate. The fact that nature errs—that not all natural couples can have, or desire to have, children, or that the characteristic sexual virtues might in some cases be in shorter supply than others—does not vitiate the rule. Nor does it alter in the slightest the interest (and we might say obligation) of civil society to have its human laws reflect the natural law.

For Christians, in particular, marriage has meant the union of a man and woman. This is because marriage refers, among other things, to the unique, God-given capacity of man and woman to enter into a covenantal relationship parallel to that between Christ and his church. It is a point of encounter between God and man. The rites of marriage are performed in the hope—with full knowledge that the reality sometimes does not live up to the hope—that each and every example of the sacramental relationship realizes its potential and purpose and therefore reflects the divine intention. The divine mind has an idea of human nature, and therefore human relationships, that does not and cannot change. "Marriage," in short, is a word that describes something particular in the divinely created natural order, something that simply cannot be replicated in a same-sex relationship. Following the pattern of so much recent jurisprudence, the nominally neutral courts that have already substituted in the public square secular religiosity for actual religion now undermine the sacramental character of marriage with their competing, profane version of that institution.

A kind of mysticism is embraced by these new deconstructionists, who insist that each "marriage" has to be considered on its own terms, independent of universals. Of course, most deconstructionists would, at this point, say that the law should not and would not sanction as marriage the union of a man and twelve women, or of a man and a sow. But they cannot, on the principles enunciated by the highest courts of Vermont or Massachusetts, say *why,* for the principles are not themselves rational. The deconstructionists are wed, apparently, to a residual prejudice—defined by where we are *now* in History—that might soon give way before autonomy's incessant march. In its anti-rationalism, theirs is a mysticism not fundamentally different from the medieval mysticisms set up in opposition to realism, or the Oriental mysticisms that emphasize the illusory character of the phenomenal world and thereby oppose themselves to Western rationalism.

But the deconstructionist mysticism differs from the medieval in one key respect: its complete substitution of progressive, liberal purposes for God's. Contemporary legal nominalists, as we have already seen, possess theological conviction in abundance: they are as pious in their own way as their medieval forebears. Impiety to medieval nominalists came from those who would purport to read the mind of God and therefore limit his freedom; to the moderns, impiety comes from limiting our own freedom.

Henry Herbert, the second Earl of Pembroke, said that Parliament can do anything but make a man into a woman. In this remark, he was pointing to the idea that some things exist in nature, and Parliament, while supreme over human affairs, was not omnipotent. Parliament is, ultimately, a human institution that lacks power when it comes to controlling the articulations of nature and nature's God—the most fundamental and self-evident of which is the man–woman distinction and the natural consequences of it. It is also worth noting that Pembroke was speaking only of Parliament, not of the far more hubristic, nominally common-law courts of America, which have come, under the influence of historicist doctrines of progress, much closer to toying with the order of nature than Parliament ever dreamed possible. We can now foresee the day when, in effect, courts will routinely declare men to be women, and vice versa, according to the political pressures of the age.

We are at a precipice, not only for constitutional law but also for thought itself. If developments continue apace, we will soon have no word to express the union of a man and woman, as it was in the beginning. Already, many, and perhaps most, American adults of college age see nothing "wrong" with the new, expansive definition of marriage and can't imagine why anyone would reject it. In such an environment, those who cleave to the notion that at least the *concept* of marriage is sacred—its boundaries not subject to deconstruction—are destined to be disappointed in the short term. But the long-term prospect is, from one point of view, better. As the silent artillery of time wreaks its inevitable havoc on the chords of memory, those who would reject the new jurisprudence will not have to fear being adjudged guilty of thoughtcrime because they will no longer have a word to express that which someone, somewhere, once meant by the union of a man and a woman. Unconsciousness will be their best defense.

Common Purposes and Temporary Alliances

We are left with an odd status quo, few parts of which point away from "progress" toward return. This book has argued that the legal and political dynamics of the regime have changed dramatically since the ascendancy of progressive jurisprudence. We now live with the apparatus of a vast administrative state dedicated to security and equality. As the state itself—especially its national component—moved toward progressive ideas, so the courts increasingly deferred to legislative judgments on economic matters. The Supreme Court has consistently cleared the way for this administrative apparatus, while creating an ever expanding catalog of rights that it, and other courts, must vindicate. With the advent of the New Deal and the New Deal Court, the institutional ground of American politics shifted decisively to the left. We should not forget that the era of substantive due process was, as Clement E. Vose writes, in some measure driven by the Court's "institutional clienteles. Before 1900, and up to 1937, judicial review was championed by businessmen and their conservative lawyers. It was opposed by Progressive reformers, the settlement-house movement and lawyers 'for the people.' . . . Between 1937 and 1944, the Supreme Court lost its business champions and gained the confidence of civil rights and civil liberties advocates."[4] The Court moved from defending business interests to extending constitutional protections to various individual and group minority claimants.

With this shift, the salience of the issues that were once central to early progressivism declined, from corporate power and labor rights and regulations, to the freedom to exercise legislatively the police power of the state. "Cumulatively, the changes scrambled and largely reversed the politico-constitutional premises and branch affinities of the half century that preceded 1937."[5] The idea became increasingly entrenched that courts would be the key progressive players in the system—the voices of "good government," efficiency, the individual, and "true" public opinion. In one sense, it was ironic that the foundations for this shift were being laid even as Woodrow Wilson was theorizing a unitary form of government under the command of strong presidential and administrative leadership. In another sense, it was not ironic; for Wilson's theoretical premises and purposes were in large measure the same as those of the people who would later attach themselves to the courts as the engines and superintendents of change.

As the Court continued to change its purposes to progressive ones, so the progressive attitude toward the Court continued to change. New cases started to do for civil liberties what the Old Court had done for property rights. "The Warren Court completed the reversal of political assumptions and branch affinities begun in 1937."[6] After the "activist-conservatism" of the substantive due-process era, the Supreme Court moved to an "activist-liberalism."[7] This phase has lasted even through decades of Republican appointments to the Court.

The term "progressive" has fallen into desuetude. "Liberal" is now the preferred designation for those individuals and institutions that have taken the lead in progressive battles, and essentially won them. The post–New Deal liberal seems more committed to national, as opposed to state, power and to civil rights and liberties—especially those concerned with the autonomy and self-expressive freedom of the individual—than the old progressive. But the seeds of this "new" orientation were sown in the social Darwinism and pragmatism that first grounded progressive thinking; the orientation itself is but another fruit of that tree of the knowledge of good and evil.

The evolution of progressivism into liberalism has been marked by concern for the individual—and by faith in courts as the institutions best suited to protect the individual from the curse of bigness. With the switch in institutional affinities, a new breed of legal theory arose, that was dedicated substantively to progressive goals but relied on courts to achieve them. Harvard's Henry M. Hart Jr., a New Dealer and clerk to Brandeis, came to see courts as the domain of principle.[8] He sounded some old-fashioned common-law notes in emphasizing the interaction of the general and particular. As Edward Purcell writes, "In the 1930s the young Progressive had depicted the courts as incompetent to formulate policy and Congress as expert; by the 1950s he portrayed the courts as refined instruments of reason and the legislature as the voice of ignorance and partisanship."[9] Judge-made law was now to be preferred to statutory law on grounds of rationality and fairness. Indeed, judges have a virtual obligation to step in where legislatures fail to act, thereby shifting the workload of politics away from legislatures.[10]

While Brandeis had dreamed of repeal of the Fourteenth Amendment in the 1920s, it proved to be the bulwark of progressive-liberal judicial activism later in the century.[11] While this might seem ironic, one progressive understanding never changed: all social understandings are in flux, and in the face of this flux, the Constitution must necessarily be plastic. In light of this view, the Constitution, and liberal constitutionalism itself, had to respond incessantly to changing social circumstances. The tactics of progressive liberalism had to change, too, in the face of shifting institutional imperatives. Progressives failed to perceive any irony because judicial restraint was never essential to their enterprise, but rather a mere tactical consideration in pursuit of a Constitution supporting social and individual change, experimentation, and growth.

Pragmatism or Nihilism?

Some critics of the progressive revolution in jurisprudence now argue for a new "conservative" judicial activism, including a reinvigorated *Lochner* approach to preserve economic liberties against dangerous majoritarian—or judicial—impulses.[12] Others argue simply for a pragmatism that does not entangle itself in the esoteric theoretical debates of the day, as if such pragmatism is an answer to all or most of what ails contemporary constitutional interpretation.

Richard Posner, in particular, argues for a "pragmatic liberalism" or "everyday pragmatism" that is skeptical of the "constraining effect of legal, moral, and political theories."[13] His understanding of pragmatism is both positive and normative: It best describes what judges actually do, and what they ought to do. "What is important is that judges and other policy-makers should think in terms of consequences without taking the rhetoric of legal formalism seriously and without bothering their heads about pragmatic philosophy either; that they should be, in short, everyday pragmatists."[14] Posner notes the legal professionals' tendency to disdain democracy as it is actually practiced in the United States, as something that is hostile to law, and particularly to rights-oriented jurisprudence. The result is that the "theoretical uplands, where democratic and judicial ideals are debated, tend to be arid and overgrazed; the empirical lowlands are fertile but rarely cultivated."[15]

According to Posner, pragmatic philosophers believe Darwin's claim that mind and body evolved together: that human beings are merely "clever animals" with a dominantly practical, rather than theoretical, reasoning capacity.[16] This inverted Platonism is, for Posner, the essence of philosophical pragmatism. Pragmatism rejects actual Platonism, which is the two-thousand-year-old search for stasis and knowledge over change and activity.[17] Metaphysical propositions might be useful to the human psyche, but they are not true, and dispute over them is inevitable in the "open, diverse, competitive culture"[18] that Darwinian pragmatists prefer. Our minds—including the minds of so many legal theorists—seek to universalize local experience, but they do so in vain. Significance lies not in purposes, but in consequences.[19] The experimental method—on the model of natural selection—is linked to pragmatism insofar as the only test of truth is what works for giving people what they want.[20] "Both *Lochner* and *Roe* can be described as activist pragmatic decisions," writes Posner, and such decisions can best be criticized on the basis that they impede useful regulatory experimentation.[21] Posner elides the question of why—there being nothing in the text of the Constitution or in case law to compel the decision in *Roe*—the Court feels itself the competent body to intervene. His concern is more with the stifling of experimentation than with constitutional structure or judicial capacity, particularly when "[p]ragmatic decisionmaking will inevitably be based to a disquieting extent on hunches and subjective preferences. . . ."[22] Homosexual marriage also can be considered an experiment in living, not to be interfered with by a statute such as the Defense of Marriage Act. A pragmatic court might well strike down such legislation.

For Posner, formalism and the "pretense" of objectivity, including the pretense that comes from theorists such as Ronald

Dworkin, must be deployed tactically. Dworkin's preferred policies—doomed to be unpopular—can be argued for on the basis of an "impressive abstraction" known as "the law." For judges, tactical deployment of the pretense of objectivity is a psychological defense mechanism, allowing them to think and publicly proclaim that they know what they are about.[23] At a more self-conscious level, it also allows them to communicate with "ordinary folk" who would be inclined to view with disdain unalloyed pragmatist rhetoric.[24]

The Constitution of the Fathers and the New Nominalism

The burden of this book has been to show, among other things, that faith in an unphilosophic pragmatism such as Posner's is a losing proposition for those who would maintain the Founders' constitutionalism. As Posner argues, judges are overwhelmingly less likely to be Dworkinians than pragmatists; nevertheless, they are also very likely to see themselves as doing the work of democracy, pragmatically, by "muddling through." But their muddling through does have a political valence. The game is rigged; pragmatism, with its indissoluble links to modern science, tends toward the dissolution of constitutional norms and, in practice, to policies that are antithetical to a regime of fixed truths and transcendent faith. It therefore also leads to the kinds of policies that Posner himself is inclined to disfavor. The gap between pragmatist informalism and principled liberalism has been bridged by progressivism.

The shift in political understanding in the United States—from Madisonian constitutionalism to twentieth- and twenty-first-century progressivism—has been dramatic. Differing understandings of nature and natural rights have been central to this shift. American political thought subsequent to Lincoln has, for the most part, amounted to an attack on Lincoln's conception of American constitutionalism and the philosophical propositions on which it rests. This transformation in political thought, commencing after Reconstruction and running through the progressive era of the early twentieth century to what is essentially the progressive era of the twenty-first, accounts for many kinds of political actions and ideas in America. It also decisively informs institutional attitudes and behaviors, particularly those of the judicial branch. This transformation began with the intellectual phenomenon of social Darwinism, which had taken hold in American intellectual circles in the last decades of the nineteenth century.

It is fair to say that the pre-progressive nineteenth-century understanding of American constitutionalism was rooted in a broad faith in democracy grounded in rational moral truths linked to religion, American history, and the ideals of the founding moment expressed in the Declaration of Independence.[26] In light of this understanding, constitutional interpretation, from one point of view, relied on "a formalistic, deductive concept of legal reasoning, a vague belief in natural law and a rigid theory of precedent [that] became the pervasive assumptions behind American jurisprudence" in the late nineteenth century.[27] From another, it is not so much formalism that defined the earlier jurisprudence as a faith in objective standards of right and wrong.[28] From still another perspective, jurisprudential thought "rested upon faith in a unified and regular natural and social order of providential design, in the close connection between the improvement of knowledge and the moral and material progress of society, and in the benefits of a republican democracy giving the greatest practical freedom to the operation of the fundamental values of moral voluntarism and individual accountability."[29] There is some truth to each of these claims, which share considerable common ground. Exponents of any of them would find unintelligible a philosophy of History and would be uncomfortable with an emphasis on the state and its principles as mere organisms that live and grow in time.

As one scholar has noted, with some sympathy, "Modern legal educators are really teaching their students . . . that as man makes himself, so lawyers make the law; but they do so only in the same degree as they desacralize both themselves and the law, for the prime obstacle to the true legal reform (which will bring about true freedom) is their lingering belief in the mysticism in themselves and the law."[30]

For the American Founders, it is impossible to get beyond, or improve upon, a self-evident truth. In the words of Calvin Coolidge—America's last president to be almost entirely devoid of progressive instincts—to move beyond such a truth is not to progress, but to regress to a time when people were not free, equal, or possessed of political rights. As he said in a speech titled "The Inspiration of the Declaration," given at Philadelphia on the July 5, 1926: "It is not so much then for the purpose of undertaking to proclaim new theories and principles that this annual celebration is maintained, but rather to reaffirm and reestablish those old theories and principles which time and the unerring logic of events have demonstrated to be sound." Coolidge went on to consider the underpinnings of American constitutionalism, noting that when we consider "the immediate conception of the principles of human relationship which went into the Declaration of Independence we are not required to extend our search beyond our own shores. They are found in the texts, the sermons, and the writings of the early colonial clergy who were earnestly undertaking to instruct their congregations in the great mystery of how to live. They preached equality because they believed in the fatherhood of God and the brotherhood of man. They justified freedom by the text that we are all created in the divine image, all partakers of the divine spirit." And with this historical analysis, Coolidge offered a warning:

Unless the faith of the American people in these religious convictions is to endure, the principles of our Declaration will perish. . . . About the Declaration there is a finality that is exceedingly restful. It is often asserted that the world has made a great deal of progress since 1776, that we have had new thoughts and new experiences which have given us a great advance over the people of that day, and that we may therefore very well discard their conclusions for something more modern. But that reasoning cannot be applied to the great charter. If all men are created equal, that is final. If they are endowed with inalienable rights, that is final. If governments derive their just powers from the consent of the governed, that is final. No advance, no progress can be made beyond these propositions. If anyone wishes to deny their truth or their soundness, the only direction in which he can proceed historically is not forward, but backward toward the time when there was no equality, no rights of the individual, no rule of the people. Those who wish to proceed in that direction can not lay claim to progress. They are reactionary. Their ideas are not more modern, but more ancient, than those of the Revolutionary fathers.

But to find such sentiments, one need not have recourse to a figure like Coolidge, whom progressive historians have labeled reactionary. Instead, one might consider the words of Martin Luther King Jr., in his "Letter from Birmingham Jail." He there reminded us that human law must always and everywhere be held up to, and judged against, the natural law, lest human beings be degraded to the status of mere creatures who respond to commands that do not deserve the name "law." Or one might reflect on his "I Have a Dream" speech, wherein he refers to the "magnificent words of the Constitution and the Declaration of Independence" as amounting to a "promissory note to which every American was to fall heir."

In the face of progressive dogma, it is perhaps a promissory note that can be read no more forever. Instead, as the new science of jurisprudence makes even language—and with it, reality itself—subject to litigation, we must wait with bated breath to see where History will take us next.

Notes

Chapter 1: The Organic Constitution

1. *Lochner v. New York*, 198 U.S. 45 (1904).
2. Clement E. Vose, *Constitutional Change: Amendment Politics and Supreme Court Litigation Since 1900* (Lexington, MA: Lexington Books, 1972).
3. See, for example, Edward A. Purcell Jr., *Brandeis and the Progressive Constitution: Erie, Judicial Power, and the Politics of the Federal Courts in Twentieth-Century America* (New Haven, CT: Yale University Press, 2000).
4. *Planned Parenthood of Southeastern Pennsylvania v. Casey*, 505 U.S. 833 (1992).
5. *John Geddes Lawrence and Tyron Garner v. Texas*, 539 U.S. 558 (2003).
6. William J. Brennan, "The Constitution of the United States: Contemporary Ratification," 27 *South Texas Law Review* 433 (1986): 438.
7. Ibid., 438–39.
8. Ibid., 440.
9. Ibid., 442.
10. *Whitney v. California*, 274 U.S. 357.
11. Brennan, "The Constitution of the United States," 443.
12. Ibid., 439–40.
13. Excepting those areas where the judge's position apparently should be "fixed and immutable"—for example, in opposition to capital

punishment as a violation, in all circumstances, of the Eighth Amendment ban on cruel and unusual punishment. See Brennan, "The Constitution of the United States," 443.

14. Brennan, "The Constitution of the United States," 444.

15. Ibid., 445.

16. Ibid., 445.

17. Thurgood Marshall, "The Constitution: A Living Document," 30 *Howard Law Journal* 915 (1987).

18. Ibid., 918.

19. Ibid., 919.

20. Ibid.

21. Ibid.

22. *Bowers v. Hardwick*, 478 U.S. 186 (1986).

23. These quotations are from Holmes's great essay, "The Path of the Law."

24. *Hurley v. Irish-American Gay, Lesbian, & Bisexual Group of Boston*, 515 U.S. 557 (1995).

25. *Boy Scouts of America v. Dale*, 530 U.S. 640 (2000).

26. For an extended discussion of the relationship of this and similar cases to the doctrine of stare decisis, see John C. Eastman, "*Stare Decisis*: Conservatism's One-Way Ratchet Problem," in Bradley C. S. Watson, ed., *Courts and the Culture Wars* (Lanham, MD: Lexington Books, 2002), 127–37.

27. *Brown v. Board of Education*, 347 U.S. 483 (1954).

28. *Cruzan v. Missouri Department of Health*, 497 U.S. 261 (1990).

29. *Washington v. Glucksberg*, 521 U.S. 702 (1997).

30. *Vacco v. Quill*, 521 U.S. 793 (1997).

31. Herman Belz, "The Constitution in the Gilded Age: The Beginnings of Constitutional Realism in American Scholarship," *The American Journal of Legal History*, vol. 13, no. 2 (April 1969): 111.

32. The reluctance of historians to deal with philosophical categories, including those of the old constitutionalism that was replaced by the new, has been noted by Mark Warren Bailey, in *Guardians of the Moral Order: The Legal Philosophy of the Supreme Court, 1860–1910* (DeKalb, IL: Northern Illinois University Press, 2004), 2–6.

33. As Belz notes, a strain of constitutional realism became evident in historical studies in the years after Reconstruction, by such pre-

progressive scholars as John W. Burgess, Herman Edward von Holst, J. Franklin Jameson, Alexander Johnston, Brooks Adams, George Bancroft, Christopher Tiedeman, and Sidney George Fisher. These men emphasized the importance of extra-constitutional influences on the practice of American politics and the development of constitutional understandings, from the growth of political parties to the particular actions of the branches of government. While they went "beyond the façade of the formal written document" and examined particular historical circumstances, they did not, for the most part, rely on a strong theory of History, or concentrate their attention on the role of the Supreme Court in promoting organic growth. See Belz, "The Constitution in the Gilded Age," passim. Woodrow Wilson would become the most prominent exponent of a theory of History that suggested evolution in a particular direction—though he saw the executive, rather than judicial, branch as primary expositor and superintendent of this evolution.

34. William James, *Pragmatism: A New Name for Some Old Ways of Thinking* (New York: Longmans, Green, 1907). "To the memory of John Stuart Mill from whom I first learned the pragmatic openness of mind and whom my fancy likes to picture as our leader were he alive today."

35. Roger Kimball, "On Liberty, Or, How John Stuart Mill Went Wrong," in Bradley C. S. Watson, ed., *Civic Education and Culture* (Wilmington, DE: ISI Books, 2005), 30.

36. Herbert Croly, *Progressive Democracy* (New York: Macmillan, 1914), 3.

37. Ibid., 368.

38. Ibid., 361.

39. Ibid., 369.

40. Edward A. Purcell Jr., *The Crisis of Democratic Theory: Scientific Naturalism and the Problem of Value* (Lexington, KY: University Press of Kentucky, 1973), 5–6.

41. Ibid., 8.

42. *Truax v. Corrigan*, 257 U.S. 312 (1921).

43. Holmes, dissenting in *Abrams v. United States*, 250 U.S. 616 (1919).

44. See, for example, Richard A. Posner, *Law, Pragmatism, and Democracy* (Cambridge, MA: Harvard University Press, 2003), 29–30 and passim.

45. Purcell, *Brandeis and the Progressive Constitution*, 40.

46. Many have traced this doctrine to *Marbury v. Madison*, although Robert Lowry Clinton has argued that Chief Justice John Marshall embraced only a very circumscribed version of judicial review in cases "of a judiciary nature." See Clinton, *Marbury v. Madison and Judicial Review* (Lawrence, KS: University Press of Kansas, 1989). Whatever the origin of judicial review, it is clear that it has come to mean something quite different from anything the Founders or Justice Marshall would have imagined.

47. See Bailey, *Guardians of the Moral Order*, 86–88, 92–99.

48. Ibid., 86.

49. Ibid., ch. 2 passim.

50. Ibid., 46.

51. Ibid., 96.

52. Ibid., 4.

53. Ibid., 60.

54. Felix Frankfurter, as quoted in Purcell, *Brandeis and the Progressive Constitution*, 13.

55. Purcell, *Brandeis and the Progressive Constitution*, 16.

56. Ibid., 19–20.

57. Vose, *Constitutional Change*, 164.

58. Purcell, *Brandeis and the Progressive Constitution*, 27.

59. Raoul Berger, *Government by Judiciary: The Transformation of the Fourteenth Amendment* (Cambridge, MA: Harvard University Press, 1977).

60. L.B. Boudin, "Government by Judiciary," 26 *Political Science Quarterly* 238 (1911).

61. Brutus, Essay XV, March 20, 1788, in *The Anti-Federalist: An Abridgement of The Complete Anti-Federalist*, ed. Herbert J. Storing, selected by Murray Dry (Chicago: University of Chicago Press, 1985), 183.

Chapter 2: The Constitution of the Fathers

1. Parts of this chapter are adapted from my article "Creed & Culture in the American Founding," *Intercollegiate Review* 41, no. 2 (Fall 2006).

2. Those who see America in creedal terms, though they disagree over

the nature and significance of the creed, include Michael Zuckert and Thomas G. West. See, for example, Zuckert's *The Natural Rights Republic* (Notre Dame, IN: University of Notre Dame Press, 1996), and his "Natural Rights and Protestant Politics," in Thomas S. Engemann and Michael P. Zuckert, *Protestantism and the American Founding* (Notre Dame, IN: University of Notre Dame Press, 2004), 21–75, and West's *Vindicating the Founders: Race, Sex, Class and Justice in the Origins of America* (Lanham, MD: Rowman & Littlefield, 2001), and his "The Transformation of Protestant Theology as a Condition of the American Revolution," in Engemann and Zuckert, *Protestantism*, 187–223. Those who emphasize cultural continuities, and particularly religious continuities, include Barry Alan Shain and Peter Lawler. See, for example, Shain's *The Myth of American Individualism: The Protestant Origins of American Political Thought* (Princeton: Princeton University Press, 1994), and Lawler's "Religion, Philosophy, and the American Founding," in Engemann and Zuckert, *Protestantism*, 165–85. James R. Stoner has made the case that there is much more to the Declaration than its most famous lines. It contains a list of grievances—not much read anymore—indicting the king for acts contrary to the common-law rights and liberties of Englishmen. See Stoner, "Is There a Political Philosophy in the Declaration of Independence?" *Intercollegiate Review* 40, no. 2 (Fall/Winter 2005): 3–11. These readings merely sit at the tip of a very large iceberg.

3.   John Locke, *Second Treatise of Government*, in Locke, *Two Treatises of Government*, ed. and int. Peter Laslett (Cambridge: Cambridge University Press, 1988).

4.   For example, the Delaware and Maryland Declarations of Rights (1776) respectively assert that "All government of right originates from the people and is founded in compact only"; the Virginia Declaration of Rights (1776) claims that "all men are by nature equally free and independent" with certain "inherent rights" that they cannot by "compact" divest themselves of; the Pennsylvania Constitution (1776) asserts "all men are born equally free and independent"; the New Hampshire Constitution (1776) claims "All men are born equally free and independent; therefore, all government of right originates from the people, is founded in consent, and instituted for the general good," while the Constitution of 1784 asserts that "All men have

certain natural, essential, and inherent rights—among which are, the enjoying and defending life and liberty; acquiring, possessing, and protecting, property; and, in a word, of seeking and obtaining happiness"; and the Massachusetts Constitution of 1780 says that "The body politic is formed by a voluntary association of individuals: it is a social compact, by which the whole people covenants with each citizen, and each citizen with the whole people, that all shall be governed by certain laws for the common good. . . . All men are born free and equal, and have certain natural, essential, and unalienable rights; among which may be reckoned the right of enjoying and defending their lives and liberties; that of acquiring, possessing, and protecting property; in fine, that of seeking and obtaining their safety and happiness."

5. The enduring importance of these principles is transparent to almost all outsiders looking in—many foreigners love nothing more than to show alleged American hypocrisy when America does not live up to its universal principles.

6. The other side of this argument is that Lockean theory as the Founders understood it serves not as an accelerant but a brake on demagogic egalitarianism or individualism—as Lincoln would argue in his Lyceum and Temperance addresses. Natural rights are *self*-limiting in that they point to *nature*. One needs to know what human nature *is*— what type of creature one is referring to—or what is appropriate to this type of creature by nature. This knowledge is necessary to begin, and ultimately end, the discussion of rights and their concomitant obligations. And these are things that can be reasoned about. They do not, and cannot, depend on mere will, or tradition, for will is fickle, and tradition sometimes indefinite and sometimes simply wrong. Even the most strident critics of some of the Founders do not accuse them of moral libertinism. One can, of course, make the case that the Founders were steeped in the notion of virtue, public and private, from their reading of the classics. But natural rights, too, provide the ground for a manly assertiveness in pursuit of something beyond individual satisfaction. See Harvey C. Mansfield, "Democratic Greatness in the American Founding," *Intercollegiate Review* 40, no. 2 (Fall/Winter 2005): 12–17.

7. Hume, too, praised the Glorious Revolution but emphasized its

moderation and conservative nature as a reassertion of established practices.

8. Henry Steele Commager, "Leadership in Eighteenth Century America and Today," in *Excellence and Leadership in a Democracy*, ed. Stephen R. Graubard and Gerald Holton (New York: Columbia University Press, 1962), 25–46.

9. I develop this argument at greater length, concentrating on its specific connection to David Hume, in my piece "Hume, Historical Inheritance, and the Problem of Founding," in Ronald J. Pestritto and Thomas G. West, eds., *The American Founding and the Social Compact* (Lanham, MD: Lexington Books, 2003), 75–94. Parts of my argument here are borrowed from that essay. The most comprehensive work on the Humean origins of America has been undertaken by Mark G. Spencer in *David Hume and Eighteenth-Century America* (Rochester, NY: University of Rochester Press, 2005) and his edited collection of primary source materials with commentary, *Hume's Reception in Early America*, 2 vols. (Bristol, UK: Thoemmes Press, 2002).

10. Stoner, "Is There a Political Philosophy in the Declaration of Independence?" 5. As Spencer notes, the combined historiography of the colonial period shows "that the colonists claimed English liberties on the ground of the historical rights of Englishmen *and* the natural rights of man. And claims of both sorts co-existed in colonial writings of the mid-1760s as well as in writing of the mid-1770s. Rigid distinctions, which many modern commentators attempt to impose, between rights claimed as natural and rights claimed as historical, did not always exist to the same degree within the eighteenth-century mind." See Spencer, *David Hume and Eighteenth-Century America*, 122.

11. This is an idea that Madison, in *Federalist* 10, borrows in part from Hume, especially his essay "Idea of a Perfect Commonwealth." The precise extent of Madison's reliance on, and agreement with, Hume is a matter of dispute. A summary of the historiography surrounding this question can be found in Spencer, *David Hume and Eighteenth Century America*, 154–87.

12. Thomas Jefferson, *Notes on the State of Virginia*, Query XIII, in *The Portable Thomas Jefferson*, ed. Merrill D. Peterson (New York: Penguin, 1975), 162.

13. Jefferson, *Notes*, in Peterson, 164. Emphasis in original.

14. For a good short summary of this conservatism, see Kevin Ryan, "Coke, the Rule of Law, and Executive Power," *Vermont Bar Journal*, vol. 31, no. 1 (Spring 2005).

15. Michael Zuckert, "Social Compact, Common Law, and the American Amalgam: The Contribution of William Blackstone," in Pestritto and West, eds., *The American Founding and the Social Compact*, 42–43.

16. See Hume, "Of the Rise and Progress of the Arts and Sciences," in *Essays, Moral, Political, and Literary*, ed. Eugene F. Miller (Indianapolis, IN: Liberty Fund, 1985), 124.

17. My interpretation of Abraham Lincoln, here and elsewhere, is indebted to the thought of Harry V. Jaffa in ways that I can no longer count. See especially Jaffa's *Crisis of the House Divided: An Interpretation of the Issues in the Lincoln-Douglas Debates* (Chicago: University of Chicago Press, 1982); *A New Birth of Freedom: Abraham Lincoln and the Coming of the Civil War* (Lanham, MD: Rowman & Littlefield, 2000); and "Equality as a Conservative Principle," in Jaffa, *How to Think About the American Revolution: A Bicentennial Cerebration* (Durham, NC: Carolina Academic Press, 1978), 13–48.

18. For a discussion of such assertiveness in the context of the American founding, see Mansfield, "Democratic Greatness."

19. Abraham Lincoln, "Address to the Young Men's Lyceum of Springfield, Illinois," originally entitled "The Perpetuation of Our Political Institutions," January 27, 1838, in Don E. Fehrenbacher, ed., *Lincoln: Selected Speeches and Writings* (New York: Vintage Books/Library of America Edition, 1992), 13–21.

20. The view that Lincoln attacks is roughly coterminous with the conception of politics put forth by the great English philosopher Thomas Hobbes, though Hobbes is not mentioned directly.

21. Abraham Lincoln, "Address to the Washington Temperance Society of Springfield, Illinois" in Fehrenbacher, *Lincoln: Selected Speeches*, 34–43.

22. Nevertheless, based on this image of Caesarism, Lincoln's critics saw, and continue to see him, as the first great orator of American government—someone who would create a centralized, uniform, egalitarian union, of which he would be the "leader."

23. Abraham Lincoln, "Speech on Kansas-Nebraska Act," at Peoria, IL, October 16, 1854, in Fehrenbacher, ed., *Lincoln*, 93–99.

24. Abraham Lincoln, "Address at Gettysburg, Pennsylvania," November 19, 1863, in Fehrenbacher, ed., *Lincoln*, 405.

25. See Frederick Douglass, "Fourth of July Oration," in Herbert J. Storing, ed., *What Country Have I? Political Writings by Black Americans* (New York: St. Martin's Press, 1970), 28–38.

26. *Dred Scott v. Sandford*, 60 U.S. (19 How.) 393 (1857).

27. Clinton, *Marbury v. Madison and Judicial Review*, 126.

28. Ibid., 140.

29. Ibid., 119.

30. See Abraham Lincoln, "Speech on the *Dred Scott* Decision at Springfield, Illinois," June 26, 1857, in Fehrenbacher, ed., *Lincoln*, 117–22.

31. Robert Lowry Clinton, "How the Court Became Supreme," *First Things*, no. 89 (January 1999): 14.

Chapter 3: The Social Darwinist Moment

1. Richard Hofstadter, *Social Darwinism in American Thought*, rev. ed. (Boston: Beacon Press, 1955 [1944]), 32. The phrase "social Darwinism" gained widespread intellectual currency as an appropriate descriptor of an amalgam of ideas only with the publication of the first edition of that book in 1944.

2. Ibid., 33.

3. Ibid., 4–5

4. Ibid., 25.

5. Ibid., 30.

6. Ibid., 107–8.

7. Ibid., 24.

8. Herbert Hovenkamp, "Evolutionary Models of Jurisprudence," *Texas Law Review* 64, No. 4 (December 1985): 645.

9. John Dewey, "The Influence of Darwinism on Philosophy," in *The Influence of Darwinism on Philosophy and Other Essays in Contemporary Thought* (New York: Henry Holt and Co., 1951).

10. The only other contender for the throne was the vigorous, pragmatic individualist frontier strain of thought associated with such figures as

Frederick Jackson Turner and Mark Twain. But this strain was never as theoretically unified as social Darwinism and never found the same acceptance among the intellectual classes. Not coincidentally, perhaps, it could not be said to have undermined, in any direct or consistent manner, the principled understanding of the American founding articulated by Lincoln.

11. There are problems with this Deweyan tendency to identify nature as final cause or form with changelessness. Such an account comes close to capturing the essence of Plato's forms, but for Aristotle there are no fixed, immutable ideas separate from matter. Rather, things develop to their natural perfection, which for human beings is happiness, relying on a combination of intellectual and moral virtue. There is a tension in Aristotle between philosophy (man as knower) and politics (man being a political animal, i.e., a virtuous actor, rather than, or in addition to, a knower). It is far from clear, in either Aristotle or Plato, how these virtues interact at all levels. But what is clear is that there is no simple teleology in Aristotle when it comes to human beings. Simple teleologies are for the lower forms, whereas for humans there are choices involving politics, ethics, and philosophy, and nature many times misses its mark. Furthermore, for Aristotle, essence is not form simply, but activity or what a thing does. In his science, repose does not represent the highest state of being. Although there is a good amount of truth to Dewey's characterization of Western science, or philosophy, as the search for the transcendent, he seems wrong insofar as he puts a Platonic gloss on Aristotle.

12. Dewey, "The Influence of Darwinism on Philosophy," 13.

13. Ibid., 15.

14. Ibid., 16.

15. Purcell, *The Crisis of Democratic Theory*, 202.

16. See, for example, John Dewey, *Reconstruction in Philosophy* (Boston: Beacon Press, 1957), passim.

17. This is the reason why we do not expect great statesmen—exercising practical and theoretical wisdom—to be young, whereas mathematicians might be.

18. Albert W. Alschuler, *Law Without Values: The Life, Work, and Legacy of Justice Holmes* (Chicago: University of Chicago Press, 2000), 49.

19. Hofstadter, *Social Darwinism in American Thought*, 51.

20. Ibid., 8.

21. Hofstadter, *Social Darwinism in American Thought*, 8.

22. William Graham Sumner, "Purposes and Consequences," in *Essays of William Graham Sumner*, vol. 1, ed. Albert Galloway Keller and Maurice R. Davie (New Haven, CT: Yale University Press, 1934).

23. William Graham Sumner, "Mores of the Present and Future," in *Essays of WG Sumner*, ed. Keller and Davie.

24. Ibid., 75.

25. Ibid., 86.

26. Ibid., 87.

27. William Graham Sumner, "The American Code," in *Essays of WG Sumner*, ed. Keller and Davie, 88.

28. William Graham Sumner, *What Social Classes Owe to Each Other* (Caldwell, ID: Caxton Printers, 1989; orig. pub. 1883).

29. Ibid., 17.

30. Ibid., 108.

31. Why social Darwinism in the United States moved in this direction is opaque; it is arguably related, however, to the very philosophical liberalism—including natural rights doctrines—which American social Darwinism pitted itself against. Edward Purcell has argued—with perhaps too much emphasis on the "democratic" character of the "old" America—that "[t]he depth and pervasiveness of democratic ideals was apparent in the discussion over the meaning of the new science. . . . [F]or neither Sumner's view of evolution nor the harsh, deterministic interpretation of man's place in the universe won general acceptance. Instead, Americans turned the new ideas to the support of the old. Led by James, Dewey, and Ward, social thinkers defined empiricism and evolution as broadly humanitarian and democratic." See Purcell, *The Crisis of Democratic Theory*, 10.

32. Sumner, *What Social Classes Owe*, 34.

33. Sumner, "The Absurd Effort to Make the World Over," in *Essays of WG Sumner*, ed. Keller and Davie, 101.

34. Sumner, *What Social Classes Owe*, 52.

35. Sumner, "Purposes and Consequences," 17.

36. Ibid., 18.

37. Lester Frank Ward, "Mind as a Social Factor," *Mind*, vol. 9, no. 36 (October 1884): 565.

38. Ibid., 566.

39. Like Sumner, Ward fails to allow that the natural sciences themselves might be historically conditioned, in the manner of Thomas Kuhn's argument that scientific ideas develop akin to Darwin's account of the evolution of organic beings—in neither case can we say that evolution is "toward" any goal or purpose. As science develops, one incompatible paradigm after another follows on what has gone before, all of which are parts of a process that does not necessarily point to the truth of things. See Thomas S. Kuhn, *The Structure of Scientific Revolutions*, 2nd ed. (Chicago: University of Chicago Press, 1970).

40. Ward, "Mind as a Social Factor," 567.

41. Ibid., 569.

42. Hofstadter, *Social Darwinism in American Thought*, 67–68.

43. Ibid., 82.

44. Ibid., 122.

45. The conference was organized by white progressives who sought, among other things, to challenge Booker T. Washington's perceived leadership of black politics, with more progressive views.

46. W. E. B. DuBois, "The Evolution of the Race Problem" (1909) in *Political Thought in America: An Anthology*, ed. Michael B. Levy (Homewood, IL: Dorsey Press, 1982), 300.

47. DuBois, "The Evolution of the Race Problem," 301.

48. Ibid., 302.

49. Ibid.

50. Ibid., 303. Emphasis in original.

51. The judicial branch is but one facet of this apparatus, albeit now a central one.

52. Charles Darwin, *The Origin of Species*, Harvard Classics, vol. 11, ed. Charles W. Eliot (New York: P.F. Collier and Son, 1909–14), 489.

53. Darwin, *The Origin of Species*, 488.

54. Ibid., 506.

55. Louis Menand, *The Metaphysical Club* (New York: Farrar, Straus, Giroux, 2001), 302.

56. Hofstadter, *Social Darwinism in the American Thought*, 125.

57. Ibid., 123.

58. Ibid., 125.

59. Hofstadter, *Social Darwinism in American Thought*, 123.

60. William James, "What Pragmatism Means," in William James, *Essays in Pragmatism*, ed. and int. Alburey Castell (New York: Hafner Press, 1948); originally delivered by James as a lecture in 1906.

61. Ibid., 142–43.

62. Hofstadter, *Social Darwinism in American Thought*, 128.

63. Ibid., 132.

64. James, "What Pragmatism Means," 153–54.

65. Ibid., 141–42.

66. Ibid., 146.

67. Ibid., 144–45; 154.

68. Ibid., 147.

69. Ibid., 150.

70. Ibid., 150. Emphasis in original.

71. William James, "The Will to Believe" (1896), in *Pragmatism: A Reader*, ed. and int. Louis Menand (New York: Vintage Books, 1997), 92.

72. James, "What Pragmatism Means," 154–55.

73. Ibid., 156–57.

74. James, "What Pragmatism Means," 157.

75. Interestingly, U.S. courts, in establishment clause jurisprudence, have come to deal with the Absolute in similarly pragmatic terms. If government celebration of or teaching about religious holidays, institutions, or symbols can be understood in purely secular terms, it passes constitutional muster. Unlike James, many judges do not appear to suffer cognitive dissonance as a result.

76. James, "What Pragmatism Means,"157–58.

77. One need only compare the constitutional rhetoric of Lincoln to virtually any recent president to see this difference in stark relief. See Jeffrey K. Tulis, *The Rhetorical Presidency* (Princeton, NJ: Princeton University Press, 1987).

78. Hofstadter, *Social Darwinism in American Political Thought*, 141–42.

79. Menand, *The Metaphysical Club*, 302.

80. Indeed, Louis Menand notes that the growth of American social-science disciplines was a consequence of the rejection of the notion that evolutionary laws govern in a way that cannot be improved upon by public policy. See Menand, *The Metaphysical Club*, 302.

81. Dewey, *Liberalism and Social Action* (Amherst, NY: Prometheus Books, 2000; orig. pub. 1935), 29.

82. Dewey, *Liberalism and Social Action*, 27.

83. This move was delayed in the United States due to the more agrarian nature of its economy and the lack of a Benthamite influence. See Dewey, *Liberalism and Social Action*, 27–28.

84. Ibid., 30–35.

85. Ibid., 24.

86. Ibid., 35.

87. Ibid., 36.

88. Ibid., 42.

89. Ibid., 40.

90. Ibid., 59.

91. Ibid., 46.

92. Ibid., 40.

93. Ibid., 80.

94. Ibid., 55–56.

95. See especially John Dewey, *Democracy and Education: An Introduction to the Philosophy of Education* (New York: The Free Press, 1966; orig. pub. 1916).

96. Dewey, *Liberalism and Social Action*, 61.

Chapter 4: Progressive Political Leadership

1. I use the phrase "intellectual and political" to distinguish the progressivism that is the subject of this study from the populist "movement" progressivism and social reform initiatives that were common in the early twentieth century.

2. Hofstadter, *Social Darwinism in American Thought*, 5.

3. See especially Herbert Croly, *The Promise of American Life*, ed. Arthur M. Schlesinger (Cambridge, MA: Belknap Press of Harvard University, 1965; orig. pub. 1909).

4. Theodore Roosevelt, "The Merit System versus the Patronage System."

5. See Theodore Roosevelt, "The New Nationalism" (1910).

6. Theodore Roosevelt, "A Remedy for Some Forms of Selfish Legislation."

7. See Theodore Roosevelt, "The New Nationalism" (1910).

8. Theodore Roosevelt, "True Americanism."

9. Theodore Roosevelt, "The Strenuous Life."

10. Friedrich Nietzsche, *Thus Spoke Zarathustra*, in *The Portable Nietzsche*, ed. Walter Kaufmann (New York: Penguin, 1982), 159.

11. Woodrow Wilson, *The State: Elements of Historical and Practical Politics* (1889), in *Woodrow Wilson: The Essential Political Writings*, ed. Ronald J. Pestritto (Lanham, MD: Lexington Books, 2005), 39. This recent volume is by far the most accessible collection of Wilson's theoretical writings. I cite it, although I have occasionally undertaken very slight amendments in wording, punctuation or italicized emphases to accord with original versions of Wilson's writings, or earlier collections of his writings.

12. Ibid., 32.

13. Woodrow Wilson, "Cabinet Government in the United States" (1879), in *Essential Political Writings*, 128.

14. Ibid., 128.

15. See especially Woodrow Wilson, *Congressional Government* (1885), in *Essential Political Writings*, 141–73.

16. Wilson, "Cabinet Government," 134.

17. Ibid., 138. Emphasis in original.

18. This is the polar opposite of ancient political thought, and indeed of all political thought prior to the historicist revolution of late modernity, which told us that *philosophy* is historically conditioned (as opposed simply to the people, or society). With the ancients and early moderns, the American Founders understood their thought to apply to all people, for all time.

19. Wilson, "The Study of Administration," in *Essential Political Writings*, 232.

20. Wilson, *The State*, 63.

21. Wilson, "The Study of Administration," 242.

22. Ibid., 243.

23. Ibid., 244–45.

24. Wilson, *The State*, 64, 69.

25. Wilson, "Leaders of Men," in *Essential Political Writings*, 215.

26. Ibid., 216.

27. Ibid., 221.

28. Ibid.

29. Ibid., 222.

30. Ibid., 224.
31. Ibid., 222–23.
32. Ibid., 225.
33. Wilson, *Constitutional Government in the United States* (1908), in *Essential Political Writings*, 176–77.
34. Ibid., 176.
35. Ibid., 178.
36. Ibid., 183.
37. Woodrow Wilson, *The New Freedom* (New York: Doubleday, Page & Company, 1913).
38. Ibid., 41.
39. Ibid., 42.
40. See Herbert Croly, *Progressive Democracy* (New York: Macmillan, 1914); see also Croly, *The Promise of American Life.*
41. Croly, *Progressive Democracy*, 20–21.
42. Ibid., 351.
43. Ibid., 361.
44. Ibid., 358.

Chapter 5: The New Science of Jurisprudence

1. See, for example, Vose, *Constitutional Change*, xxiv–xxv.
2. Dewey, *Liberalism and Social Action*, 86.
3. Ibid., 86.
4. John Dewey, "Logical Method and the Law," 10 *Cornell L.Q.* 17 (1924), 17–27.
5. Ibid., 26.
6. Alschuler, *Law Without Values*, 9.
7. Richard A. Epstein, *How Progressives Rewrote the Constitution* (Washington, D.C.: Cato Institute. 2006), 12.
8. Ibid., 135.
9. Bailey, *Guardians of the Moral Order*, 23.
10. Christopher Wolfe, *The Rise of Modern Judicial Review: From Constitutional Interpretation to Judge-Made Law*, rev. ed. (Lanham, MD: Rowman & Littlefield, 1994), 3.
11. Ibid., 18.
12. Ibid., 4.

13. Ibid., 6.
14. Ibid.
15. Ibid., 203.
16. Ibid.,158.
17. Ibid., 395
18. Hofstadter, *Social Darwinism in American Thought*, 46–47.
19. Ibid., 50.
20. Epstein, *How Progressives Rewrote the Constitution*, 135.
21. Vose, *Constitutional Change*, 164.
22. Epstein, *How Progressives Rewrote the Constitution*, 52.
23. *Northern Securities Co. v. United States*, 193 U.S. 197 (1904).
24. *Swift & Co. v. United States*, 196 U.S. 375 (1905).
25. *Champion v. Ames*, 188 U.S. 321 (1903).
26. *McRay v. United States*, 195 U.S. 27 (1904).
27. *Standard Oil v. United States*, 221 U.S. 1 (1911).
28. Justice Brandeis laid out factors to be considered in *Chicago Board of Trade v. United States,* 246 U.S. 231 (1918).
29. *Howard v. Illinois Cent. R.R.*, 207 U.S. 463 (1908).
30. *Adair v. United States*, 208 U.S. 161 (1908).
31. *Lochner v. New York*, 198 U.S. 45 (1905).
32. *Hammer v. Dagenhart*, 247 U.S. 251 (1918).
33. *Dagenhart* was overruled by *U.S. v. Darby*, 312 U.S. 100 (1941).
34. *Muller v. Oregon*, 208 U.S. 412 (1908).
35. Though it would again be relied on, subsequent to *Muller.*
36. Bailey, *Guardians of the Moral Order*, 127.
37. Ibid., 163–64.
38. See especially Bailey, *Guardians of the Moral Order*, passim.
39. Epstein, *How Progressives Rewrote the Constitution*, 48.
40. Purcell, *Brandeis and the Progressive Constitution*, 123. As Purcell shows, Brandeis's advocacy of various jurisdictional doctrines to limit judicial power served the same ends.
41. See, e.g., *The Curse of Bigness: Miscellaneous Papers of Louis D. Brandeis*, ed. Osmond K. Fraenkel (New York: Viking Press, 1934).
42. Vose, *Constitutional Change*, 175–77.
43. *Brown v. Board of Education*, 347 U.S. 483 (1954).
44. Louis Brandeis, as quoted in Purcell, *Brandeis and the Progressive Constitution*, 137.

45. Purcell, *Brandeis and the Progressive Constitution*, 137.

46. *Burns Baking Co. v. Bryan*, 264 U.S. 504 (1924).

47. *New State Ice Co. v. Liebmann*, 285 U.S. 262 (1932).

48. Alpheus T. Mason, "Louis Dembitz Brandeis," *International Encyclopedia of the Social Sciences*, vol. 2, ed. David L. Sills (New York: Macmillan, 1968), 144.

49. Philippa Strum, *Brandeis: Beyond Progressivism* (Lawrence, KS: University Press of Kansas, 1993), 54.

50. Ken I. Kersch, *Constructing Civil Liberties: Discontinuities in the Development of American Constitutional Law* (Cambridge, UK: Cambridge University Press, 2004), 149n40.

51. Strum, *Brandeis: Beyond Progressivism*, 57.

52. Ibid.

53. Ibid., 69.

54. Ibid.

55. Ibid., 118.

56. Ibid., 116.

57. If we may assume for the sake of argument that such a distinction is tenable. It is hardly clear that it is, on many very diverse grounds, including Lockeanism, classical liberalism, or Marxism.

58. *Schenk v. U.S.*, 249 U.S. 47 (1919).

59. In *Schenck*, the test had been used interchangeably with clear and present danger, thus muddying waters that would later have to be cleared.

60. *Whitney v. California*, 274 U.S. 357 (1927).

61. Vincent Blasi, "The First Amendment and the Ideal of Civic Courage: The Brandeis Opinion in *Whitney v. California*," 29 *William and Mary L. Rev.* 653, at 668 (1988).

62. Dewey, *Liberalism and Social Action*, 70. In contrast to Dewey, for Blasi these words are nothing more than an affirmation of Brandeis's belief in self-government. See Blasi, "The First Amendment and the Ideal of Civic Courage," 672.

63. Dewey, *Liberalism and Social Action*, 90.

64. Blasi, "The First Amendment and the Ideal of Civic Courage," 677.

65. Ibid.

66. Blasi, "The First Amendment and the Ideal of Civic Courage," 690–91.

67. David M. Rabban, "Free Speech in Progressive Social Thought," *74*

Texas Law Review 951 (1996), 958.

68. *Gilbert v. Minnesota*, 254 U.S. 325 (1920).

69. *Gitlow v. New York*, 268 U.S. 652 (1925).

70. Louis Brandeis orally to Felix Frankfurter, recorded in 1923 memorandum of Frankfurter's, as reproduced in Strum, *Brandeis*, 124.

71. *Olmstead v. United States*, 277 U.S. 438 (1928).

72. See Hadley Arkes, *Beyond the Constitution* (Princeton: Princeton University Press, 1990), esp. ch. 1.

73. Purcell, *The Crisis of Democratic Theory*, 88.

74. Alschuler, *Law Without Values*, 2.

75. Ibid.

76. Ibid., 2–3.

77. Ibid., 140.

78. Ibid., 2.

79. Oliver Wendell Holmes, "The Path of the Law," in Holmes, *Collected Legal Papers* (New York: Peter Smith, 1952), 167.

80. Alschuler, *Law Without Values*, 8.

81. Ibid., 171.

82. Holmes, "The Path of the Law," 167–68.

83. Ibid., 179.

84. Strum, *Brandeis*, 186n74.

85. Holmes, "The Path of the Law," 181.

86. Posner, *Law, Pragmatism, and Democracy*, 359.

87. Alschuler, *Law Without Values*, 4.

88. *Abrams v. United States*, 250 U.S. 616 (1919).

89. Compare Holmes's reasoning with that of Charles Sanders Peirce, "The Fixation of Belief" (1877), in *Pragmatism: A Reader*, ed. Louis Menand (New York: Vintage Books, 1997), 7–25 passim. Peirce concludes by writing, "The person who confesses that there is such a thing as truth, which is distinguished from falsehood simply by this, that if acted upon it will carry us to the point we aim at and not astray, and then, though convinced of this, dares not know the truth and seeks to avoid it, is in a sorry state of mind indeed" (25).

90. This reasoning is quite consonant with his earlier writings that "offered Darwinian and militaristic images of clashing ideas." See Alschuler, *Law Without Values*, 79 passim.

91. Wolfe, *The Rise of Modern Judicial Review*, 186.

92. Ibid., 189.

93. Posner, *Law, Pragmatism, and Democracy*, 360.

94. Ibid., 360–61.

95. Ibid., 361–62.

96. Ibid., 362.

97. Alschuler, *Law Without Values*, 5.

98. Ibid.

99. Alschuler, too, suggests the possibility that his later free-speech and criminal-procedure jurisprudence marked a change in Holmes insofar as "individuals may prevail over seemingly dominant forces and that there is more to life than survival of the fittest" (83)—though he draws back from this conclusion in a footnote where he suggests that Holmes's life is remarkable precisely for his lack of growth over time. See Alschuler, *Law Without Values*, 246n244. In another take on *Abrams*, Alschuler suggests, "[t]he issue that most obviously divided Holmes and the *Abrams* majority was an issue of statutory construction. The Espionage Act used words like 'willfully' and 'with intent,' and the simplest explanation of Holmes's endorsement of a subjective standard is that he was better at reading English than his brethren" (75); alternatively, "[a]lthough later opinions on the freedom of expression are compatible with a progressive, republican vision of society, they are also compatible with skepticism" (79). As I have suggested, there is more to the story than either a change of heart or a generalized skepticism.

100. Alschuler, *Law Without Values*, 6.

101. Ibid., 67.

102. *Gitlow v. New York*, 673.

103. Henry J. Abraham and Barbara A. Perry, *Freedom and the Court: Civil Rights and Liberties in the United States*, 6th ed. (New York: Oxford University Press, 1994), 12.

104. Epstein, *How Progressives Rewrote the Constitution*, 137 passim.

105. Oliver Wendell Holmes, "Ideals and Doubts," in Holmes, *Collected Legal Papers*, 304–5.

106. Oliver Wendell Holmes, "Natural Law," in Holmes, *Collected Legal Papers*, 310.

107. Vose, *Constitutional Change*, 6.

108. Ibid., 8.
109. Hofstadter, *Social Darwinism in American Thought*, 164.
110. Ibid., 169.
111. *Buck v. Bell*, 274 U.S. 200 (1927).
112. Vose, *Constitutional Change*, 17.
113. Alschuler, *Law Without Values*, 67.
114. It is worth noting, too, that Holmes's dissents were in some cases to be adopted by later Courts. In *West Coast Hotel v. Parrish*, 300 U.S. 379 (1937), freedom of contract was repudiated; Holmes's view of freedom of speech was accepted in *Herndon v. Lowry*, 301 U.S. 242 (1937); *Katz v. United States*, 389 U.S. 347 (1967) overruled *Olmstead*, 277 U.S. 438 (1928) in which Holmes had asserted, in dissent, a broad conception of Fourth Amendment protections.
115. Alschuler, *Law Without Values*, 10, 94.
116. Ibid., 94.
117. Ibid.
118. Ibid., 95–97.
119. Ibid., 98.
120. Ibid., 99.
121. Ibid., 100.
122. Ibid., 101.
123. Though this might be changing with the increasing imposition, by treaty, of European Union mandates on English courts.
124. Alschuler, *Law Without Values*, 102.
125. See John Dewey, "The Influence of Darwinism on Philosophy," and *Liberalism and Social Action*.
126. Alschuler, *Law Without Values*, 135.
127. Ibid., 20.
128. Ibid., 23.
129. Christopher Wolfe, *The Rise of Modern Judicial Review*.
130. *Macpherson v. Buick Motor Company*, 217 N.Y. 382 (1916).
131. *Ultramares Corporation v. Touche*, 255 N.Y. 170 (1931).
132. *Jacobs and Young v. Kent*, 230 N.Y. 239 (1921).
133. Benjamin N. Cardozo, *The Nature of the Judicial Process* (New Haven and London: Yale University Press, 1921).
134. Ibid., 12.
135. Ibid., 16.

136. Ibid., 28.

137. *Griswold v. Connecticut*, 381 U.S. 479 (1965).

138. Cardozo, *The Nature of the Judicial Process*, 43.

139. Ibid., 66

140. Ibid.

141. Ibid., 108.

142. Ibid., 108–9.

143. Wolfe, *The Rise of Modern Judicial Review*, 239.

144. Ibid., 240.

145. *Carter v. Carter Coal Company*, 298 U.S. 238 (1936).

146. *Steward Machine Company v. Davis*, 301 U.S. 548 (1937).

147. *Helvering v. Davis*, 301 U.S. 619 (1937).

148. *Helvering v. Davis*, 640.

149. *Palko v. Connecticut*, 302 U.S. 319 (1937).

150. *Roe v. Wade*, 410 U.S. 113 (1973).

151. Purcell, *Brandeis and the Progressive Constitution*, 35.

152. Ibid., 36–37.

153. Alschuler, *Law Without Values*, 23.

Chapter 6: Academic Progressivism

1.   Purcell, *The Crisis of Democratic Theory*, 15.

2.   See Bradley C. S. Watson, "Who Was Francis Lieber?" *Modern Age* 43, no. 4 (Fall 2001).

3.   John S. Dryzek, "Revolutions Without Enemies: Key Transformations in Political Science," *American Political Science Review* 100, no. 4 (November 2006): 487.

4.   See Dennis J. Mahoney, *Politics and Progress: The Emergence of American Political Science* (Lanham, MD: Lexington Books, 204), 8.

5.   "College Professors and the Public," *The Atlantic Monthly* 89 (1902), as quoted in Sandra P. Epstein, *Law at Berkeley: The History of Boalt Hall* (Berkeley, CA: Institute of Governmental Studies Press, 1997), 54.

6.   Mahoney, *Politics and Progress*, 53.

7.   Peter N. Ubertaccio and Brian J. Cook, "Wilson's Failure: Roots of Contention about the Meaning of a Science of Politics," *American Political Science Review* 100, no. 4 (November 2006): 576.

8. Mahoney, *Politics and Progress*, 10–11.

9. Dryzek, "Revolutions Without Enemies," 488.

10. Purcell, *The Crisis of Democratic Theory*, 35 passim.

11. John G. Gunnell, "The Founding of the American Political Science Association: Discipline, Profession, Political Theory, and Politics," *American Political Science Review* 100, no. 4 (November 2006): 480.

12. Gunnell, "The Founding of the American Political Science Association," 483.

13. Mahoney, *Politics and Progress*, 13.

14. See, for example, Purcell, *The Crisis of Democratic Theory*, esp. ch. 5, and Alschuler, *Law Without Values*, passim.

15. Laura Kalman, *Legal Realism at Yale: 1927–1960* (Chapel Hill, NC: University of North Carolina Press, 1986), 15.

16. Ibid., 7.

17. See, for example, Jerome Frank, *Law and the Modern Mind* (New York: Coward-McCann, 1949). This book was still required reading at Harvard Law School as late as the 1960s.

18. Purcell, *The Crisis of Democratic Theory*, 74.

19. Robert Stevens, *Law School: Legal Education in America from the 1850s to the 1980s* (Chapel Hill, NC: University of North Carolina Press, 1983), 23.

20. Ibid.

21. Ibid., 56.

22. See Purcell, *The Crisis of Democratic Theory*, 75.

23. Benjamin Cardozo, *The Growth of the Law*, 4, as quoted in Stevens, *Law School*, 132.

24. Stevens, *Law School*, 64.

25. Ibid., 62–63.

26. Oliver Wendell Holmes, "The Use and Meaning of Law Schools, and Their Methods of Instruction," as quoted in Stevens, *Law School*, 122.

27. Stevens, *Law School*, 123.

28. G. Edward White, "From Sociological Jurisprudence to Realism: Jurisprudence and Social Change in Early Twentieth-Century America," *Virginia L. Rev.* 58, no. 6 (September 1972): 999.

29. Stevens, *Law School*, 156.

30. White, "From Sociological Jurisprudence to Realism," 1025.

31. Herman Belz, "The Realist Critique of Constitutionalism in the Era of Reform," *The American Journal of Legal History* 15, no. 4 (October 1971): 288.

32. Belz, "The Realist Critique of Constitutionalism," 292.

33. Wolfe, *The Rise of Modern Judicial Review*, 217–18.

34. Belz, "The Realist Critique of Constitutionalism," 294.

35. Wolfe, *The Rise of Modern Judicial Review*, 325.

36. G. Edward White has argued that progressivism differed from realism in the former's faith in progress, both political and moral, and the latter's lack of such faith. This seems to be an overstatement, or an underestimation of the continuing influence of historical categories on many of the realists. See White, "From Sociological Jurisprudence to Realism," 1023. The strongest version of his claim—that "the conflict between the Progressives and the New Dealers, like that between the Sociological Jurisprudes and the Realists, came down to one between a relativistic or absolutist approach to morals" (1026)— is unconvincing.

37. Belz, "The Realist Critique of Constitutionalism," 304.

38. Calvin Woodward, "The Limits of Legal Realism: An Historical Perspective," *Virginia Law Review* 54, no. 4 (May 1968): 693–94.

39. See Cardozo, *The Nature of the Judicial Process*, especially lectures 2 and 3.

40. Purcell, *The Crisis of Democratic Theory*, 76.

41. Ibid., 77.

42. Roscoe Pound, "Mechanical Jurisprudence," 8 *Columbia Law Review* (December 1908): 609.

43. Hovenkamp, "Evolutionary Models in Jurisprudence," 650.

44. Ibid., 651.

45. Purcell, *The Crisis of Democratic Theory*, 77.

46. Ibid., 91.

47. Purcell, *The Crisis of Democratic Theory*, 78.

48. Kalman, *Legal Realism at Yale*, 3.

49. Of course, many of the tendencies that seemed so marked in the leading law schools of the era—Columbia, Harvard, and Yale— disappeared entirely in the ensuing decades, to the point where nowadays it hardly seems meaningful to speak of fundamentally different approaches to legal education across these schools or

many others. See Kalman, *Legal Realism at Yale*, xii. Schools are restrained in their desire to emulate the perceived "better" schools only by the availability of resources.

50. Kalman, *Legal Realism at Yale*, 164.

51. Purcell, *The Crisis of Democratic Theory*, 82–83.

52. Ibid., 85.

53. Stevens, *Law School*, 135. Columbia in the 1920s also made tentative moves in this direction.

54. The differences between institutions and the academics who inhabited them were, in many cases, matters of degree. Pound had been an early critic of Langdell's case method, arguing that it ignored ways in which cases were, and ought to be, decided. In the early part of the twentieth century, he argued for a sociological jurisprudence that took account of a variety of social forces and factors rather simply an examination of the endogenous logic of legal decision-making. See Pound, "Mechanical Jurisprudence," 605–23.

55. Epstein, *Law at Berkeley*, 103.

56. Stevens, *Law School*, 158. Kalman, *Legal Realism at Yale*, 78–92.

57. Purcell, *The Crisis of Democratic Theory*, 86.

58. With respect to administrative law, Harvard tended to play catch-up to Columbia, Yale, and Chicago.

59. Stevens, *Law School*, 141.

60. Kalman, *Legal Realism at Yale*, 130.

61. Epstein, *Law at Berkeley*, 139.

62. Kalman, *Legal Realism at Yale*, 157.

63. Myres McDougall and Harold Lasswell, "Legal Education and Public Policy: Professional Training in the Public Interest," *Yale Law Journal* 52 (1943): 203–9.

64. McDougall and Lasswell, "Legal Education and Public Policy," 248–51.

65. See, for example, Woodard, "The Limits of Legal Realism."

66. Stevens, *Law School*, 274.

67. Mahoney, *Politics and Progress*, 54.

68. Alschuler, *Law Without Values*, 2.

69. Ibid., 30.

70. Vose, *Constitutional Change*, 188.

71. *West Coast Hotel Co. v. Parrish*, 300 U.S. 379 (1937).

72. *Adkins v. Children's Hospital*, 261 U.S. 525 (1923).

73. Vose, *Constitutional Change*, 237.

74. *Erie Railroad Co. v. Tompkins*, 304 U.S. 64 (1938).

75. *Swift v. Tyson*, 16 Pet. (41 U.S) 1 (1842).

76. Purcell, *Brandeis and the Progressive Constitution*, 67.

77. Ibid., 79.

78. Ibid., 79–80.

79. Robert H. Jackson, *The Struggle for Judicial Supremacy* (New York: Alfred A. Knopf, 1941), 311–12.

80. Felix Frankfurter and Henry M. Hart Jr., "The Business of the Supreme Court at October Term, 1933," *Harvard Law Review* 48 (1934): 238.

81. Purcell, *The Crisis of Democratic Theory*, 88.

82. Ibid., 94.

83. Ibid., 95.

84. Ibid., 95, 99–104.

85. Ibid., 109.

86. Ibid., 110.

87. William Y. Elliott, "Mussolini, Prophet of the Pragmatic Era in Politics," 41 *Political Science Quarterly* (June 1926), and also *The Pragmatic Revolt in Politics* (New York, 1928).

88. Purcell, *The Crisis of Democratic Theory*, 140.

89. Robert Maynard Hutchins quoted in Purcell, *The Crisis of Democratic Theory*, 146. For a full expression of Hutchins's views, see Hutchins, *The Higher Learning in America*.

90. Frankfurter and Hart, "The Business of the Supreme Court," 280.

Chapter 7: The Future Is Now

1. Portions of this chapter on same-sex marriage and the judicial manipulation of language first appeared as "Love's Language Lost," *Claremont Review of Books* 5, no. 2 (Spring 2005). I am grateful to the *Claremont Review* for permission to adapt my arguments here.

2. *Baker v. State of Vermont*, 744 A.2d 865 (Vt. 1999).

3. *Goodridge v. Mass. Department of Public Health*, 440 Mass. 309, 798 NE2d 941 (Nov. 18, 2003).

4. Vose, *Constitutional Change*, xxv.

5. Purcell, *Brandeis and the Progressive Constitution*, 199.

6. Ibid., 258.

7. Vose, *Constitutional Change*, xxiv–xxv.

8. Henry M. Hart Jr., "The Relations Between State and Federal Law," 54 *Columbia Law Review* 489 (1954).

9. Purcell, *Brandeis and the Progressive Constitution*, 240.

10. Henry M. Hart Jr., "Comments on Courts and Lawmaking," in Monrad G. Paulsen, ed., *Legal Institutions Today and Tomorrow* (New York: Columbia University Press, 1959).

11. Purcell, *Brandeis and the Progressive Constitution*, 257.

12. See especially Bernard H. Siegan, *Economic Liberties and the Constitution* (Chicago, 1982). Richard Epstein has made similar arguments.

13. Posner, *Law, Pragmatism, and Democracy*, ix.

14. Ibid., 55.

15. Ibid., 3–4.

16. Ibid., 4.

17. Ibid., 29–30.

18. Ibid., 5.

19. Posner sketches the various elements of pragmatic adjudication in *Law, Pragmatism, and Democracy*, 69–85.

20. Ibid., 9.

21. Ibid., 79.

22. Ibid., 126.

23. Ibid., 42.

24. Ibid., 48.

25. Ibid., 55.

26. Purcell, *The Crisis of Democratic Theory*, 5.

27. Ibid., 74.

28. Alschuler, *Law Without Values*.

29. Bailey, *Guardians of the Moral Order*, 7–8.

30. Woodard, "The Limits of Legal Realism," 731.

Index

ABOUT THE AUTHOR

Bradley C. S. Watson holds the Philip M. McKenna Chair in American and Western Political Thought at Saint Vincent College, where he is also Fellow in Politics and Culture at the Center for Political and Economic Thought. He is also a fellow of the Claremont Institute for the Study of Statesmanship and Political Philosophy and the author or editor of several books, including *Civil Rights and the Paradox of Liberal Democracy, Courts and the Culture Wars, Civic Education and Culture* (available from ISI Books), and *The West at War*. A former civil litigation attorney, Watson writes and speaks frequently on Progressive jurisprudence, liberalism and communitarianism, Western political thought and the American regime, same-sex marriage, and immigration law and policy.